Fun with the Family™
in Wisconsin

"Bound to lead you and your kids to fun-filled days, those times that help compose the memories of childhood."
—Dorothy Jordon, Publisher, *Family Travel Times*

"Enables parents to turn family travel into an exploration."
—Alexandra Kennedy, Editor, *FamilyFun*

Help Us Keep This Guide Up-to-Date

Every effort has been made by the authors and editors to make this guide as accurate and useful as possible. However, many things can change after a guide is published—establishments close, phone numbers change, facilities come under new management, and so on.

We would love to hear from you concerning your experiences with this guide and how you feel it could be improved and kept up-to-date. While we may not be able to respond to all comments and suggestions, we'll take them to heart, and we'll make certain to share them with the authors. Please send your comments and suggestions to the following address:

The Globe Pequot Press
Reader Response/Editorial Department
P.O. Box 480
Guilford, CT 06437

Or you may e-mail us at: editorial@globe-pequot.com

Thanks for your input, and happy travels!

FUN WITH THE FAMILY™

in WISCONSIN

HUNDREDS OF IDEAS
FOR DAY TRIPS WITH THE KIDS

THIRD EDITION

By MARTIN HINTZ
and
STEPHEN V. HINTZ

The
Globe
Pequot
Press

Guilford, Connecticut

Cover and text design by Nancy Freeborn
Cover photograph by Julie Bidwell
Maps by M.A. Dubé

Library of Congress Cataloging-in-Publication Data

Hintz, Martin.
    Fun with the family in Wisconsin : hundreds of ideas for day trips with the kids / by Martin Hintz and Stephen V. Hintz.—3rd ed.
        p. cm. — (Fun with the family series)
    Includes index.
    ISBN 0-7627-0631-7
        1. Wisconsin—Guidebooks. 2. Family recreation—Wisconsin—Guidebooks.
I. Hintz, Stephen V. II. Title. III. Series.

F579.3.H55 2000
917.7504'44—dc21   99-087974

Manufactured in the United States of America
Third Edition/First Printing

To the family, again . . . travelers, all

Contents

Acknowledgments

The authors thank all the Wisconsinites whose hospitality, patience and good cheer, fun-loving nature, and keen insights laid the groundwork for this book over the years. There were fishing guides, convertible drivers, trolley operators, store clerks, bike repairmen, waitresses, desk clerks, balloonists, campground managers, forest rangers, highway patrolmen, and kids on in-line skates.

Their love of Wisconsin and their home communities always made our traveling, researching, and writing a much more pleasant task.

Special thanks go to good friends Gary Knowles and Don Davenport, all the state's travel professionals, the Wisconsin Restaurant Association, the Wisconsin Hotel and Motel Association, and to Gary Bellamy for his assistance in reworking and updating this guide.

The prices and rates listed in this guidebook were confirmed at press time. We recommend, however, that you call establishments to obtain current information before traveling.

Introduction

"On Wisconsin, On Wisconsin . . . ," the strains of the university's fight song echo from the northern pine glades rimming frosty Lake Superior to the rolling farm fields of the alpinelike southern counties. Wisconsin is a state for "doing things," whether your family fare consists of festivals, baseball, waterslides, hiking, ballet, or beaches. There is a delightful menu of attractions and events from which to choose fun for all seasons.

The Badger State celebrates heartily, with plenty of down-home zest, all of which takes advantage of geography, ethnic heritage, contemporary lifestyles, and person-made wonders. You can tour a House on the Rock, sit in the mouth of a giant muskie (statue, of course), climb into a kettle (a depression in the ground caused by melting glacial ice), take in a rainbow of cultures from Haitian to Hmong, and generally kick back and enjoy.

The state is made for families looking for the offbeat, as well as the traditional. You want to waterslide? Wisconsin has 'em. You want to drive? The state has 108,000 miles of roads to meander. You want to fish? Try angling in Lake Michigan off Algoma, which is the "Trout and Salmon Capital," or dipping a line into a stream near Birchwood, the "Bluegill Capital."

In 1998 the state proudly celebrated its 150th birthday with pomp and circumstance, flag waving, fireworks, and all-around fun. Communities and organizations across Wisconsin organized concerts, parades, festivals, and comprehensive celebrations of all kinds. The hoopla confirmed one thing: No one runs out of activities in Wisconsin. For more than a century and a half, the state has expanded on its attractions, services, and commitment to helping visitors enjoy themselves. There is always more to do. Each visit turns into something new and exciting. So we encourage you to make the best of it.

Be sure to have lots, loads, tons, and multitudinous amounts of fun while exploring the Badger State. Venture down the rustic roads, stop in villages and explore their back streets, and hit the cities and soak in their cultural life, restaurants, and neighborhoods. Absorb the glitter and glitz, to be sure. Remember, though, to pause occasionally on a hill overlooking a meadow, to dangle a foot in a slow-moving stream, or to count Wisconsin's stars. Now that's a challenge!

With all that we've done, and with the promise that more good things are yet to come, it is no wonder that the Hintz home turf of Wisconsin will always remain a favorite in our hearts.

Attractions Key

The following is a key to the icons found throughout the text.

 Swimming

 Animal Viewing

 Boating / Boat Tour

 Food

 Historic Site

 Lodging

 Hiking / Walking

 Camping

 Fishing

 Museums

 Biking

 Performing Arts

 Amusement Park

 Sports/Athletic

 Horseback Riding

 Picnicking

 Skiing/Winter Sports

 Playground

 Park

 Shopping

North and Northeast Wisconsin

Wisconsin's travel pundits say that this pine- and oak-carpeted landscape is north of the Tension Line. The promos promise a world of bottomless, mud-free lakes where muskie are ready to leap into your boat. Azure skies are clear on every vacation day. Crisply scented air is heady and fresh. Deer gambol and beaver splash happily. There is a sunset to match every dream and a sunrise guaranteed to pull off the morning blankets.

Okay, okay. That's the stuff of marketing. But reality? Hmmm. Take it from us, a family that has seen almost everything in the Badger State. There's truth in most of those words in the preceding paragraph when it comes to northern Wisconsin (except for the one about the muskie; we're still trying to figure that out). And so what if it does sprinkle—well, maybe actually rain—once or twice. Or who cares if the raccoons run off with the chocolate chip cookies left out overnight on the picnic table (leaving them

Hintz's Top Picks

- Hiking in Vilas County
- Watching the sunset on the Flambeau Flowage
- Cross-country skiing anywhere in the Chequamegon Forest
- Climbing the observation tower at Timm's Hill, the highest point in Wisconsin
- Listening for bugling elk or howling wolves in the North Country
- Stopping in for steak and pie at a North Woods eatery
- Snowmobiling along the rim of Lake Superior
- Watching a flight of blue herons
- Taking in a small-town museum
- Attending a Native American powwow

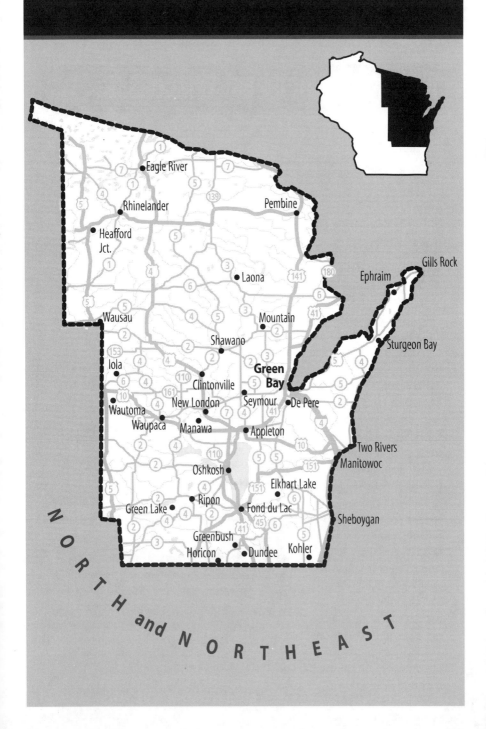

NORTH and NORTHEAST

Customized Trips John

Bales of **Trails North** formed his tour firm to help nature lovers understand and appreciate life in the North Woods. He can fashion custom trips along the nature trails, rivers, and lakes throughout the Northland. Weekly trips are also scheduled if you want to join a group. Contact Bales at Trails North, 2263 State Highway 47, Mercer, WI, 54547; (715) 476–2828.

there is a real woodsy no-no, anyway). Or the sunset is hidden by the glare from the neighboring camper's lantern. Or . . . aw, enough of this.

There is enough great opportunity in the state's north and northeastern neighborhoods so you actually don't need hyperbole. Just accept the challenging reality of family travel in the wood, kick back, and have a good time.

Upper Wisconsin is tailor-made for a get-out-and-go adventure. That's why raincoats, maps, stout boots, and walking sticks were invented. We've camped, hiked, museum-hopped, antique-rummaged, vista-sat, fished, eaten beans, watched rabbits, canoed, and gotten lost on rustic roads enough times to say that we wouldn't have it any other way.

That's the attitude you should have when roaming the back trails and rural vastness of Wisconsin's northern rim. Yet don't lose sight of the trees when thinking of the forest up here. Every bend in the highway opens to a new potential, whether dropping by the local bait shop—the one tucked in behind the gas station—or settling down for steak, salad, and pie at a log cabin eatery after a full day of ridge running and waterfall watching.

So, as the brochures suggest, check your cares and woes at the imaginary border between Wisconsin's northern clime and the rest of the world. You don't even need a passport.

To enjoy our woodsy get-aways, we tried to be flexible enough to accommodate the various family vacation needs—within reason, of course. One son (elder Dan) and his mother (long-patient Sandy) enjoyed hardcore fishing, so we built time for that into the program. Son number two (yours truly, Stephen V.) went swimming, and the World's Best Daughter (Kate) marched out on her usual frog and bug hunt. Yours truly (Hintz the Elder) appreciated dockside loafing under the sun with an adventure tale to read, along with a can o' tonic and the chance to doze when the mood struck.

We then gathered for a picnic or met for supper to relate the day's

Weather or Not When

traveling in Wisconsin, check the weather reports. As resident Badgers say, "If you don't like the weather now, just wait an hour." For the latest National Weather Service reports in Madison, call (608) 249–6645; for Milwaukee, try (414) 744–8000.

tales. Other times, we jointly planned a town excursion where everyone had the chance to rummage: Best Daughter to the souvenir shops, Elder Son and Mother to the bait stores, and the two Yours Trulys to whatever struck their respective fancies. We then did the *de rigueur* tours of ye olde ice cream, card, and fudge shoppes en masse.

Wisconsin Trees

Wisconsin is heavily forested, with dense tree growth covering about half the state, mostly in the north. Softwood tree species include white cedar, pine, spruce, fir, and hemlock. Ash, aspen, elm, maple, basswood, ironwood, and oak are among the hardwoods.

In the evening we visited a local church carnival, enjoyed a band concert on the town hall lawn (never forgetting bug repellent), listened to a ranger lecture in camp, or paddled out on a late-night boat ride (with life preservers) to admire the stars.

Somehow it always seemed to come together.

Options—that's the North Woods game.

Eagle River

Start your excursion in Wisconsin's north country at Eagle River. Eagle River is at the heart of Wisconsin's North Woods vacation country, with a strong emphasis on outdoor adventure and loads of fun with a family twist. Regardless of the season, there is always plenty to keep everyone occupied, whether summertime fishing and loafing dockside or wintertime snowmobiling and cross-country skiing.

THE WORLD CHAMPIONSHIP SNOWMOBILE DERBY
(ages 10 and up)

For dates, times, and ticket information, contact the Derby, 1311 North Railroad Street, P.O. Box 1447, Eagle River, WI 54521; (715) 479–4424 or (715) 479–2764; fax: (715) 479–9711; e-mail: snopros@derbytrack.com; www. derbytrack.com. Races are held the third week in January.

Loud, racy, explosive, and cold: that's the World Championship Snowmobile Derby, held on an oval of ice where speeds topping 100 mph can be reached. Tell the kids to wear their long johns and extra wool socks, because the wind chill at the town track can go far down into the double digits. Don't forget the mufflers, not only for the warmth but also to soften the sound of hundreds of snowmobiles revving at top speed. Yet sled drivers from around the world don't seem to mind the nip in the air. In fact, the frostier the better, because all that snow and ice provide plenty of danger and real-life adventure.

The behind-the-scenes work is just as fascinating, from the busy pit crews to the water truck struggling around the track to spray another coat of glaze over the ice. The vehicle looks like Old Man Winter incarnate, with its frozen hoses and icicles hanging from every knob and pipe. Don't worry about frostbite, however. Plenty of concession stands are on hand to keep funnelling explosive chili and marshmallowy hot chocolate down the throats of the young 'uns.

SNOWMOBILE RACING HALL OF FAME (ages 5 and up)

The Hall of Fame is on Highway 70 West, St. Germain; call (715) 542–4463 for hours.

Derby artifacts, oodles of photos, and racing machines are displayed in the hall. After a visit here, kids can dream about their future on the track someday.

Be Prepared

Be Prepared Being prepared makes for a better time in the woods. Here's some hints that will ease your trip, especially when bringing the family:

- Stick a few board games and card decks into a special box (just in case a few drops do fall and indoor or in-tent quiet time is required).

- Bring some of those novels you claimed you never had time to read over the past year. No excuses now.

- Put plenty of candles and extra matches in a watertight container for illuminating late-night ghost storytelling.

- Pack with potential weather changes in mind. A sunny beginning might end up in a cold rain. Weather can change quickly in northern Wisconsin. If your family is prepared, grumpy weather is only a diversion from the general fun.

- Anything forgotten during the home packing process—whether wriggling worms or snug sweatshirts—can always be purchased "Up North."

DECKER'S SNO-VENTURE TOURS (ages 10 and up)

*1311 North Railroad Street, P.O. Box 1447, Eagle River, WI 54521; (715)
479–2764.*

The company has led caravans of sledders over hill and dale in Yellowstone National Park and Iceland as well around the upper Midwest. Thousands of miles of groomed track loop around Eagle River, the firm's home base. Decker's takes visitors of all ages on runs up to the Lake Superior shoreline, across the forest land to neighboring counties, and generally wherever there is a trail link. Some trips last up to a week. Safety first is the Decker motto, with each rider in line responsible for the driver on both front and back. No one is ever left behind to confront the vast, frozen land alone. Novice sledders, including kids, can enjoy the trips.

CARL'S WOOD MUSEUM (ages 5 and up)

*230 Sundstein Road; (715) 479–5117. Open late May through Labor Day,
10:00 A.M. to 6:00 P.M. Monday through Saturday; after Labor Day through
early October, 10:00 A.M. to 5:00 P.M. Closed Sunday.*

This is the place to go to if the jokester in the backseat of the family caravan wants to "knock on wood" or if Dad needs to see a real chip off the old block. For a rip-roaring sight, take a gander at Carl's chainsaw carvings whacked from huge logs. There's even a 2,000-pound fierce-looking grizzly sculpture.

Night 'mobiling

Night 'mobiling Taking a predawn Decker Sno-Venture Tours snow run between Bayfield on the Wisconsin mainland to Madeline Island makes the winter especially exciting. Only the bright stars illuminate the way on the groaning ice across the north channel of Lake Superior to the island. The route is marked with old Christmas trees, stuck at irregular intervals in snowbanks plowed up on either side of the trail. The harsh air is crisp and cold, which makes breathing come hard from behind your ski mask and snowmobile windshield.

The trip takes barely thirty minutes, but it is a step through a wonderful doorway into a frosty winter world where there are no other vehicles other than the line of sleds on your tour. Scooting around the snow-stilled island, past buildings shuttered for the season, is eerie . . . as if traveling through a movie set. Then it's back to the mainland for breakfast.

Amazing Wisconsin Facts Wisconsin has five major land regions. They are the Lake Superior Lowland, the Northern Highland (sometimes called the Superior Upland), the Central Plain, the Western Upland, and the Eastern Ridges and Lowlands (or Great Lakes Plains).

The Lake Superior Lowland slopes gently southwards from Lake Superior. The flat plain ends from 5 to 20 miles inland. The Northern Highland encompasses most of northern Wisconsin, also gradually running downward toward the south. The state's highest point, Timm's Hill, rises 1,952 feet above sea level in the Price County portion of the Highlands.

The Central Plain arcs across the central portion of Wisconsin, where glaciers once crunched as shortly as 10,000 years ago. The Wisconsin River here has carved out the scenic Wisconsin Dells. The Western Upland consists of steep ridges and deep valleys that were untouched by the glaciers. The sandstone bluffs of the Mississippi River in this portion of the state are among the most scenic sections of Wisconsin. The Eastern Ridges and Lowlands extend from Green Bay southward to Illinois. These are easily navigated plains of glacial leftovers and limestone ridges. This is the best agricultural land in the Dairy State.

Places to Eat

Aerio Club. *1540 Highway 45 North; (715) 479–4695.* For good down-home eats in the North Country, you can't go wrong at the Aerio Club. $

Chanticleer Inn. *1458 East Dollar Lake Road; (715) 479–4486.* This is a great resort, one popular for generations. The dining room is one of the best in the Eagle River area. $$

Hunan Chinese Restaurant. *4351 Highway 45 South (Wall Street); (715) 479–4141.* For those who still need their fried-rice fix, the Hunan will satisfy every eating need. $

For More Information

Eagle River Chamber of Commerce Information Center, *116 Railroad Street, Eagle River, WI 54521-0218; (715) 479–8575 or (800) 359–6315.*

Woodruff

From Eagle River, drive 20 miles west on State Highway 70 to Woodruff.

Once a rough 'n' ready lumberjack town, Woodruff has all the accompanying wild stories about the good old days. Life is much calmer now, except for the summertime traffic on the main drag. Get a block off the main street or tuck yourself into a cabin in the woods, though, and all that hectic life disappears. Woodruff provides the chance for the family catch up both on suntans or snowmen. Take your pick. Or come in every season.

WOODRUFF STATE FISH HATCHERY (ages 5 and up)

8770 County Highway J (take State Highway 47 south to County Highway J and turn east); (715) 356–5211 or (715) 358–9215. Open from 8:00 A.M. to 4:30 P.M. Monday through Friday (with tours at 11:00 A.M. and 2:00 P.M.), Memorial Day through Labor Day.

The world's largest fish hatchery was set up in 1900 and has produced millions of fingerlings for muskie, pike, and walleyes in the years since. For a real show-and-tell fish story when everyone gets back to school, bring the kids pondside with their cameras to watch the leaping and splashing. (Keep the worms at home, though.) There are plenty of mounted fish displayed in the main building, as inspiration for little anglers.

SCHEER'S LUMBERJACK SHOWS (ages 5 and up)

State Highway 47, downtown Woodruff; (715) 356–4050. Open June through August with performances at 2:00 P.M. on Wednesday, Thursday, and Friday and at 7:30 P.M. Tuesday, Thursday, and Saturday.

Watch the lumberjacks climb poles, saw wood, and battle for supremacy by rolling logs in huge tanks of water. It's the rough-and-ready days of the Wisconsin logger frontier all over again.

Places to Eat

Ma Bailey's Supper Club. *8591 Woodruff Road; (715) 356–6133. From U. S. Highway 51 North, go to Highway J, then 2 miles east to Woodruff Road. This* fine lakeside dining palace is in a historic former bordello (don't tell the kids) on the Minocqua Chain o' Lakes. $$

Indian Shores/Shoreline Inn. *7750 Strongheart Road; (715) 356–5552.* With its beautiful views overlooking the woods, this restaurant has long been a popular drop-by for visitors who are visiting resorts or camping in the area. Steak and potatoes and lots more! $$

Places to Stay

Indian Shores Camping & Cottages. *State Highway 47 East, Box 12C, Woodruff, WI 54568-0012; (715) 356–5552.* The resort has a swimming pool, sandy beach, mini-golf, tennis, game room, and marina to accommodate the vacation needs of its guests. $$

Madeline Lake Resort. *8902 West Madeline Lake Road; (715) 356–7610.* The resort is open May 1 through mid-October, with lakefront cottages, trailer sites, and dock spaces. A playground is open for the kids. This is the only resort on Madeline and Carroll Lakes, with miles of shoreline from which to fish. Madeline Lake is only 2 miles east of Minocqua and Woodruff. $$

For More Information

Minocqua–Arbor Vitae–Woodruff Chamber of Commerce, *Box 1006, Minocqua, WI 54548; (800) 446–6784.*

Minocqua

Minocqua is adjacent to Woodruff's south side, so you don't have to travel far for fun. U.S. Highway 51 leads right to the heart of it all.

Minocqua couldn't be much farther north or it would sneeze itself into Vilas County. Nicknamed the Island City for good reason, Minocqua is surrounded by more than 2,000 acres of water with more than 3,000 lakes, ponds, and puddles in the immediate vicinity. This is a land tailor-made for outdoor recreation opportunities. The town offers 𝐅𝐫𝐞𝐞 waterskiing shows each afternoon throughout the summer, with a semi-pro troupe of brilliantly smiling beauties who certainly earned their water wings. They flip, fly, twirl, and turn on two skis, one ski, and no skis in an exciting display that keeps even the most jaded teen interested. For booted landlubbers, the city is also at the end of the Bearskin State Trail, built on 19 miles of an abandoned railroad bed that takes hikers and bikers through truly scenic countryside. There are dozens of boat ramps on the 3,000 lakes in the immediate neighborhood, where anglers, water-skiers, and swimmers have a field day. A kid can stay immersed in water and wrinkled all summer.

Minocqua's **"Parade of Beef"** is an experience that has to be seen and enjoyed for its fun. Local civic groups provide sides of beef to area businesses, which then come up with exotic recipes for their preparation. Most roast their concoctions outside, where the delightful scents mingle with the crisp September air. At noon, all the chefs strut with their culinary delights down the main street to the city park where the meat is cut and made into hefty sandwiches. Proceeds go to local charities. Country-western bands play up a storm in the background.

CONNIE'S TOY BOX (ages 5 and up)

320 Milwaukee Street; (715) 356–9893.

Kids love dropping by Connie's Toy Box in Minocqua. Here they can play with wooden animals, trains, and other neat goodies . . . sort of a test run before Mom and Dad plunk down the dollars.

MINOCQUA WINTER PARK (ages 5 and up)

12375 Scotchman Lake Road; (715) 356–3309. Open December 1 through March 31.

Even when winter freezes everything with its Jack Frost hammerlock, there is plenty to do. The Minocqua Winter Park presents 58 kilometers of groomed ski trails located only a few minutes outside of town. There are even lighted sections for nighttime fun, a special treat after a fresh snow when the landscape is diamond-dazzling. When toes are numb and noses are red after a run along the trails, a stop at the park's chalet-shaped warming hut is more than welcome. Food service, child care, and a ski shop are also on the site, which makes it an all-around package when Ol' Man Winter breathes down on the land. If you want to use more power to swoosh along the slopes, there are several hundred miles of snowmobile trails that loop in and out of the land around the city.

HOLIDAY ACRES (ages 10 and up)

7994 U.S. Highway 51 South; (715) 356–4400. Open daily May through September.

Bumper cars, two go-cart tracks, horseback riding, and four-wheeler trail rides keep kids going when the attention span wanders lakeside.

A Hintz Adventure

After one long-distance trip downstate from a weekend in Minocqua, Steve, Kate, one of Kate's friends, and I paused to look at Timm's Hill. Steve and Kate slept through the stop while I climbed the observation tower and hiked nearby trails for more than an hour. The sleepyheads, who were in their preteens at the time, haven't been back since, at least that I know of.

Sport Rentals

Sport Rentals No need to worry if you forgot some outdoor gear back home in the garage. Outlets in the Minocqua area can provide everything from sailboats to bicycles to fishing poles to cross-country skis.

Arbor Vitae Marine, 11015 State Highway 70 East, Arbor Vitae; (715) 356- 5367. Get marine gear here.

B. J.'s Sportshop, 917 Highway 51 North, P.O. Box 1008, Minocqua; (715) 356–3900. All sports fans served.

Minocqua Sport Rental, 9568 State Highway 70 West, P.O. Box 965, Minocqua; (715) 356–4661. Think water.

Minocqua Winter Park Ski Shop, 12375 Scotchman Lake Road, Minocqua; (715) 356–3309. Accommodates your skiing needs.

 FUN ZONE (ages 5 and up)

10295 Highway 70 West; (715) 356–4441. Open May through September; call for hours.

Mini-golf, train rides, a water slide, kiddie rides, horseback riding, bumper boats, and go-carts keep the family active.

 JIM PECK'S WILDWOOD (ages 5 and up)

10094 State Highway 70 West; (715) 356–5588. Open 9:00 A.M. to 5:30 P.M. daily from May through mid-October. Handicap accessible.

Looking for a llama in the North Woods? There are several at Jim Peck's Wildwood, where the fuzzy Andean creatures seem as much at home as the porcupines, white-tailed deer, bears, and other more-native species. Kids can pet and feed the smaller noncarnivorous beasties.

 NORTHWOODS WILDLIFE CENTER (ages 5 and up)

8683 Blumstein Road; (715) 356–7400. Call for tour appointments.

For more animal connections, the Northwoods Wildlife Center is a hospital for wounded critters. Injured animals can be brought to the shelter for rest, recuperation, and a healing touch before being returned to the the wild. Kids can watch how injured wildlife are helped by the resident medical staff. Tours and educational programs are regularly scheduled from spring through summer, when the intricacies of returning animals to the wild are explained.

BEARSKIN STATE TRAIL (ages 5 and up)
County Highway M; (715) 385–2727.

Hikers can find their way in and out of Minocqua on the 18-mile-long Bearskin State Trail. It runs over an abandoned railroad right-of-way that can be picked up behind the post office. For more information on what to expect along the Bearskin, contact the trail offices at the Department of Natural Resources, 4125 Highway M, Boulder Junction, WI 54512.

Places to Eat

The Belle Isle. *In downtown Minocqua, the Belle Isle is in the historic Landmark Building. 301 Front Street; (715) 356–7444.* The grill opens at noon and closes at 7:00 P.M., but the bar stays open until around midnight. $

Bosacki's Boathouse. *At the Bridge; (715) 356–5292.* Family dining is offered from 11:00 A.M. to midnight. The Boathouse is one of the first restaurants spotted on the drive into town from the south. It's a welcome sight, especially with its fudge shop. The place is crowded with stuffed and mounted fish, some displays dating back to when the restaurant first opened. $$

MaMa's Supper Club. *10486 State Highway 70 West; (715) 356–5070.* Since the 1950s, MaMa's has been serving fantastic Italian food, mostly of the robust Sicilian variety. The dining room overlooks Curtis Lake. This is a place to take the family for the big night out. $$

Paul Bunyan's Lumberjack Cook Shanty. *8653 U.S. Highway 51 North; (715) 356–6270.* The Cook Shanty has been a favorite of Minocqua visitors since it opened in 1961. It is famous for its huge camp breakfasts and is open from May through September. $

Places to Stay

Best Western Lakeview Motor Lodge. *311 East Park Avenue (U.S. Highway 51 North); (715) 356–5208 or (800) 852–1021.* This lodge is popular because of its main strip location on Minocqua Lake. Nonsmoking rooms are available. Children under twelve stay **Free**. $$

New Concord Inn of Minocqua. *320 Front Street; (715) 356–1800 or (800) 356–8888.* Many of the fifty-three rooms and suites have great lakefront views. Some of the units have whirlpools; perfect for after skiing or hiking. Children under twelve stay **Free**. $$

Pine Hill Resort. *8544 Hower Road; (715) 356–3418.* This is a great family place with two- and three-bedroom cottages. All are carpeted, with automatic gas heat for those cool North Country evenings. Reduced rates for spring and fall. $$

For More Information

Minocqua–Arbor Vitae–Woodruff Chamber of Commerce, *Box 1006, Minocqua, WI 54548; (800) 446–6784.*

Hazelhurst

Hazelhurst is 6 miles south of Minocqua on U.S. Highway 51.

NORTHERN LIGHTS PLAYHOUSE (ages 10 and up)

5611 Highway 51 South; (715) 356–7173. Productions are at 8:00 P.M. from May through Labor Day, with shows at 7:30 P.M. from September through October. Call ahead for schedule.

Located 10 miles south of Minocqua on U.S. Highway 51, the playhouse has children's theater performances at 11:00 A.M. on Wednesday as well as musicals and comedies. The productions are staged rain or shine, with regular theater seating. Professional actors from around the country are regularly booked for the summer season.

WARBONNET ZOO (ages 5 and up)

5610 U.S. Highway 51; (715) 356–5093. Open daily 9:00 A.M. to 7:00 P.M. May through September and 1:00 to 5:00 P.M. on Saturday in October.

This is an all-around adventure land with a petting zoo, go-carts, trail rides for horse lovers, and pony rides for tykes.

Rhinelander

Rhinelander is about a 15-mile drive south of Hazelhurst. Leave the city on U.S. Highway 51, cut across County Highway D to State Highway 47, then turn south.

Tell the kids to watch out for "hodags" when driving along dark forest roads in Oneida County around Rhinelander. The fearsome, long-toothed beasts were known for their stomping around in the woods, tickling loggers, and generally raising havoc with the rabbit population. Don't push the point too much, though; the hodag is actually a mythological critter. It was dreamed up at the turn of the twentieth century by some young pranksters who wanted to pull wool over the eyes of gullible visitors. The hodag, however, has taken on a dimension that those jokesters probably never imagined, from being the name of the high school mascot to becoming statues on the roofs of restaurants.

RHINELANDER LOGGING MUSEUM (ages 10 and up)

Pioneer Park, Oneida Avenue and Kemp Street (downtown); (715) 369– 5004. Open 10:00 A.M. to 5:00 P.M. from mid-May through mid-September.

The city's woodsy history is exemplified at the Rhinelander Logging Museum. This reproduction of a nineteenth-century logging camp is complete with appropriately costumed interpreters. They tell about the rugged life in the forests, show off original equipment, and describe all the personalities who opened the North Woods to development. Also on the grounds is an 1879 narrow-gauge railroad engine, a rural school, and Civilian Conservation Corps museum, as well as a Soo Line depot.

RHINELANDER PAPER COMPANY (ages 12 and up)

West Davenport Street; (715) 369–4100. Open for tours Tuesday through Friday 10:00 and 11:00 A.M. and 1:30 and 2:30 P.M. No children under twelve.

On a more contemporary level, tours are available at the Rhinelander Paper Company plant between June and August. Guides show how wood pulp and other wood products are made. There is also a self-guided, 17-mile-long, two-hour tour of the company's "industrial forest." The first stop is the company's pine seedling greenhouse on U.S. Highway 8 near Monico. Then drive past the 95,000-acre forest to see modern forest logging and preservation practices. The lands are open to the public and offer hiking and ski trails.

Rhinelander-Area Beaches

- **Buck Lake.** This is a great public beach 3 miles south of Rhinelander on County Highway C. Turn right on Lassig Road, then take another right on Hixon Lake Road and follow the brown signs. The lake is in the Almon Recreation Area.

- **Hodag Park.** The park is off Thayer Street in downtown Rhinelander.

- **Lake George.** The lake is easily reached 5 miles east of Rhinelander on U.S. Highway 8. Turn left on East Lake George Road and go ½ mile. The beach is on the left.

- **Town Line Lake.** Go north of Rhinelander 2 miles on State Highway 47, turn left on County Highway K. After ½ mile, you'll see the the lake on the right.

Places to Eat

Bernie's Bakery & Deli. *151 Brown Street; (715) 365–3355.* Danger zone! Don't say you weren't warned about Bernie's. Check your calorie counters at the door, podner. Sugar, frosting, butter—well, winter is coming, and we all need some extra layers for protection. $

Peking Chinese Restaurant. *825 Lincoln Street; (715) 369–1556.* Tired of burgers, mosquitoes, and burnt marshmallows? Go inside for fried rice and more from a grand assortment of Cantonese, Mandarin, and Szechuan munchies. $$

Rhinelander Cafe & Pub. *Downtown Rhinelander, adjacent to the J. C. Penney building at 33 North Brown Street; (715) 362–2918.* The restaurant has been serving American food to North Woods vacationers since the turn of the twentieth century. $$

Places to Stay

There are dozens of resorts, campgrounds, motels, and other lodging possibilities in a variety of price ranges throughout the Rhinelander area. A few of the top lodgings are listed here.

Holiday Acres. *South Shore Drive on Lake Thompson 4 miles east of Rhinelander (take State Highway 8 and follow signs); (715) 369–1500.* Operated by the Zambon family, the resort won the Wisconsin Innkeepers property of the year award in 1988. Its standards have remained high. There are twenty-eight motor-lodge rooms and thirty cottages, dining room, cocktail lounge, coffee shop, and jazz shows on weekends. Holiday Acres is on Lake Thompson. $$$

Miller's Shorewood Vista. *4239 West Lake George Road; (715) 362–4818.* The resort has get-acquainted specials as well as preseason deals with an American Plan. Three tennis courts, shuffleboard, and ping-pong augment the outdoor sports. Pets are allowed if leashed. $$$

Three G's Resort. *4134 Business 8 East; (715) 362–3737.* The resort is tucked into a bay on Lake George. There are one- to five-bedroom cottages as well as a fieldstone lodge with three baths, five bedrooms, family room, fireplace, and private two-acre lakefront adjacent to the resort. $$$

For More Information

Oneida County Visitors Bureau, *450 West Kemp, P.O. Box 795, Rhinelander, WI 54501; (800) 236–3006; www.oneidacountry-WI.org.*

More Things to Do in Oneida County

- **Min-Aqua Bat Water Ski Show,** downtown Minocqua in the Aqua Bowl. Wednesday and Friday at 7:00 P.M., mid-June through mid-August.

- **Hodag Water Ski Show at Hodag Park,** Rhinelander. Thursday at 7:30 P.M., mid-June through mid-August.

- **Free summer music concerts.** A different band plays each week on Thursday at 7:00 to 8:30 P.M. at the First Financial Bank drive-in. Call (715) 362–7157 for information.

- **World Championship Snowshoe Baseball.** Thursday at 7:00 P.M. from the end of June through August. Call (715) 277–2602 for details.

- **Rhinelander Knights of Columbus Fish Buffet,** 5490 Riverview Drive, Rhinelander. Friday from 5:00 to 8:00 P.M. through the summer. Call (715) 362–2768.

Wausau

Wausau is 58 miles south of Rhinelander. From Rhinelander, take U.S. Highway 8 to U.S. Highway 51. Turn south and go through Tomahawk, Irma, and Merill. Wausau is next.

Originally called Big Bull Falls, Wausau's name was changed in 1850 when a local businessman thought the Indian term for "far away" had more of an exotic ring than its former handle. This Marathon County city went into its adolescence in Wisconsin's logging boom that followed the Civil War. Today it is one of the major metro areas of northern Wisconsin, with its paper

Amazing Wisconsin Facts Wisconsin has forty-seven state parks, ten state forests, and twenty-four state trails. For information on the park and forest system, contact the Wisconsin Division of Tourism, P.O. Box 7606, Madison, WI 53707 (800–372–2737 or 800–432–TRIP).

factories, shopping malls, and recreational opportunities. While those 150 years or so of urban growth may seem impressive, consider the age of the surrounding geological landscape.

RIB MOUNTAIN STATE PARK (ages 10 and up)

Take U.S. Highway 51 to County Highway N to the park entrance. A state-park sticker is required; (715) 842–2522. Open daily year-round.

Rib Mountain, which overlooks the city on its west side, is estimated to be one billion years old. Surviving the crunch of the Ice Age, which flattened most of the neighborhood under its refrigerator grip, the mountain remains the third highest point in the state at 1,940 feet. Only 12 feet behind the front runner (Timm's Hill in nearby Price County), Rib Mountain is still tops for the longest downhill ski runs in the upper Midwest. An observation tower at the peak provides an amazing view for miles around, and the kids can almost see forever on a clear day. The mountain is now a state park with camping, hiking, and mountain biking, along with winter skiing.

The Arts in Wausau

Wausau's **Artrageous Weekend,** held in early September, features a festival of arts on the downtown pedestrian mall. More than one hundred juried artists represent a variety of media from glass to graphics and everything in between. Many of the artists demonstrate their production processes. There is also a hands-on area for children that gives them the chance to "throw" a pot, paint, and work with clay. There is no need to go hungry either because dozens of local restaurants and ethnic organizations set up booths along the brick- and tree-lined mall, serving everything from the standard burger to more exotic fare from the Far East, Latin America, and Europe.

In the city's Marathon Park, which is located between Twelfth and Seventeenth Avenues on the west side of the Wisconsin River, the Wisconsin Valley Art Association sponsors *Art in the Park.* This is a permanent exhibit where 130 artists who specialize in woodcuts, weaving, stained glass, and other crafts show off their wares.

For more information on the Artrageous Weekend, contact the Wausau Area Convention and Visitors Bureau at (888) 948–4748.

HSU'S GINSENG GARDEN (ages 10 and up)

Located on County Highway W, about 5 miles north of Wausau; (715) 675–2325. Tours by appointment only.

While driving along the side roads of the county, motorists often wonder about the racks of wooden frames either covered by netting or slates that shade the ground. These are growing beds for ginseng, an herb highly treasured by Oriental cultures for its curative potency. Wisconsin is the world's largest producer of the weirdly shaped root, with buyers from China, Korea, Japan, and other Asian nations making Wausau a center of the ginseng-buying world. Tours of one farm can be arranged in advance by calling Hsu's Ginseng Garden.

Wheeling Around Wausau Other opportunities abound for outdoor fun in the Wausau vicinity. Loops northwest of Wausau originate from the city's Marathon Park, taking a cyclist on runs from 6 to 36 miles long. Rides to the southwest side of the city begin at Bluegill Park and meander through town toward Rib Mountain, ranging from 12 to 35 miles. You can ride alone, with the family, or with the Wausau Wheelers Bicycle Club, which sponsors weekly rides.

The club also sponsors workshops, seminars, weeknight rides, tours, and racing events. On the menu each year is the Spin into Spring Ride and Spring Mountain Bike Ride in May; Hammerdown Tour, June; Fat Tire & Flat Footed Biathlon, July; Tour of the Eau Claire River Dells Century Ride, August; and Gear Grinder Classic and Fall Mountain Bike Tour, September. With all this pumping, is it any wonder that Wausau folks have husky thighs and calves? For more information write the Wausau Wheelers Bicycle Club, P.O. Box 138, Wausau, WI 55402-1381.

LEIGH YAWKEY WOODSEN ART MUSEUM (ages 10 and up)
North Twelfth Street, Wausau; (715) 845–7010. Open year-round Tuesday through Friday from 9:00 A.M. to 4:00 P.M. and Saturday and Sunday from 12:00 to 5:00 P.M. **Free**.

At the Leigh Yawkey Woodsen Art Museum, the annual *Birds in Art* exhibit brings together one hundred noted wildlife painters and sculptors the weekend after Labor Day. The museum is a fancy old mansion that was once the home of an old-time lumberman. Tell the kids the place is for the birds, and they'll get into the swing of things. Usually, a master artist such as Richard Sloan will present a lecture during festival time.

NINE-MILE RECREATION AREA (ages 10 and up)
On Red Bud Road off County Highway North. Contact the Marathon County Forestry Department, 500 Forest Street, Wausau, WI 55401; (715) 693–3001.

The area around Wausau provides excellent mountain biking opportunities for daredevil dads, moms, and gang. Nine-Mile Recreation Area is a maze of logging roads that are used as hiking and mountain-bike paths in the summer and cross-country ski runs in the winter. None of the paths are marked only for bikers, so riders should be aware of hikers. So whether by foot or pedal power, the dips and ridges of the heavily forested region are challenging (this is especially true in the mud, which the kids will absolutely *love*). Trail maps are necessary so you don't get lost.

Wausau-Area Cross-Country Skiing

In the winter, the Wausau region is a skiing paradise.

The **Nine-Mile Recreation Area** is tops, with 19 miles of loops kicking off from a ski lodge that offers rentals and instructions (715–693–5844). Season and day passes are required.

Big Eau Pleine Park Trail loops for 7 miles on machine-set double tracks on a peninsula of a county park of the same name. Take State Highway 153, 7½ miles west of U.S. Highway 51 (the Mosinee exit). Turn south on Big Eau Pleine Park Road and follow it 3½ miles to the park entrance. Continue in the park 1 mile to a parking area on the left side.

The **Sylvan Hill/American Legion Trail** is frequently groomed and is adequate for beginners and intermediates. The lane swoops along the hills of the American Legion Golf Course hills, located on the northeast side of Wausau.

DELLS OF THE EAU CLAIRE PARK (all ages)

Drive 15 miles east from Wausau on State Highway 29 and turn north on County Highway Y at the village of Hatley. Go 7 miles to the first park entrance. An alternative route is via County Z east from Wausau's north side to Highway Y, where the park entrance is only 1 mile to the left. The second park entrance is ¼ mile up the road. The park is open between May 1 and October 31. Except for registered campers, the area closes at 11:00 P.M.

Take time to relax once in awhile. The best place in Marathon County for a leisurely picnic is at the Dells of the Eau Claire. The term *dells* does not refer to the "farmer in the . . . " but is a corruption of a French word, *dalles,* which means "gorge." Ancient volcanic rock was eroded by the Eau Claire River over the eons to form fantastic shapes. Several hiking trails through the park eventually lead to the river, which still bubbles and foams around the base of the massive stones. One of the paths leads over a dam from the forest on the south side of the river to a camping/swimming area on the north. Swimming below the dam is not recommended because of the rocks and current. In fact, signs warn of the danger, so stick to the approved dunking site well upriver. Potholes in the cliffs, formed by rocks swirled around by glacial runoff, can be seen along the riverbanks festooned with wildflowers.

More Things to See and Do in Wausau

JANUARY
Wausau Curling Club, Marathon Park. Fans of this Scottish sport use a broom to push a "stone" down an ice aisle in attempt to touch a special marker and score points.

FEBRUARY
Candlelight snowshoe walks, Rib Mountain State Park. Nighttime schlepping in the snow adds extra excitement to an outing.

MARCH
Hockey, Marathon Park Multi-Purpose Building. Cheer and applaud for the locals.

APRIL
Children's Festival, Wausau West High School Fieldhouse. Sports, games, and activities for youngsters make this fest a special event.

MAY
Musical productions, Grand Theater. There's nothing like a night out on the town.

JUNE
June Dairy Kick-Off all-you-can-eat dairy breakfast, Marathon Park. Ham 'n' eggs in the outdoors. What a way to greet the day!

JULY
Wisconsin Valley Fair, Marathon Park. Kick tractor tires. Munch corn dogs. Check out the pigs. Admire the rabbits. This is fair time.

AUGUST
YMCA Wausau Triathlon, Sunnyvale Park. Run, bike, and swim. But be sure you are in shape.

SEPTEMBER
Wausau Festival of the Arts, downtown Wausau Pedestrian Mall. Purchase a painting.

OCTOBER
Ice Age Trail Hikeathon, Dells of the Eau Claire County Park. Wander where mastadons once roamed.

NOVEMBER
Annual Marathon Craft Show, Marathon Area Elementary School. Pick up a little something for Aunt Tessie or Grandma.

DECEMBER
Twelve Days of Christmas, downtown Wausau. Ho-ho-ho your way through town for loads of shopping bargains.

Places to Eat

Back When Cafe. *606 Third Street; (715) 848–5668.* Remember the days when food meant Grandma in the kitchen serving up her world-famous blue-plate special? Oh, you don't recall that? Don't worry, the Back When will take you to a place where hearty food is just as delicious today. Ask for pie. $$

Blue Willow Cafe. *1111 North Fourth Avenue; (715) 675–4543.* Simple eats . . . good and fresh. What more do you need on a trek into the back country? $

Carmelo's Italian Restaurant. *3607 North Mountain Road; (715) 845–5570.* When our taste buds roar for pasta satisfaction, Carmelo's fulfills our needs for rich sauce and oodles of noo-dles. $$.

Lozzo's Italian Food. *3115 Camp Phillips Road; (715) 848–2202.* Okay, so more spaghetti? You bet. Lozzo's does things with pasta that would make the Romans jealous. Tuck a napkin into your shirt collar and dig in. $$

For More Information

Wausau Area Convention and Visitors Council, *Box 6190, Wausau, WI 54402-6190; (888) 948–4748 or (715) 355–8788.*

Wisconsin Valley Art Association, *c/o Marathon County Parks Department, 500 Forest Street, Wausau, WI 54403; (715) 261–1570.*

Laona

To get to Laona from Wausau, head east 20 miles on State Highway 52 to U.S. Highway 45, turn north, and drive 10 miles to pick up State Highway 52 again. Take 51 and go about 40 miles north to Laona.

LUMBERJACK SPECIAL & CAMP FIVE MUSEUM & ECOLOGY COMPLEX (ages 5 and up)

R.F.D. 1, U.S. Highway 8, and State Highway 32, Laona; (715) 674–3414. Open mid-June through late August, train rides at 11:00 A.M., noon, and 1:00 and 2:00 P.M.; fall color tours, last Saturday in September through first Saturday in October.

The Lumberjack Special & Camp Five Museum & Ecology Complex is more than a simple highway crossing. It is a trip into the past, where kids can see huge stacks of cut timber and touch rough lumber. For decades, as the nineteenth century moved into the twentieth, the vast white-pine forests of northern Wisconsin gave up their treasures to the logging crews. Tens of thousands of board feet of wood fed the appetite of a growing America. No wonder Forest County got its name.

The Lumberjack Special, a 1916-era steam train, takes visitors from the Laona Depot through the woods to the Camp Five Museum Complex, where the tough life of the logging camp is highlighted. The museum features audiovisual exhibits, a working blacksmith shop complete with brawny smith and roaring forge, a harness-making shop, and a country store. Surrey rides through the woods are also available, as are pontoon-boat excursions on the nearby Red River.

Amazing Wisconsin Facts A divide running in an easterly-westerly direction slashes across northern Wisconsin. The rocky hills and ridges that can be found here separate the water that flows north to Lake Superior (Nemadji and Bad Rivers, among others) and those that meander south like the St. Croix River. A north-south line of hills divides the eastern third of the state from the western portion. Westward rivers, such as the Black and Wisconsin, flow into the Mississippi. The eastbound flowages aim toward Lake Michigan. These include the Fox, Peshtigo, and Milwaukee.

MOUNTAIN OPEN PITCHING TOURNAMENT (all ages)

One and one-half miles south of Mountain on State Highways 32 and 64, adjacent to the village community center. Call (715) 276–6041. **Free**.

"For the want of a shoe . . ." the old ditty goes. In horseshoe pitch, the want of a strong arm is needed. Especially during the first full weekend in August, when this tiny town hosts the Mountain Open Pitching Tournament. Rounds begin at 8:00 A.M. and end whenever the last clink is heard on Sunday. Several hundred pitchers gather from around the state, making it the largest such event in the region. There are several classes, accommodating teens to old-timers. Trophies and cash prizes are awarded to the winners. A baseball tournament and flea market complete the activities.

Shawano

After Laona, visit Shawano, which is 50 miles to the south. Take State Highway 52 south from Laona to State Highway 55, which will provide a straight run to Shawano.

SHAWANO'S HERITAGE PARK (all ages)

On Wolf River Pond at the north end of Franklin Street in Shawano; (800) 235–8528. Tours are given from 1:30 to 4:30 P.M. Wednesday and Sunday, June through September.

Tucked into a bend of the roaring Wolf River at the dead end of Franklin Street is a cluster of restored historic structures that includes a country schoolhouse (stick the kids at their desks and help them recite the day's poetry lesson), barns and outbuildings, and a log cabin. Costumed interpreters help with all the background. Sunset Island next door has picnic shelters, a fishing dock, and boat ramp.

Spawning Sturgeon If a family is motoring through town anytime between mid-April through early May, Lake Michigan sturgeon can be seen on their spawning runs from Lake Winnebago up the Wolf River. The best place to watch the fish, some of which are 6 feet long, is from the observation platforms on the Shawano Dam on Richmond Street.

Places to Eat

The Daily Grind & More. *130 South Main Street; (715) 524–5958.* Great coffee and desserts make the Daily Grind a pick-me-up stopover. $

Main Cafe. *132 South Main Street; (715) 524–6240.* Come for breakfast, stay for lunch, and hang around for dinner. $

Torch Lite. *1276 East Green Bay Street; (715) 526–5680.* Wash the kids behind the ears and take them to the Torch Lite for some fine dining, a far cry from camp cooking. Best behavior, now. $$

For More Information

Shawano Area Chamber of Commerce, *1413 East Green Bay Street, Shawano, WI 54166-0038; (715) 524–2139 or (800) 235–8528.*

Hit the Water

The Wolf is one of the better Wisconsin rivers for **canoeing, kayaking, and rafting.** Plenty of white water means that life jackets and helmets are absolute necessities, so some stretches of the river would be inappropriate for very little youngsters. Older kids, however, would have a wonderfully wet field day on any such excursion. Don't forget the Red River near Gresham, either. That one is for kayakers and white-water canoeists. The toughest is the Red, especially between the Gresham dam to Zlemer's Falls. This is rugged enough that the American Canoe Association has held its downriver and slalom races here.

Numerous outfitters along the river offer tours, rentals, and equipment:

- **Shotgun Eddy,** N2797 Highway 55 and W, White Lake, WI 54491; (715) 882–4461 or (414) 494–3782. Twenty-five miles north of Shawano.

- **Jim and Mary Ann Stecher, River Forest Rafts,** White Lake, WI 54491; (715) 882–3351 or (813) 481–6365. Four miles north of Shotgun Eddy Rapids, 30 miles north of Shawano on Highway 55.

- **Herb's Wolf River Rafting,** N2580 Highway 55, White Lake, WI 54491; (715) 882–8611 or (715) 882–8612. Twenty miles north of Shawano.

Clintonville

To get to Clintonville from Shawano, take State Highway 22 south 14 miles.

Loads of activities are always going on in Clintonville. The Winter Whirl, a family-oriented winter celebration on the last weekend in January, includes a bowling and pizza party and chili cookoff. Leaping ahead to the first weekend in June, there's the Classic Wheels and Wings Show, an air show at the Clintonville Municipal Airport. On the third weekend in August, the city hosts a Civil War encampment and skirmish.

FOUR-WHEEL DRIVE MUSEUM (ages 5 and up)

Eleventh Street, Clintonville; (715) 823–2141. Open Saturday and Sunday afternoons from Memorial Day through Labor Day.

Anyone into muscle machines will love meandering through the Four-Wheel Drive Museum in Clintonville, the town where the first 4x4 was engineered in 1908. Built to get through the area's thick forest-lands, whether in mud or snow, the original vehicles are among a collection of high-powered trucks, tractors, and other vehicles that can withstand almost any terrain.

PIONEER PARK (ages 5 and up)

Open Sunday and holidays 1:00 to 4:00 P.M. from Memorial Day to Labor Day. **Free**.

Vacations are a time for rock collecting, but don't try to walk off with a section of the Great Wall of China, which is among the stones gathered from around the world and exhibited in the town's Pioneer Park. Rocks from Jerusalem, Yellowstone National Park, the Dakota Badlands, and Arizona's Petrified Forest are among the pieces on display.

For More Information

Clintonville Area Chamber of Commerce, *18 South Main Street, Clintonville, WI 54929; (715) 823–4606.* Open 9:00 A.M. to 5:00 P.M. Monday through Friday.

Iola

If you see a line of old cars leaving Clintonville, they are probably on their way to Iola. Drive south from Clintonville on U.S. 45. Turn west on State Highway 22 and pick up State Highway 161 at Symco. From here, it is just another 11 miles or so.

IOLA OLD CAR SHOW AND SWAP MEET (ages 10 and up)

The car show is held at a site ¼ mile east of Iola on State Highway 161; watch for signs. First weekend after the Fourth of July. Call (715) 445–4000.

The annual Iola Old Car Show and Swap Meet is considered one of the largest such antique auto shows in the world. As many as 2,500 flivvers flock to the event, which attracts 100,000 people. Collectors in the family can pick up hubcaps, crank handles, rumble seats, hood ornaments, steering wheels, transmissions, and, of course, entire cars. So no one becomes lost, be sure to set a meeting time and place for the kids, who naturally want to scoot around the grounds on their own to check out tailpipes and ignition systems.

Places to Eat

Crystal Cafe. *126 Main Street; (715)*
445–9227. This is food like Mom used
to fix. Eggs over easy and strong, black
coffee will set your day off right. $

New London

New London is only 9 miles south of Clintonville on U.S. 45.

WOLF RIVER TRIPS AND CAMPGROUND (all ages)

*Two miles west of New London. Take County Highway X west from New London or
County Highway X east from Weyauwega. Either way, travelers are not far off highways Wisconsin 54, Wisconsin 110, U.S. 45, or Wisconsin 22. Floaters can take
as many trips as they can cram in between 9:00 A.M. and 5:00 P.M. daily during
the summer. Rental rates are generally higher on Friday, Saturday, and Sunday
($6.00, plus $1.00 deposit) than on weekdays ($5.00, plus $1.00 deposit). Call
(920) 982–2458.*

"A-tubing we will go, a-tubing we will go. Hi, ho, the derry-o, a-tubing
we will go." Okay, so the song isn't much, but the fun is there. The
smooth flowage of the Wolf River is great for a leisurely float trip on a
hot summer afternoon (just bring sunscreen lotion, because the sun
reflecting from the water can make for fiery pink skin). One of Wisconsin's finest river beaches for tube launching, canoeing, and swimming is
found at Wolf River Trips and Campground.

There is a definite tubing technique that sets the tyros apart from
the pros. To make it into the upper echelons from the lower ranks, take
this advice: Toss the tube into the water, yell, jump into the tube, bob
around to get used to the cool water, then start drifting downstream.
Sounds easy enough, right? It's the yelling and amount of bobbing that
makes the difference. Wolf River makes sure moms and dads won't have
to worry about kids because life preservers are provided for the smaller
floaters. A 𝓕𝓻𝓮𝓮 shuttle picks up drifters several miles down river.

The property also has canoes for more of a frontier experience;
excursions run from 9:00 A.M. to 4:00 P.M. daily, including two-hour,
four-hour, and one-day expeditions wiggling their way south from the
campgrounds. The Wolf is as curvy as Dolly Parton, so some amount of

steering and paddling is necessary. Beginners can have just as much fun as old hands, though. Float fishing is allowed.

After all that whooping on the river, suntanned (burned) families appreciate easing into the cool, dim interiors of the Pine Tree, Rainbow, or any of the other supper clubs throughout the New London vicinity. Afterward, campers at Wolf River can take in shuffleboard, horseshoes, tennis, swimming in the river, volleyball, and softball. It's enough to have vacationers return home for a rest.

Symco

Visiting Symco from New London is a breeze. Simply travel west on State Highway 54, turn north on State Highway 22, and go 11 miles.

German settlers established this tiny community, which is located 15 miles north of Waupaca, 11 miles east of Iola, and 2 miles north of Manawa on State Highway 22. Originally called Unionville, the village makes a point of being in the dead center of the township of Union, Waupaca County.

THRESHEREE (ages 5 and up)
Call the Manawa city hall at (920) 596–2577 for dates.

Explicit directions are not needed each July, when the noise coming from town is enough of a directional pull. Symco's claim to fame is its annual Thresheree. Old steam engines, threshing demonstrations, and an antique tractor pull provide enough screeching, roaring, smoke, grease, and dust to delight any kid who loves to play with toy tools and trucks.

The Union Threshermen, a group of collectors of the huffing, puffing, old-time machinery, can answer all sorts of questions about boilers, steam pressure, turn-of-the-twentieth-century harvesting techniques, and the superiority of one muscular tractor line over another. There are usually a few side bets whether Case will win out over John Deere.

FERG'S BAVARIAN VILLAGE (all ages)
Five miles north of Symco, 1 mile west of the intersection of State Highways 110 and 22, just off 161. Christmas display is lighted from dusk until 10:00 P.M. Thanksgiving through Christmas. The lights are left on until 1:00 A.M. on Christmas Eve for any wide-eyed kid still awake. Call (920) 596–2946.

On a quieter note, the Bavarian Village puts up a three-acre lighted Christmas display each year. Get the toddlers to count the amazing number of cut-out camels marching across the wintery Wisconsin land-scape.

The Ferg Haus Inn bed-and-breakfast on the property is operated by Lloyd and Sherley Ferg. In keeping with the German theme, the Fergs also operate the Alpen Haus Gift Shop and the Adelweiss Beer Garden.

Manawa

To reach Manawa, return south on State Highway 22.

MID-WESTERN RODEO (ages 5 and up)
The rodeo grounds are on a sixteen-and-a-half-acre site in southwest Manawa. Held annually on Fourth of July weekend.

Although Manawa was established by lumbermen and evolved into an agricultural center, the folks who live in Manawa are enamored of all things having to do with the Wild West. On Fourth of July weekend, Manawa plays host to the annual Mid-Western Rodeo, which went into its fortieth year in 1998. Sanctioned by the Professional Rodeo Cowboys Association, the three-day hee-haw includes bareback and saddle bronc riding, calf roping, steer wrestling, bull riding, team roping, and girls' barrel racing. Competitors come from around the country and Canada, eyeing the almost $10,000 in cash prizes for the cowpokes who can make the time limit.

Visitors cheer for their favorite cowgirls in the Miss Rodeo Wisconsin Pageant, sponsored by the Manawa Lions Club, and take in the parade that kicks off the festivities. There are also Free dances (for all ages) on the Friday and Saturday nights of the rodeo weekend, a chicken barbecue, prize drawings, and pony rides.

Places to Eat

John's Steak House. *960 Depot Street; (920) 596–2811.* The name says it all. Vegetarians can eat salad. $$

For More Information

Manawa Chamber of Commerce, *431 South Bridge (P.O. Box 308), Manawa, WI 54949-0221; (920) 596–2495.*

Waupaca

Waupaca is 21 miles south of Manawa on State Highway 22. Waupaca County, which is in the heart of Wisconsin, has 759 square miles of woods, 240 lakes, 79 rivers, and 35 trout streams.

J. R.'S SPORTSMAN'S BAR AND CHILDREN'S ZOO (all ages)

J. R.'s is ⅛ mile west of U.S. Highway 10 on State Highway 54. Open 9:00 A.M. to 8:00 P.M. daily from Memorial Day to Labor Day. Call (715) 258–9605 or (414) 295–3007 in the off-season.

J. R.'s Sportsman's Bar and Children's Zoo has more than thirty species of critters and birds, while the bar has dozens of mounted animals, including an amazing thirty-two-point buck. Sensitive kids might question the why of that particular display, especially after touring the zoo with its live residents; parents should be prepared to answer questions.

TOM THUMB MINIATURE GOLF (ages 5 and up)

N2494 Whispering Pines Road; (715) 258–8737.

Tom Thumb Miniature Golf is tucked into the scenic Chain of Lakes area about 3 miles west of Waupaca on County Highway Q. The course features eighteen interesting hazards themed around fairy tales.

DING'S DOCK (ages 5 and up)

N2498 West Columbian Lake Drive; (715) 258–2612. To get to Ding's, take State Highway 22 to County Highway Q. Then go east about 3 miles. Open April through autumn.

Ding's Dock canoe trips journey down the calm, 3-foot-deep Crystal River, which comes off what is called Wisconsin's Chain of Lakes. From the air, the string of beautiful blue water looks like a necklace tossed into the forest. Canoeists first take a larger excursion boat on Columbia Lake, chug through Long Lake, and eventually arrive at the mouth of Crystal River, where they pick up their smaller two-person craft. A canoeing expedition takes about three hours and is not recommended for kids under six years although older kids could easily make the trip. The Crystal meanders east and south through bright green timberland and Holstein-filled pastures to conclude at a pickup location. Don't worry about being abandoned—contemporary *voyageurs* are always rescued by a bus that will take them back to their cars.

For some indoor fun, **Indian Crossings Casino and Entertainment Center** is also located at Ding's Dock. Originally a dance hall, the old roadhouse used to feature touring big bands during the 1920s and 1930s. Today, after a canoe excursion, visitors wolf down burgers and fries and play pinball there. Through the summer, teen dances are held at least twice a month with live bands or DJs.

HARTMAN CREEK STATE PARK (all ages)

N2480 Hartman Creek Road; (715) 258–2372. Motor-vehicle admission sticker required year-round.

Follow a state-designated Scenic Rural Road 6 miles to the northwest from Waupaca to Hartman Creek State Park. The park has more than 1,300 acres of forestland, beaches, and picnic areas. Winter fans love the 10 miles of groomed snowmobile tracks, while summer lovers can stroll the 17 miles of marked hiking trails. State rangers also give guided hikes and evening nature programs at Hartman Creek during the height of off-school vacation season.

Picnicking

- **Brainards Bridge Park.** On the Waupaca River at North Bailey Street. There is a shelter house, fishing, canoe access, grills, and playground.

- **Lions Park.** On the Waupaca River, east of North Main Street, off Division Street. Playground and fishing are popular diversions.

- **Oakwood Park.** Located at an ancient Native American crossing on the Chain o' Lakes on County Highway Q. Grills, playground, and hiking trails available.

- **South Park.** On Mirror and Shadow Lakes at the south end of Main Street. Shelter house, swimming beach, bathhouse, fishing dock, grills, and boat landing.

Places to Eat

Foxfire Golf Club. *215 Foxfire Drive; (715) 256–1700.* After eighteen holes, a shower, and a couple of lemonades, you probably feel hungry enough to eat a North Woods bear. Well, come on in, sit down, and relax. Elegant dining. $$.

Simpson's Restaurant. *222 South Main Street; (715) 258–2330.* TV's Bart Simpson is not working behind the cash register. So you can be sure that this comfortable family place will take care of all your culinary needs. And topped off with good desserts, too. $

Wheelhouse Restaurant. *State Highway Q at Indian Crossing; (715) 258–8289.* In the summer, eat outside on the deck overlooking the lakes. Live concerts are regularly scheduled. A pizza smorgasbord every Monday night is a guaranteed delight for anyone who likes to eat. The restaurant also makes it own soups. Adjacent to the Wheelhouse, Scoopers Ice Cream & Cookies is open for after-dinner treats from April to September. Ask the bartender to show how he sticks dollar bills to the ceiling way above his head. $$

Places to Stay

Thomas Pipe Inn. *11032 Pipe Road; Waupaca, WI 54981; (715) 824–3161.* Kids are usually welcome (but call first) in this Portage County landmark built in 1855. Four rooms are available in the building, which is a former stagecoach stop and is now on the National Register of Historic Places. $$

Green Fountain Inn. *604 South Main Street, Waupaca, WI 54981; (715) 258–5171.* Four rooms are open to guests, plus one cottage for getaways. The inn is decorated in a 1920s decor. $$

Rustic Woods Campground. *E2585 South Wood Drive, Waupaca, WI 54981; (715) 258–2442.* The campground has 70 miles of groomed snowmobile trails, as well as trout fishing, mini-golf, a game room, a swimming pool, and canoe rentals. There are more than fifty tent and RV sites. $$

For More Information

Waupaca County Chamber of Commerce, *c/o Parks and Recreation, 221 South Main Street, Waupaca, WI 54981; (715) 258–7343.*

King

King is 5 miles south of Waupaca on State Highway 22.

 ***CHIEF WAUPACA* OR *LADY OF THE LAKES* (ages 5 and up)**
Board at Clearwater Harbor in King, 2 miles southwest of Waupaca; (715) 258–2866.

A tour aboard the old sternwheeler *Chief Waupaca* or *Lady of the Lakes* on northeast Wisconsin's Chain of Lakes is a restful way to drift away an afternoon. *Chief Waupaca* was originally owned by Chief Oshkosh Brewery as a floating palace for company management and their guests. Kids can pretend they are Mark Twain, riding the waters into adventure.

Places to Eat

King's Table Restaurant. *County Highway QQ, King, WI 54946; (715) 258–9150.* A fish boil is held every Friday throughout the summer, where whitefish, potatoes, and onions are boiled in a huge outside kettle. A complete Mexican menu is offered seven days a week, or take carry-out chicken. The restaurant's jumbo cinnamon rolls must be the size of an eighteen-wheeler semi. Ahhhh, good. $$

Wautoma

From Waupaca, drive southwest on State Highway 22 to Wautoma.

 MH RANCH (all ages)
On County Highway Y, just off State Highway 22. Mailing address: Route 1, P.O. Box 398, Westfield, WI 53964; (608) 296–2171.

Kid-size horses graze in the fields at the MH Ranch, homestead of McHugh's Miniature Horses. McHugh's has some one hundred tiny horses, none of which are more than 34 inches tall. Equestrian-minded tykes, therefore, can almost see eye-to-eye with the miniatures. When born, the horses only weigh about 13 pounds and are 13 inches high. An exhibit hall shows off the dozens of trophies that the horses have won in shows around the country.

Oshkosh

To reach Oshkosh, drive east 40 miles on State Highway 21.

 PRIME OUTLETS (ages 10 and up)
3001 South Washburn Street; (920) 231–8911.

Yes, Oshkosh is the home of the big B'Gosh, the casual clothing manufacturer whose brand name is famous around the world. Parents with an eye on the budget can stop at the 230,000-square-foot

Oshkosh B'Gosh factory outlet, the Oshkosh B'Gosh Superstore (920–231-3134). Clothes there range from the traditional striped coveralls to toddlers' wear. Another sixty stores in the mall provide innumerable choices in which to roam.

 ### EAA AIR ADVENTURE MUSEUM (ages 10 and up)
Poberezny Road; (920) 426–4818. Easily accessible off U.S. Highway 41. For a landmark, look for the Sabre jet on its pedestal near the exit from the highway.

The EAA Air Adventure Museum shows the progress made in air transportation over the years. Each summer, the EAA stages the largest "fly-in" in the world, with hundreds of planes coming and going like so many gnats. The planes range from the supersonic Concorde to home-made lighter-than-air devices that look as though they can't get off the ground. In 1994, celebrating the twenty-fifth anniversary of the U.S. space program, several dozen astronauts, including many of the original contingent of spacemen, were on hand to meet the crowds. Workshops and lectures round out the program for the thousands of guests who come to admire the civilian and military aircraft that come from around the world.

Places to Eat

Butch's Anchor Inn. *225 West Twenti-eth Avenue; (920) 232–3742.* Steak, pasta, and seafood grace the menu. Amid gurgling fish tanks, Chef Butch Arps displays his large collection of sailing memorabilia. Try the Treasure Island buffet for a great treat. $$

The Granary Restaurant. *50 West Sixth Avenue; (920) 233–3929.* The restaurant is located in a restored nineteenth-century stone flour mill. A fantastic staircase leads up to a bal-cony dining room. There is a children's menu, but hearty eaters go for the Alaskan king crab, Australian lobster, and Canadian scallops. Country-western, folk, and jazz are regularly per-formed. $$

Robbins. *1810 Omro Road; (920) 235–2840.* Go for the homemade sausage on the Bavarian Plate, a tradi-tion since the restaurant opened in 1928. Robbins is heavy on German food, with Wiener schnitzel, potato dumplings, and smoked pork chops. Remember, it's cheaper than taking the kids to Berlin. $$

Wisconsin Farms. *2450 Washburn; (920) 233–7555.* Kids know this is the place. All they need to see is the herd of glass-fiber cows on the front lawn. Homemade cheesecake, burgers, soups, and steaks round out the menu. Take the youngsters into the gift shop that peddles items of a "cow" nature, from T-shirts to cow dolls.

Ripon

Ripon is quickly reached from Oshkosh by driving southwest 20 miles on State Highway 44.

LITTLE WHITE SCHOOLHOUSE (ages 10 and up)

Located on Blackburn Street, just down the hill from Ripon College; (920) 748–6764. Open for tours 10:00 A.M. to 4:00 P.M. Monday through Saturday and 10:00 A.M. to 4:00 P.M. Sunday, Memorial Day to Labor Day; 10:00 A.M. to 4:00 P.M. Saturday and 10:00 A.M. to 4:00 P.M. Sunday, October through May.

Personal voting preference and politics aside, take the kids to see the Little White Schoolhouse. The building is considered the birthplace of the Republican Party, which was organized in 1854. Some upstart communities outside Wisconsin have claimed the same honor, however. Naturally, Riponites pooh-pooh them as specious latecomers. If the building is closed, visitors can peek in the windows and see lots of pictures of bewhiskered old gents on the walls, plus party artifacts in glass display cases. The windows are low enough so Junior and Missy can even sneak a gander at this GOP gestation site.

FARMER'S DAUGHTER DAIRY FARM (ages 5 and up)

County Highway E to W12835 Locust Road; (920) 748–2146.

The Farmer's Daughter Dairy Farm gives the kids a prime opportunity to see a Guernsey up close (they are very large with very bony hip-behinds; ah, that's the cows, not necessarily the kids). For something "udder" to do at the Farmer's Daughter, hayrides are available.

LARSON'S FAMOUS CLYDESDALES (ages 5 and up)

Route 1, Reed's Corner Road; (920) 748–5466. The stable is open daily from May 1 through October 31. A 1:00 P.M. show is staged Monday through Saturday, with reservations required.

Larson's Famous Clydesdales is another chance to meet animals up close and to pet Clydesdale colts. Covered bleacher seats allow guests to watch a harness show in relative comfort, even on the hottest summer days. The huge horses are surprisingly light-footed as they go through their intricate paces. The Larson family also has a large collection of antique wagons and similar horse-drawn equipment.

Brandon

Brandon is just a 10-mile jump south of Ripon on State Highways 44/49.

WILLIE'S WILDLIFE FARM AND ZOO (ages 5 and up)

Take State Highway 49 west and north through Brandon, turn north to Sunny Knoll Road, and then go east to Willie's. Open from 9:30 A.M. to 5:30 P.M. daily from May 1 through November 1; (920) 346–2675.

Wille's Wildlife Farm and Zoo is a petter's paradise, with dozens of animals to stroke and snuggle. The facility also rents birds and animals to other zoos and for commercials and movies.

Green Lake

Take the circle route around Green Lake from Brandon to reach the city of Green Lake. Drive west on State Highway 44 about 18 miles to State Highway 73. Turn north and skirt the western edge of the lake to pick up State Highway 23. Turn back east and travel the 10 miles into town.

Green Lake is known as the "oldest resort community west of Niagara Falls." As early as 1867, folks were coming to the village to rest and recuperate from the rigors of big-city living. By the turn of the twentieth century, several large hotels were catering to the Chicago crowd and visitors from back East. They were drawn to the deep, clear lake, which is 7½ miles long and 2 miles wide. The waters still offer opportunities for boating, fishing, and swimming.

YACHTS OF FUN (all ages)

Heidel House, 643 Illinois Avenue; (920) 294–3344 or (800) 444–2812. Tours are given daily from June through August and on Saturday and Sunday in May, September, and October.

The 1,001-acre American Baptist Green Lake Center has extensive camping, swimming, and golfing options and is open to the public. While there, take a cruise on the *Yachts of Fun*. The excursion vessel is boarded from the Heidel House Resort docks (see Places to Stay, p. 36).

Places to Eat

Alfred's Supper Club. *506 Hill Street; (920) 294–3631.* For upscale eating, Alfred's is among those with the best ambience in the Green Lake region. And good food, too!

Hinky Dinks. *304 South Lawson Drive; (920) 294–3150.* Great place to drop by for a munch, lunch, or dinner. A real neighborhood place.

Little Corporal Restaurant, Ltd. *499 Hill Street; (920) 294–6772.* Marshall your forces, march right in, and have a grand time at the table.

Norton's Marine Dining Room. *380 South Lawson Drive; (920) 294–6577.* Norton's has an extensive menu with reasonable prices, so bring the munchkins.

Places to Stay

Green Lake Campground. *W2360 State Highway 23; (920) 294–3543. Located 1½ miles west of Green Lake.* The campground offers 365 shaded grass sites, full hook-up, electricity, and water. Included at the facility are a fishpond and a nine-hole, par-three golf course. $

Heidel House Resort and Conference Center. *643 Illinois Avenue; (920) 294–3344 or (800) 444–2812.* The resort overlooks Green Lake and offers rooms, suites, and separate buildings. There are indoor and outdoor pools in which the kids can splash, sauna and whirlpools, a fitness center, game room, and walking trail. While there is formal dining, don't worry about the kids; the resort offers plenty of opportunities for youngsters to enjoy themselves. $$$

McConnell Inn. *497 Lawson Drive (Box 639, Green Lake, WI 54941); (920) 294–6430.* Children over fifteen are welcome at the inn, which was built in 1900. Full breakfast starts off the day, followed by a dip in the lake across the street if one is athletically inclined. There are five bedrooms, and one suite has a Jacuzzi. A fireplace makes for snug winter getaways. $$

Montello

To reach Montello, drive west 20 miles from Green Lake on State Highway 23.

Once there, walk down the hill from the Marquette County courthouse, not far from the intersection of State Highway 23 and Park Street. Bring a camera, because there on the corner is Wisconsin's largest tree, a 138-foot-tall cottonwood. The trunk measures 23.2 feet. The city is also the home of the Montello Waterfall, at the corner of State Highways 22 and 23. The falls are adjacent to a red granite quarry that has provided rock for buildings and tombs around the world.

Fond du Lac

Backtrack 30 miles east to Fond du Lac from Montello via State Highway 23.

TALKING HOUSES (ages 5 and up)
Fond du Lac Information Center, 19 Scott Street; (920) 923–3010 or (800) 937–9123. The center has maps and details on how the system works.

The tykes will be amazed at Fond du Lac's Talking Houses. The city has prepared a neat tour around town; the car radio can pick up a special program that describes eleven of twenty-three historic sites. Driving slowly past the Victorian-era homes is a fun excursion, especially while on the way to **Lakeside Park** and a ride on the antique carousel there. Bike rentals and boat-launch ramps are in the park, too. Visitors can also climb the steps inside an old lighthouse for a look out over Lake Winnebago. At Christmas, the trees are decorated with thousands of glowing lights and dazzling ornaments that pick up the reflections in the snow.

FOND DU LAC LIGHTHOUSE (ages 5 and up)
At the north end of Main Street (State Highway 175) in Lakeside Park. Self-guided tours are available from 8:00 A.M. to dusk. Closed in winter.

The lighthouse was built in 1932, overlooking the rolling waters of Lake Winnebago. The structure is one of the most impressive lighthouses on the state's inland waters.

KRISTMAS KRINGLE SHOPPE, LTD. (ages 5 and up)
Exit U.S. Highway 41 at Main Street (Highway 175). 1330 South Main Street; (800) 937–9123.

The Shoppe has the state's largest collection of Christmas ornaments and seventy themed trees. Kids especially love the train displays, but everyone oohs and aahs over the displays of handicraft globes and figures from Italy, Bavaria, and other countries. Owners Grace and Jerry Mielke regularly travel overseas to pick up the best display items for their shop. As Jerry says, "My grandkids always love coming to visit the grandfolks." The Mielkes are always glad to tell the stories behind each piece. Ask about the ornamental pickles or the doll collectibles.

SCHREINER'S RESTAURANT (all ages)
Schreiner's is located at 168 North Pioneer Road, Fond du Lac; (920) 922–0590; www.fdchowder.com.

Anyone traveling to the North Woods knows about Schreiner's, the traditional midway stop between southern and northern Wisconsin for breakfast, lunch, or dinner since 1938. The restaurant, after being moved from several locations around Fond du Lac, is now located at the junction of U.S. Highway 41 and State Highway 23. Schreiner's is noted for its comfort food: chicken and dumplings, chowder, malts, home-made pie, and other goodies. Some of its staff have been on hand for twenty or more years. For a yearly dietary wrap-up in honor of the Dairy State, Schreiner's uses 4,100 gallons of milk, 3,000 pints of heavy whip-ping cream, 7,000 pounds of cottage cheese, plus 9,000 cups of butter a week. The place serves 600,000 persons a year, a testimony to its award-winning reputation. Current owner Paul F. Cunningham started work at Schreiner's as a busboy and dishwasher in his high-school days.

Cross-Country Skiing

Fond du Lac County has excellent cross-country ski opportunities. All are close to urban centers, so warmth is close at hand when chill-out occurs. For informa-tion on trails, contact the Fond du Lac Convention and Visitors Center (see For More Information, this page. Here are two of the best:

- **Eldorado Marsh Wildlife Area.** Take State Highway 23 west 4 miles from Fond du Lac. The 5,968-acre site is very primitive, with loops of varying lengths through the marsh. The area opens for skiing at 6:00 A.M. and closes at dusk.

- **Hobbs Woods Nature Study Area.** From U.S. Highway 41, take the west frontage road called Rolling Meadows Drive. Drive 1 mile to Hickory Road, then go south about 3½ miles. The area is open for skiing from 6:00 A.M. to 10:00 P.M.

For More Information

Fond du Lac Convention and Visitors Center, *19 Scott Street, Fond du Lac, WI 54935; (920) 923–3010 or (800) 937–9123.*

Horicon

The rural splendor of Horicon is straight south of Fond du Lac on State Highway 175, which parallels U.S. Highway 41. At Theresa, pick up State Highway 28 and meander down to Goose Country.

HORICON MARSH (all ages)

The area is administered by the Wisconsin Department of Natural Resources from its office at N7725 State Highway 28 in Horicon; (920) 387–7860. The marsh is also a National Wildlife Refuge, so the feds are involved, too. Their offices are at W4279 Headquarters Road in nearby Mayville; (920) 387–2658. Horicon Marsh's 31,653 acres are located in east-central Wisconsin. It is bordered on the south by State Highway 33, on the west by State Highway 26, on the north by State Highway 49, and the east by State Highway 28 and County Highways TW and Z. It is 13 miles west of U.S. Highway 41. For more information log onto www.horiconmarsh.com.

The best bullhead **fishing** in the state can be had at Horicon Marsh. Grassy banks lead to the water's edge, which also makes it a great spot for tiny first-time fisherfolk. **Canoeing** is another good way to get far back into the reeds and brush to **bird-watch,** fish for bass, and generally get away from the rush of daily life. You can put in near the John Deere Horicon Works plant on North Vine Street or in the parkland north of the bridge there.

The marsh comes most alive in autumn. Tens of thousands of Canada geese pause there each season on their way to goose condos farther south, far away from the upper Midwest's winter chill. The

- **Horicon Marsh Redhead Trail.** A 2½-mile loop that takes about two hours to hike. The parking area for the trail is on the north side of the marsh along State Highway 49. The trail can be boggy in the spring, so have the kids wear boots.

- **Marsh Haven Nature Center.** There are several loops at the facility, which is on State Highway 49 north of the marsh. Admission to the forty-seven-acre nonprofit center is $1.00. The site is great for watching yellow-winged blackbirds, Canada geese, and other birds. Call (920) 324– 5818 for details.

31,000-acre site is a veritable vacation resort for the feathered flocks as they zoom in overhead, honking and beeping in their V formations. Local farmers groan when the birds arrive, because they often take snack time in nearby cornfields. Yet watching the flocks is easy. Any road around the marsh is a prime viewing area. In fact, after awhile, the sheer numbers of birds can be overwhelming. Be sure to watch where you step if you get out of the car for a closer look. Goose droppings are large and stinky, not the thing to be smushed underfoot and carried back into the close confines of an auto.

To keep up the kids' interest, combine a **goose-counting tour** while looking for your **Halloween pumpkin.** After all, Halloween isn't far behind the southern flight of the geese, and the obligatory purchase of pumpkin, squash, and Indian corn is easier on the wallet earlier on in the season. Almost every farm has a wagonload of vegetable bounty on its front lawn just waiting for folks to buy up a dozen or so of the giant golden globes for jack-o'-lanterns.

BLUE HERON TOURS (ages 5 and up)

State Highway 33 at the bridge; (920) 485–2942. Tours are available from April through October, running at 2:00 P.M. daily from May through September and weekends only in October. Ask for the special heron and egret rookery tours for an extra punch. For more information log onto www.horiconmarsh.com.

The tours run into the marsh aboard houseboats, offering an up-close view of the watery haven for all sorts of wildlife.

Cycling the Wild Goose Trail

The easy, 34-mile-long Wild Goose Trail rolls over a crushed limestone-rock surface from State Highway 60 in the center of Dodge County to the south side of the city of Fond du Lac. The trail crosses State Highway 49 on the north side of Horicon Marsh, near the hiking trailhead. No trail fees are required, but donation boxes are posted along the route, so be generous. The money helps with trail upkeep.

Dundee

Leaving Goose Country behind, take State Highway 33 east to West Bend and turn north on U.S. Highway 45. The wide freeway ends at just south of Kewaskum, but proceed north for another 7 miles to Dundee.

HENRY W. REUSS ICE AGE INTERPRETIVE CENTER (all ages)
Campbellsport, WI 53010; (920) 533–8322. Five miles east of U.S. Highway 45 on State Highway 67.

The Henry W. Reuss Ice Age Interpretive Center is the hub of information on the glaciers that once held Wisconsin in their frosty grip. Part of the thousand-mile-long Ice Age Trail, the center has exhibits on how the rugged contemporary landscape was formed. Have the kids look out the huge picture windows at the center building and identify a *moraine,* a ridge of rubble that marked the end point of a glacier; or a *drumlin,* another geographical feature that is now topped by maples and pines. It might be difficult to encourage them to stretch leg muscles, but get the gang out on the trail to spot black-eyed Susans, feel the wind in their hair, and experience first-hand the living land. Reuss was a Wisconsin congressman who advocated the establishment of the trail and has subsequently worked tirelessly to ensure its completion.

Greenbush

Experience the rolling Kettle Moraine countryside on your way from Dundee to Greenbush. Take State Highway 67 north out of Dundee to County Road G. Turn east on State Highway 23, and you'll find Greenbush about 4 miles down the road.

WADE HOUSE STAGECOACH INN & WISCONSIN CARRIAGE MUSEUM (ages 5 and up)

W7747 Plank Road, P.O. Box 34, Greenbush, WI 53026; (920) 526–3271. Open 9:00 A.M. to 5:00 P.M., May 1 through October 31.

The Wisconsin State Historical Society operates the Wade House Stagecoach Inn & Wisconsin Carriage Museum, which takes guests back in time to the nineteenth century. Built in 1850, the refurbished Wade House, an old stagecoach inn, has three floors now open to the public. The nearby carriage museum has one hundred horse-drawn carts, wagons, sleds, and farm implements from generations past. A dirt road links the carriage museum to the Wade House; visitors are transported in a horse-drawn shuttle to keep them in the proper mood. A blacksmith shop and smokehouse are included in the outbuildings. Each September, Civil War reenactors fill the grounds and turn the entire site into a real-life camp. On a field behind the buildings, Union and Confederate forces stage mock battles, complete with cavalry charges, blasting cannons, and bayonet charges. The fighting takes place along an original sunken road and stone wall, reminiscent of many actual battles in the horrific War Between the States.

Crowds six to ten deep line the periphery of the action, which sometimes makes it hard for smaller kids to see. (Wiggly ones, though, could squirm through legs to the front of the audience for a better look.) Military encampments, with sutlers offering clothing, muskets, and other nineteenth-century items for sale, are nearby, where youngsters can talk with the reenactors about their uniforms and lifestyles.

Many take on the persona of actual soldiers, researching their lives and coming up with stories to tell guests about America of the mid-1800s. Their wives and youngsters scurry about in typical clothing of the era, in a real history lesson. It is a must that kids have cameras to record the "daily lives" of the participants, because the photographs make a fantastic show-and-tell. Be sure they ask lots of questions about why and how things were done more than a century before they were born.

Kohler

Kohler is about 17 miles east of Greenbush via State Highway 23. At the outskirts of Sheboygan are signs for Kohler at the intersection with State Highway 32. Kohler is about 4 miles south on 32.

KOHLER DESIGN CENTER (ages 10 and up)

101 Upper Road; (920) 457–3699. Tours all year. The center is open 9:00 A.M. to 5:00 P.M. Monday through Friday and 10:00 A.M. to 4:00 P.M. Saturday, Sunday, and holidays.

The most fun is to stroll through the main room, which showcases all the firm's latest bathroom technicalities: from bathtubs with side doors to climate-controlled booths for a sense-around sensation. Noted interior designers vie for the opportunity to showcase their work in a series of model rooms around the center, which demonstrate how fancy one's shower room can really be. Kids will get a kick out of the Great Wall of China, an intricate two-story-tall pattern made by multicolored toilet bowls.

Places to Eat

American Club. *Highland Drive, Kohler, WI 53044; (920) 457–8000.* The club is the only five-diamond resort property in Wisconsin, and it has all the accompanying amenities. Just before Thanksgiving, a chocolate-tasting party is

hosted at the American Club, present-
ing enough caloric delights to turn the
head of anyone within 20 miles who
has a sweet tooth. This latter event is
not kid-oriented, but it gives parents a
swishy night out on the town, with
glowing candles, glittering silver,
romantic music, and—why not—maybe
even an overnight getaway in a gra-
cious, spacious room with bath facilities rivaling those in a Kuwati palace.
There are several restaurants on-site,
with a range of prices. The most casual
for children is poolside in the health
club with excellent sandwiches and
soups. $$$$

52 Stafford, An Irish Guesthouse.
52 Stafford, Plymouth, WI 53073; (920)
893–0552. 52 Stafford is about 10
miles west of Kohler on State Highway
67 and features a more intimate getaway than the bigger American Club
resort. Rooms are named after Irish lit-
erary and political leaders, with regularly scheduled Irish music in the
downstairs bar. A restaurant is
attached. Hiking and cross-country ski-
ing opportunities are in the area. $$

Kohler Land

Kohler Land Home of the famous **Kohler Company,** whose
bathroom fixtures grace castles, airports, and residences around the
world, Kohler was originally a planned village for the company's work-
ers. Today, the main building, which once housed immigrant employees,
is now the American Club Resort. Black Wolf Run, one of the toughest
golf courses in the country, is adjacent to the American Club.

A short walk north of the Kohler Design Center, featuring the
company's products, is a mall emphasizing additional decoration and
construction elements for the home. These range from mosaics to
woodwork. Individual shops cater to highly refined tastes and to folks
who appreciate quality.

The Kohler Corporation also sponsors artists in a grant program, so
they can develop their skills in various media while working alongside
regular laborers. The resulting sculptures dot the Kohler Company fac-
tory and grounds. Even mistakes can be turned into a successful chal-
lenge at the plant. One artist made a cast-iron deer, but the sculpture's
back collapsed in the foundry. Rather than dump the piece, the artist
cut off the offending iron and made the rest of the deer into a life-size
charcoal grill. Have the kids look for the grizzly bear rearing up on its
hind legs.

The firm sponsors a real down-home Fourth of July, with rousing
band concerts that would make march composer John Philip Sousa
want to rise up again with his baton at the ready. Of course there are
fireworks, plenty of bunting and fluttering flags, and kids' activities to
round out the holiday.

Sheboygan

From Kohler, take State Highway 28 east into Sheboygan. The two cities are adjacent, so you can't go wrong.

 BRATWURST DAY (ages 5 and up)
For dates and details about Brat Day, contact the Sheboygan Area Convention & Visitors Bureau, 631 New York Avenue, Sheboygan, WI 53081; (920) 457–9495. First Saturday in August.

Here's a hint for getting along well in Sheboygan: Never, never ask for a wiener when you really mean a brat (and that is not the grumpy thirteen-year-old who just pounded her younger sister in the back of the van). The term is braaaaat, with a short "a." The difference between the two is akin to the difference between a gourmet meal and a bowl of dry corn flakes. Sheboygan is also home to Bratwurst Day in August. This is a real family festival, where the city's downtown tree-shaded Fountain Park hosts folk singers, hands-on crafts for kids, and tons of brats cooked over open fires. This picnic feast, held on the first Saturday in August, is not complete without roasted corn-on-the-cob and vanilla ice cream sundaes lathered with strawberries.

Let Junior try a **brat pizza** and Mom a **brat taco** while Dad and Sis stick to **traditional brats** hidden in their monster buns, dolloped with nose-tickling German mustard and layered with onions and/or sauerkraut. Out at Kiwanis Park, on the northwest side of town, nationally known musical entertainment, acrobats, elephant trainers, and clowns from Walker Brothers Circus put on $\mathcal{F}$ree shows. **Polka bands** do their foot-stomping, twirl-around routine, as well. True to the family nature of things, no beer is served downtown but is available at the outlying park.

A **parade along Main Street** kicks off Brat Day, where it seems everyone in town marches along, happily waving to friends. Participants include the county coroner, politicians of every stripe and party, kids on unicycles, grandmas on in-line skates, and donors to the Red Cross blood bank. Perch anywhere along the downtown route for the procession that sometimes lasts as long as two hours (little kids watching might become antsy). That's no time problem for most locals, though, because they know that plenty of brats await them at either park.

"We've never run out of brats," assert well-fed organizers from the sponsoring Jaycees. And even if there was ever a hint of such a calamity, the city is the home headquarters of the Johnsonville Sausage Company, which makes links by the tons every day.

JAYCEE PARK (ages 5 and up)

Sheboygan's north side off Business Highway 42; (920) 459–3366.

There is hardly anything better on a broiling summer day than to swoosh down the Aqua Avalanche water slide at Jaycee Park. Family fun in the park also includes fishing, boating, and a swimming beach. If the kids have already loaded up on brats, wait an hour to digest the goodies before attempting an Aqua-experience.

WISCONSIN STATE CHARTER FISHING ASSOCIATION (ages 8 and up)

Membership roster available from Doug Carlstrom, 1625 North Fourth Street, Sheboygan, WI 53081; (920) 459–7905.

Try a Lake Michigan charter-fishing jaunt in search of the elusive lake trout or giant German brown trout. Even little kids can have a heyday out on the waves. Everyone aboard gets a turn at hauling in a fish, as well. Be sure to ask if you need to pack a picnic lunch when contracting with a vessel. The rumble from empty young stomachs is disconcerting to fish. If there are enough fisherfolk in one family, rent the whole boat for a morning or afternoon cruise. Otherwise the captain will fill up a charter with other fishing fans. Sheboygan is a center for the state's charter fishing fleet, with dozens of qualified guides ready to help bring in the lunkers. To find a captain and crew, obtain a copy of the Wisconsin State Charter Fishing Association roster. There are some 150 members in the organization.

KOHLER-ANDRAE STATE PARKS (all ages)

1520 Old Park Road; (920) 451–4080. Open 6:00 A.M. to 11:00 P.M. year-round. State-park vehicle admission pass required.

The adjacent parks are only 4 miles south of Sheboygan, with a mile-long beach perfect for castle construction, loafing, volleyball, and burying Dad up to his chin in the sand. Nature lovers will want to know that the wind off Lake Michigan creates intricate dunes that seem to change almost daily. Public rest rooms, expanses of grass, and playing fields are on the bluff above the lake, and don't forget the charcoal for a picnic. Shuttles take swimmers down to the beach from a central parking lot on crowded days, so some patience is warranted. Bring a Frisbee to keep the kids occupied while waiting for a ride. A brisk stroll to the swimming area takes only about fifteen minutes, though. Give the loudest complainer the ice chest to carry.

Nature Walks

- **Black River Trail.** This trail is about 1½ miles north of Kohler-Andrae. On the trail's eastern rim is the Black River, separating the reserve from the private Kohler Company Wildlife Refuge. There are 2½ miles of trails off County Highway V.

- **Kohler Dunes Cordwalk.** This 2½-mile trek will take about two hours from the parking lot directly after the entrance near the Visitor Information Center. Or start behind the park office or from the group campsite to the south. The walk is fairly easy, even for little kids, as it moves up and down over the prehistoric dunes. Stick to the cordwalk because of the fragile ecosystem.

- **Plank Road Trail.** This trail follows a pioneer plank road for 17 miles west, from Sheboygan to near Greenbush, at the junction of State Highway 23 and Plank Road.

- **Woodland Dunes Nature Trail.** This 1½ mile, forty-five-minute jaunt strolls through heavily wooded areas near Lake Michigan. It begins just south of the park's campground area.

Places to Eat

Citystreets Restaurant. *712 Riverfront Drive; (920) 457–9050.* Cruise the city streets of Sheboygan and then pull into the Citystreets Restaurant for some great grub. Stay until the streets are empty that evening. $

Culvers. *641 South Taylor Drive; (920) 451–7150.* The kids will love the butter burgers and ice cream treats served up at one of the premier quick-food restaurants in the area. $

Ella's Dela Delicatessen & Restaurant. *1113 North Eighth Street; (920) 457–3034.* Ella sure knows how to throw together a fresh deli turkey sandwich. Sit down or carry out any of the healthy dishes served up at this "one of a kind." $

For More Information

Sheboygan Area Convention and Visitors Bureau, *712 Riverfront Drive, Suite 101, Sheboygan, WI 53081; (920) 457–9495.*

Elkhart Lake

To get to Elkhart Lake from Sheboygan, take State Highway 23 west to State Highway 67. Turn north and drive north for about fifteen minutes.

ROAD AMERICA (ages 10 and up)

For dates call Road America at (920) 892–4576 or (800) 365–RACE. Follow County Highway A from Greenbush to Glenbeulah to Elkhart Lake.

The rolling hills and ridges were formed by glaciers 10,000 years ago, making the Road America course at Elkhart Lake a twisting, turning racer's nightmare. This is, of course, why fans and drivers love the 4-mile-long fabled track, tucked into the woods just off State Highway 67. Film star and race hound Paul Newman often shows up here to demonstrate that he still has the right stuff. In fact, portions of his movie *Winning* were filmed here. The race season extends through the summer and into the autumn with a full complement of events for formula cars and high-powered machinery of other styles. Any event here is a social extravaganza with champagne and canapés on the grassy hummocks where most folks sit to watch the action. Kids, of course, are welcome.

Places to Eat

The Osthoff Resort. *101 Osthoff Avenue; (920) 876–3366.* This new property hasn't yet been fully discovered, so you won't have to stand in line. It is a great getaway place in the rolling hills of the Kettle Moraine. $$

Point Drive In. *636 Leawens Avenue; (920) 467–3382.* Burgers, fries, hot dogs, onion rings, and root beer should help keep the backseat crowd contented . . . at least for the next 60 miles of your trip through Wisconsin. $

Sal's at the Elkhart Inn. *91 South Lincoln Street; (920) 876–3133.* Try Sal's for a special evening out. Candlelight, romance . . . leave the kids at home for this one. $$

Manitowoc

Manitowoc is the next stop on your North County tour. From Elkhart Lake, drive north on State Highway 67 through the Dutch town of Kiel and go another 7 miles to U.S. Highway 151. Turn east, and Manitowoc is about 18 miles toward Lake Michigan.

MANITOWOC MARITIME MUSEUM (all ages)

Maritime Drive; (920) 684–0218. Open 9:00 A.M. to 6:00 P.M. daily year-round.

A submarine in Wisconsin? Sure enough, twenty-eight subs were built in the city's factory during World War II. On display is the U.S.S. *Cobia,* berthed in downtown Manitowoc. The deadly vessel saw heavy action in World War II and was later moved to the city to augment the museum's burgeoning collection. Although not one of the city's home-built subs, *Cobia* is now considered a National Historic Landmark, typical of the many submarines built in the city's shipyards during the war. Visitors can crawl along the narrow passageways, look into wardrooms, scramble up ladders to hatches that open to a glimpse of the sun, and generally marvel that fighting men actually lived aboard the craft for months at a time. The museum, with its 21,000 square feet of exhibit space, is the largest such facility on the Great Lakes and even includes an entire nineteenth-century waterfront scene inside its main building.

ZUNKER'S ANTIQUE CAR MUSEUM (ages 5 and up)

MacArthur Drive; (920) 684–4005. Open 10:00 A.M. to 5:00 P.M. daily, May through September. By appointment after September.

Tour Zunker's Antique Car Museum to marvel at how autos caught on in the public's imagination. A few of the early cars seem as if they couldn't make it up a small bump with a strong tailwind. Some eighty years of transportation history unfold at the museum, with lively exhibits and knowledgeable staff who keep young people alert and not thinking about simply getting to their sixteenth birthdays and snaring a license to drive.

BERNSTEEN'S CONFECTIONARY (all ages)

North Eighth Street; (920) 684–9616. Open 10:00 A.M. to 10:00 P.M. daily. $

While strolling the streets of this historic lake town, take the gang into Bernsteen's Candies for some eye-filling wonders. Homemade chocolate and other temptations fill shelf after shelf in this tiny store, which has the ambience of an old-time soda shop. Bernsteen's has been a traditional gathering place in Manitowoc for several generations, but there has never been a Weight Watchers meeting held at the shop, at least to anyone's recent knowledge. Dentists smile as they pass by, too, looking in the great front windows at the kids munching away inside. But who cares? Sit in one of the old booths and order something totally sinful in the dietary sense. There are plenty of napkins to wipe messy little faces and sticky hands. They say light lunches are available—sure, only if you skip the hot fudge.

 NATURAL OVENS OF MANITOWOC (all ages)
County Highway CR, Manitowoc; (920) 758–2500 or (800) 558–3535. Open 8:00 A.M. to 5:00 P.M. Monday through Friday; 8:00 A.M. to 3:00 P.M. Saturday. Tours at 9:00, 10:00, and 11:00 A.M. on Monday, Wednesday, Thursday, and Friday, June through August.

The bakeries of the Natural Ovens of Manitowoc feature lusciously crusty bread and rolls. No one will find mushy fake bread here, only heavy stuff with whole grains and a great crunchy texture that tastes and sounds like real bread should. Follow your nose.

Food seems to be on everyone's mind in Manitowoc, so before visiting the ovens, swing the family over to the **Pine River Dairy** (920-758-2233) at 10115 English Avenue to watch butter being made. Come early in the morning, although the plant is open until 4:00 P.M.

Places to Eat

Toby's Diner. *1424 Washington Street; (920) 682–8757.* Broasted chicken, the house specialty, is super fine, and the barbecue ribs aren't bad, either. $

Tony's Pizza. *2204 Washington Street; (920) 682–TONY.* For the biggest pizza in Manitowoc, call Tony. The restaurant also serves subs, buffalo wings, lasagna, and other Italian goodies. $

Places to Stay

Birch Creek Inn. *4626 Calumet Avenue; (920) 684–3374 or (800) 424–6126.* Twenty rooms ensure privacy here. They are all on one floor, too, so no kids will tumble down any stairs. The motel is close to the city's attractions. $$

Inn on Maritime Bay. *101 Maritime Drive (State Highway 42); (920) 682–7000 or (800) 654–5353.* This is the only lakefront hotel in Manitowoc. It offers 107 rooms, and suites are available. There is also an indoor swimming pool, whirlpool, and sauna. $$$

Two Rivers

To reach Two Rivers, Manitowoc's northern neighbor, drive along State Highway 42, which skirts the shore of Lake Michigan. The cities are adjacent.

POINT BEACH ENERGY CENTER (ages 5 and up)

6600 Nuclear Road; (920) 755–4334.

No, the folks who work at the Point Beach Energy Center do not glow in the dark. (Although there were some safety problems in 1997 noted by the Nuclear Energy Commision. And Bart Simpson's dad does not work here, either. The nuclear power plant, 10 miles north of Two Rivers, is one of the largest along the Great Lakes and provides electricity up and down the western shore of Lake Michigan. Guests are welcome to tour the facility's exhibition area that tells of nuclear power's role in energy generation. There are plenty of audio-visual displays, hands-on computer games, and videos to engross the kids, so alert them to that fact while driving up to the front entrance. There is even a nature trail outside the plant where anyone can take a quick stroll. Nearby **Point Beach State Forest** has plenty of camping sites along its beach and in the surrounding forest. To get to both, look for appropriate exit signage along U.S. Highway 43.

Places to Eat

Copper Kettle. *1600 Washington Street; (920) 794–1110.* The restaurant's relaxed, comfortable atmosphere ensures a good time out for the family. $

Lighthouse Inn/Seymour's Ice Cream Parlor. *1515 Memorial Drive, Two Rivers; (920) 793–4524 or (800) 228–6416.* Open 6:30 A.M. to 10:00 P.M. The ice cream parlor is attached to the inn, as part of its dining room. Bring a crane to lift the huge cones and bowls. Two Rivers is adjacent to Manitowoc. $

Lighthouse on the Lake. *1515 Memorial Drive; (920) 793–4524.* You won't be able to eat high atop this old structure, but the view is great from anywhere in the Lighthouse restaurant. Lake Michigan laps right up to the seawall near the windows. The main floor dining area has fish dishes fit for any sailor. $$

Machut's Supper Club. *3911 Lincoln Avenue; (920) 793–9423.* Elegant dining doesn't mean you always have to dress up. Machut's serves a healthy variety of steaks, chops, and seafood in a fancy setting, but ties are not required. $$

Algoma

Algoma is about 30 miles north of Two Rivers along State Highway 41. The views of Lake Michigan to the east are magnificent.

DOLL AND TEDDY BEAR SHOW AND SALE (ages 5 and up)

Algoma's Youth Club, 620 Lake Street; (920) 487–5480.

During early July of each year the city annually hosts its Doll and Teddy Bear Show and Sale with toys galore for sale, trade, and simple admiring. Historical and modern dolls, stuffed bears, miniature doll houses and furniture, doll parts, books, and other accessories pack the club. It's a perfect stop for any youngster who loves to hug and cuddle.

AHNAPEE STATE TRAIL (ages 10 and up)

Take youngsters who want to trek along the Ahnapee State Trail, on Algoma's northwest city limits via County Highway M. The pathway was built over an abandoned railroad bed. It extends 15 miles along the slow-moving Ahnapee River to Sturgeon Bay. The landscape along the route consists of grassy farmland, duck-filled marsh, and pine forests.

Places to Eat

Breakwater. *527 Fourth Street; (920) 487–3291.* Solid menu offerings of steak, seafood, and lighter fare are presented at the Breakwater. $$

Captain's Table. *133 North Water Street; (920) 487–5304.* Watch the fishing fleet come in and out of the harbor near the restaurant. Algoma is one of the main communities on Lake Michigan with a large charter industry. $$

For More Information

Algoma Chamber of Commerce, *1226 Lake Street, Algoma, WI 54201; (920) 487–2041.*

Door County

Door County is the thumb of land on Wisconsin's geographical mitten. On the east is Lake Michigan and to the west is Green Bay. The county has 250 miles of scenic shoreline, which cartographers say is more than any other single county in the United States. The region is made up of the towns Sturgeon Bay, Egg Harbor, Fish Creek, Ephraim, Sister Bay, Bailey's Harbor, and Washington Island and has been a tourist attraction for generations. At long last, zoning laws are controlling what had been rampant development, which was taking away the views and the quiet that so many visitors sought. Consequently there is now a better balance between getaway cottages, condos, and attractions and landscapes and parks.

From Sturgeon Bay, head north for **biking, cherry picking, perusing art galleries, charter fishing, camping, cross-country skiing, golf,** and **amusement parks.** While in the county, sample a **traditional fish boil,** which restaurateurs perform with great gusto and flair. Potatoes, onions, and Lake Michigan whitefish or trout are boiled in a huge kettle over an open flame. As the mixture comes to a magnificent head, kerosene is poured on the flames to produce an explosive boil-over that removes the fat from the liquid in the pot. While the little ones should see how the process is done, be sure they don't get too close to the fire. Singed eyebrows on holiday is no one's idea of fun.

Eating picnic style is not only best but perfect for vacationing families who need the informality. Most places use paper plates and provide plenty of napkins because mounds of butter atop the potatoes mean messy mouths and fingers. An authentic fish-boil meal is always—repeat *always*—topped off with freshly made cherry pie made from Door County fruit. Some interlopers (probably from back East) have attempted to substitute warm Door County apple pie and vanilla ice cream, with a piece of Wisconsin's sharp cheddar cheese on the side, in lieu of the cherry pie. But even teens who know the score turn up their noses at that offering (well, sometimes). You can't fool a true fish-boil aficionado, no matter what his or her age.

Sturgeon Bay

Continue along State Highway 42 to State Highway 57. The two roadways link about 6 miles south of Sturgeon Bay.

The city is the entryway to Door County, a vacation playground that has lost some of its pristine charm due to developers and their malls and big resorts. (The major part of the peninsula is safe for the moment.) Sturgeon

Bay is an old waterfront town that has been scrubbed and spruced up for its second hundred years.

DOOR COUNTY MARITIME MUSEUM (ages 5 and up)

120 North Madison Avenue; Sturgeon Bay, WI 54235-0406; (920) 743–5958. The park is at the foot of Florida Street next to Sunset Park.

Here your crew can get a sense of regional history, with pictures of steamers and stories of sunken vessels to keep up the interest.

Places to Stay

Anchor Inn. *7568 State Highway 57; (920) 856–6652.* Here you can talk about the one that got away after a day of fishing on Green Bay or Lake Michigan. The waitresses at the Anchor Inn have heard them all. They still serve with a smile. $$

Cherry Hills Lodge & Golf Course. *5905 Dunn Road; (920) 743–3240.* There is hardly a better place in Door County to come after a round of eighteen holes. Just check your cleats at the door. Cherry Hills also welcomes the nongolfer. This place consistently makes a hole-in-one with its menu. Any of the meat dishes are excellent. $$

Mr. G's Supper Club. *5890 State Highway 57; (920) 823–2112.* Mr. G's has been a popular Sturgeon Bay eatery for years. Hungry diners can get everything from salads to fish to hearty meat dishes. $$

Egg Harbor

Egg Harbor is 11 miles north of Sturgeon Bay on State Highway 42, which rims Green Bay on the west side of the Door County peninsula. Travel north on State Highway 42 between Fish Creek and Egg Harbor on the scenic peninsula.

BIRCH CREEK MUSIC PERFORMANCE CENTER (ages 12 and up)

3821 County Highway E; (920) 868–3763; http://birchcreek.org.

For a summer of relaxing and fun concerts, the Birch Creek center makes the slow evenings drift past easily. From late June through mid-August, the theater offers a broad range of music, from jazz to blues to classical. On tap in recent years have been World Music samplers, Big Band shows, tunes of Count Basie, and regular pops renditions.

Fish Creek

Fish Creek is 6 miles north of Egg Harbor on State Highway 42.

For more Door County summer theater, there's the **American Folklore Theatre** (P.O. Box 273, Fish Creek, WI 54212; 920–868–9999; www. folkloretheatre.com). In June and July the troupe presents original drama at Peninsula State Park, followed by shows in September and October at the Door County town hall in Ephraim. The **Peninsula Players Incorporated** (4351 Peninsula Players Road; 920–868–3287) presents a series of five plays from June through mid-October. These are usually on- and off-Broadway-style productions.

Ephraim

Continue north along State Highway 42 for another 5 miles to Ephraim.

This tiny fishing village has long been a favorite of water-sports fans. Located on the windy Green Bay side of Door County, sailors and sailboarders appreciate the fresh breezes that rip around the point from the north on their blusterly way southward.

Sister Bay

Sister Bay is about 4 miles north of Ephraim on State Highway 42.

There are more galleries here than you could shake assorted paintbrushes at. Kids should like the **Hanverks Music and Harp Center,** 1055 State Highway 52 (just north of County Road Q, 2 miles south of the village). The center has loads of unusual musical instruments, from ocarinas to hammer dulcimers.

Bailey's Harbor

From Sister Bay, turn south on State Highway 57 for the 9 miles to Bailey's Harbor.

Antiques lovers enjoy poking around this tiny town, with its wide open lakeside spaces, but kids will probably enjoy the **Ridges Sanctuary** (920–839–2802) much better. The site's forty acres is open year-round, but the nature center is open from 9:00 A.M. to 4:00 P.M. daily from May through October. There is **great hiking, bird-watching,** and **nature study.** Take State Highway 57 north from Bailey's Harbor and turn right on County Highway Q. Enter the first driveway on the right.

Amazing Wisconsin Facts *Wisconsin* is a Native American word with several possible meanings. Interpretations range from "gathering of the waters" and "wild-rice country" to "homeland."

Washington Island

WASHINGTON ISLAND FERRY LINE (all ages)

Located on Washington Island. The ferry departs from Northport Pier at Gills Rock for year-round service to the island off the tip of Door County. Schedule varies. Reservations are required from January through March. For information write or call Washington Island Ferry, Washington Island, WI 54246; (920) 847–2546 or (800) 223–2094 in Wisconsin only.

Sailing, Sailboarding

- **Ephraim Sailing Center.** *South Shore Pier, State Highway 41, Ephraim; (920) 854–4336.* This is Door County's sailing and sailboarding headquarters, with rentals by the day or hour. Private and group lessons are available.

- **Shoreline Charters.** *921 Cottage Road, Gills Rock; (920) 854–4614.* This is a good spot from which to do some sportfishing for salmon and brown trout.

- **Stilleto Catamaran Sailing Cruises.** *P.O. Box 500, South Shore Pier, Ephraim, WI 54211; (920) 854–SAIL.* Charters and instructions available here for cruising the shores and bays of Door County.

Places to Eat

Elquists Door County Market. *State Highway 42 and Townline Road, Ephraim; (920) 854–2552.* Pies! Plus great sandwiches and soups. $$

Shoreline Restaurant. *12747 State Highway 42, Gills Rock; (920) 854–2950.* Located in the Shoreline Resort, the restaurant's site is one of the best around for a sunset view during supper. Even the squirmiest youngster is often stilled by the sight. $$

Square Rigger Galley. *6332 State Highway 57, Jacksonport; (920) 823–2408.* The restaurant overlooks its own sand beach. $$

Village Cafe. *7918 Egg Harbor Road, Egg Harbor; (920) 868–3342.* Homemade soups are the specialty. $

 # Door County State Parks

- **Newport State Park.** *County Highway NP, Ellison Bay; (920) 854– 2500.* This 2,700-acre semiwilderness is great for hiking, skiing, camping, cross-country skiing, and snowshoeing on the 28 miles of trails near and along the 11 miles of lake shoreline.

- **Peninsula State Park.** *P.O. Box 218, Fish Creek, WI 54212; (920) 868– 3258.* This is one of Wisconsin's most popular parks due to its location on a bluff towering over the dark rugged waters of Green Bay. Camping is possible, both in the crowning woods as well as near the beach. The park is open year-round, so it is a constant haven for cyclists, hikers, snowshoers, skiers, and snowmobilers during their respective seasons. It also has the only state-owned golf course, an eighteen-holer where Ma can catch up on her hole-in-one form while Pop takes the gang to the lighthouse at Eagle Bluff for a look over the water.

- **Potawatomi State Park.** *Park Drive, Sturgeon Bay; (920) 746–2890.* For a landlubber's view of Door County, climb up the observation tower at Potawatomi State Park. When the sky is a rich azure and the sun is brightly shining, visitors can spy Marinette across Green Bay to the west and Chambers Island 20 miles to the northeast. On a foggy day, you're lucky to spot the hand in front of your face. A trip to the tower is worth it, though, regardless of the weather.

- **Rock Island State Park.** *Washington Island; (920) 847–2235.* The 906-acre island is 1 mile northeast of Jackson Harbor on the larger Washington Island. Rock is reached only via ferryboat. There are 10 miles of hiking trails, plus swimming, fishing, and camping. French explorers paused here in 1679.

- **Whitefish Dunes State Park.** *Clark Lake Road, Sturgeon Bay; (920) 823–2400.* The park comprises 847 acres of forest on the lakeside of the peninsula. This is the chance to see the state's highest sand dunes as well as hike, ski, swim, and fish.

For More Information

The **Door County Chamber of Commerce** is the fount of all knowledge when it comes to fish boils, galleries, hiking opportunities, scenic overlooks, park rates, and resort openings. Contact the folks there at Box 406, Sturgeon Bay, WI 54235-0406; (920) 743-4456 or (800) 52-RELAX.

Green Bay

Leave Door County via State Highway 57, which runs directly into the northern outskirts of Green Bay.

The city proudly calls itself the Birthplace of the Midwest, dating its Westernized history from 1634 when explorer Jean Nicolet beached his canoe and said "howdy" (actually *bonjour*) to the Winnebago Indians who had already been living there for generations. According to legend, the Frenchman apparently thought he was at some outpost of the Chinese empire, because he lept from his canoe wearing a handmade silk damask robe with colorful hand-stitched birds and flowers. He then proceeded to fire two pistols into the air to announce his arrival. This was probably a rather puzzling custom in the eyes of the locals, but they invited him to a dinner of beaver tails and wild rice anyway, the first of several feasts that attracted thousands of curious Native Americans from throughout the area. Nicolet then paddled off to claim more territory for France, supposedly taking his sartorial splendor with him.

Today Green Bay is more noted for being the **Toilet Paper Capital of the World.** This is a dubious distinction for one of Wisconsin's major, and oldest, cities, but one that youngsters—with their affinity for discussing bodily functions at the most inappropriate times—would certainly find amusing. Actually, the title is well earned, but add on other paper products, as well. Wood-processing plants, mills, and paper-company offices form the core of the city's business world.

The folks here, however, don't just eat, drink, and chew on newly made toothpicks. For many, the **Green Bay Packers football team** is *it,* especially with its Super Bowl win in 1996. World champions—at various times—the Pack is monetarily, emotionally, and spiritually community owned. Green Bay is the country's oldest professional football team, organized in 1919 and receiving a pro franchise in 1921. It was the first to win three NFL championships in a row, the first Super Bowl champ, and the first team to have its own Hall of Fame. The team received its name because its first corporate sponsor was the Acme Packing Company, a major Green Bay employer at the time.

GREEN BAY PACKER HALL OF FAME (ages 5 and up)

Lombardi Avenue; (920) 499–4281. Open 9:00 A.M. to 6:00 P.M. daily from June through August; 10:00 A.M. to 5:00 P.M. from September through May. The museum is across the street from Lambeau Field, where the team's gladiators have battled their enemies for more than a half century.

Few kids in Wisconsin, except for several on the western fringes of the St. Croix River Valley, which abuts Minnesota (who might be stray Vikings fans), or one or two along the border of Illinois (who have a predilection toward the Chicago Bears), would ever dream of not wearing the Packers' green and gold. The Pack's Hall of Fame has a hushed meccalike quality about its polished halls and glassed displays of shoulder pads, trophies, shoes, and autographed pigskins. Row after row of football greats, from renowned players such as Bret Favre and Bart Starr to fabled coaches such as Vince Lombardi, peer down from their portrait frames. Their eyes follow visitors everywhere.

The backseat squad can help dads (or moms) keep their driving eyes peeled for the giant player leaping atop a football, the sculpture that indicates the museum's entrance. Tours can also be arranged to tour the field and to survey all the behind-the-scenes action from the press box to the skyboxes.

NATIONAL RAILROAD MUSEUM (ages 5 and up)

2285 South Broadway; (920) 435–7245. Open 9:00 A.M. to 5:00 P.M. daily from May 1 through October 15. Regularly schedule rides around the grounds.

Railroad fans in the family will love all the steel and muscle shown by the old-time locomotives at the National Railroad Museum. More than eighty pieces of rolling stock, including monster engines, oil tankers, a refrigerator car, and tail-ending cabooses, are displayed on tracks ringing the facility's grounds. Puffing, huffing steamers and sleek diesels show the technical progression in this fabulous annal of transportation history. Included is Gen. Dwight D. Eisenhower's World War II traveling staff car, which operated under the code name "Bayonet." Take the littlest kid in the family and place him or her alongside the Union Pacific "Big Boy" for a photograph. Shutterbugs will need wide-angle lenses, because the 1941 engine is the largest locomotive ever built. It weighs more than 600 tons and is 133 feet long, almost half the length of a football field.

The heart of nineteenth-century America was the railroad depot, so it is appropriate that the hub of activity at the train museum is also a depot. Thousands of pieces of memorabilia are displayed in the Hood Junction Depot, a replica of such a structure at Langley, South Carolina.

Everyone should trek through the displays in the main museum building and watch the slide-video presentation to pick up a sense of background. Then run outside, where hands-on, all-aboard climbing is allowed on some of the bigger locomotives. Just watch your head. Any youngster working on a school paper will want to know that the museum has an excellent library of railroad materials.

NEVILLE PUBLIC MUSEUM (ages 5 and up)

210 Museum Place; (920) 448–4460. Open noon to 4:00 P.M. Sunday; 9:00 A.M. to 4:00 P.M. Tuesday, Thursday, and Friday; and 9:00 A.M. to 9:00 P.M. Wednesday. Closed Monday.

Brown County's Neville Public Museum takes a look at more than 10,000 years of Green Bay–area history from the Ice Age to contemporary life. A far-reaching exhibit of local Native Americans is a great resource for more schoolwork research. One display shows a prehistoric warrior attacking a mastodon with a spear. That should make the gang appreciate today's simple task of strolling to the corner grocery store to buy a pound of hamburger. Traveling shows, as well as permanent displays, make return visits a little bit different and always interesting each time. Everything a kid ever wanted to know about bears, sharks, and other toothy critters is right at hand. Looking at all those teeth is a perfect opportunity to remind everyone to brush after each meal. The museum is along the Fox River on Green Bay's west side.

BAY BEACH WILDLIFE SANCTUARY (ages 5 and up)

Sanctuary Road; (920) 391–3671. To get to Bay Beach from I–43, take exit 187 (Webster Avenue) and go east. Just look for the signage.

Moving from indoors to outside, the Bay Beach Wildlife Sanctuary on Green Bay's far north side is the place to put nature into perspective. Some 700 acres of nature and cross-country ski trails are available for silent pursuits. A wildlife observation platform allows the littlest child to see above the brush and trees, in the hopes of spotting a deer.

BAY BEACH AMUSEMENT PARK (all ages)

1313 Bay Beach Road; (920) 448–3365. Open 10:00 A.M. to 6:00 P.M. Saturday and Sunday from mid-April through Memorial Day; 10:00 A.M. to 9:00 P.M. daily through August 15; 10:00 A.M. to 6:00 P.M. daily through August 22; and 10:00 A.M. to 6:00 P.M. Saturday and Sunday from September 1 through September 27, after which the park closes for the season. The park is closed August 23–31.

Once the gang gets tired of counting hawks, swallows, woodpeckers, rabbits, chipmunks, and other feathered or furry denizens of the wild, take everyone down the road to the Bay Beach Amusement Park. The **Free** park has softball fields, horseshoe pits, volleyball courts, and kiddie rides (most still only cost a dime).

Places to Eat

50 Yard Line Sports Bar. *1049 Lombardi Access Road; (920) 496–5857.* When in Title Town, do as the Title Towners do. Head to the 50 Yard Line for Packer action and typical pub grub: burgers, dogs, etc. It really helps to wear the green and gold team colors. $

Townline Sports Pub & Grill. *1773 Cardinal Lane; (920) 434–7865.* This is one of the best places in town to watch the Green Bay Packers battle their gridiron foes. Beer, burgers, and shouting. You can't go wrong. $

DePere

DePere is a suburb of Green Bay and is home to **St. Norbert College.** On the grounds of the ivy-covered campus is **White Pillars** (920-336-3877), built in 1836 as the first bank building in the state, which now houses the **DePere Historical Society Museum.** The building is at 403 North Broadway and is open from noon to 4:00 P.M. Tuesday through Friday and 1:00 to 5:00 P.M. Saturday. Closed Sunday.

A̲mazing Wisconsin Facts Explorer Jean Nicolet was told by French governors in Canada to make peace with the Huron Indians and a mysterious people more to the west known as the *Puants* ("Stinkers" or "People of the Stinking Water"). This "stinking water" actually referred to salt water and was not a politically incorrect term, even for those days. Today, historians think that phrase referred to what the French hoped would be residents of eastern China. Actually, the people he found were the Ho-Chunk of Wisconsin.

ONEIDA NATION MUSEUM (ages 5 and up)
Brown County Highway EE; (920) 869–2768. Open year-round 9:00 A.M. to 5:00 P.M. Tuesday through Friday and 10:00 A.M. to 5:00 P.M. Saturday. Closed Sunday and Monday.

The Oneida Nation Museum is the repository of materials donated by the "People of the Standing Stone," who came to Wisconsin in the 1880s. The museum includes a replica of a wood-and-bark longhouse where tribal members used to live. Guides and interpreters are on staff to point visitors in the right direction and talk about the tribe's proud heritage.

Places to Eat

A's Dockside Grill. *112 North Broadway; (920) 336–2277.* Burgers, fries, and related munches fills hungry tummies. $

Bilotti's Pizza Garden. *113 North Broadway; (920) 336–1811.* If you and the kids have a hankerin' for pizza, Bilotti's serves it with green peppers, mushrooms, cheese, sausage, red peppers, pepperoni, and all the other add-ons. Pick and choose. $

Country Express. *2601 Monroe Road; (920) 336–6402.* The Country Express offers simple, hearty fare for the budget-conscious traveler . . . from soup to pie. $

Seymour

Take State Highway 174 northwest to State Highway 54 to Seymour, a distance of about 10 miles.

 HAMBURGER CELEBRATION (all ages)
Downtown Seymour on Depot Street; (920) 833–9522 or (920) 833–2663. Held the first Saturday in August, starting at noon.

Snug in a harness suspended from an overhead crane, the chef at Seymour's Hamburger Celebration swings back and forth across hundreds of sizzling patties. Sprinkling careful doses of salt and pepper, he sweeps over the giant fry pan. "It's a hot job, but it's gotta be done, well done," he says, wiping the sweat from his brow after the Peter Pan routine. This routine, accompanied by laughs and plenty of applause from onlookers, is part of the fun at the festival. The feast-fest celebrates the birth of the burger. According to town legend, a local meatball salesman named Charlie Nagreen fried up a batch of patty-shaped ground meat at the Outagamie Fair in 1855. By squishing his meatballs and slapping them between buns, the momentous occasion supposedly introduced the first real hamburger to a hungry pre-McDonald's public.

A parade, led by Hamburger Patty and Bunard, launches the celebration as it meanders down Main Street at midday. A Hamburger Olympics, open to all comers, concludes the afternoon with events such as a ketchup slide.

North and Northwest Wisconsin

When viewed from the air, Wisconsin's lakes are diamonds sprinkled on a velvet green mosaic of rich pine green. Shell, Rice, Red Cedar, Long, Spooner, Grindstone, Chippewa, Big Round, Clam and all the other bodies of water dapple the land in their glittering finery. Ribbons of braided silver—the rivers and streams—spiderweb their convoluted journeys through the textured scenery. St. Croix or Red Rivers, Montgomery and Little Bear Creeks—the names are rich with history. Native Americans, *voyageurs* and explorers, frontier wives and camp cooks, timber cutters, trappers, farmers, and herdsmen have touched the earth with their presence.

We touched the earth, as well, on our explorations of this part of Wisconsin. Our family has drawn both spirit and

Hintz's Top Picks

- Competing in cross-country ski marathons
- Telling fibs about the biggest fish that got away
- Telling the truth about the bass caught for a campfire supper
- Canoeing the St. Croix River
- Talking to a Department of Natural Resources ranger
- Counting the white-tailed deer grazing along the forest edge
- Mountain biking
- Camping for a week
- Coming home well rested after a week of camping
- Appreciating the open spaces

Superior
Cornucopia
Bayfield
Red Cliff
Ashland
Odanah
Cable
Glidden
Danbury
Manitowish
Waters
Webster
Hayward
Couderay
Minocqua
Grantsburg
St. Croix Falls
Rice Lake
Ladysmith
Prentice
Amery
Rib Lake
Spirit
Medford
Chippewa Falls
Abbotsford

NORTH and NORTHWEST

excitement from the living ground. It is easy to feel the past here if you remain open to that richness.

Take out a copy of the most recent *Wisconsin Atlas and Gazetteer* (Box 298, DeLorme Mapping Co., Freeport, MA 04032) or a Wisconsin Department of Transportation road map and set out on a journey of your own discovery. The time of year doesn't make any difference. Look for spring's profusion of jack-in-the-pulpit and fern along the Gandy Dancer Trail. Revel in the summer's simmering midday heat while canoeing the St. Croix National Scenic Riverway. Admire the crimson, ochre, and vermilion splendor of autumn around Little Bohemia. Break out the cross-country skis or snowshoes for a wintry trek deep into the heart of a snow-softened Chequamegon National Forest. Regardless of the season, there is always an opportunity to tuck falling stars into children's pockets. How's that for memories?

Alert the kids to the little things that will add to their enjoyment while visiting Wisconsin's north and northwest. Hone the senses, tune into the delightful world of nature. Listen for the cry of a night owl near Potato River Falls. Look high overhead toward the graceful flight of herons above the Powell Marsh Wildlife Area. Feel your bones rattle while four-wheeling near Dead Horse Slough. Be the first to spot the glint of Lake Superior through the cathedral pines from atop St. Peter's Dome. On the Cornucopia beach, roll lake-polished rocks around in your hand and feel their smooth heaviness.

Amazing Wisconsin Facts

The Wisconsin state bird is the robin. The state flower is the wood violet and the state tree is the sugar maple.

Savor a tart cranberry muffin and revel in a sweet slice of homemade apple pie from any of the multitudinous North Woods eateries.

Tell the kids to pull all their senses into play when jaunting through this corner of Badgerland. Sight, sound, smell, feel—they will bring alive the stuff of memories for years to come. Just open yourselves to it all.

Danbury

Begin a tour around Wisconsin's north and northwest by starting in Danbury, at the intersection of State Highways 77 and 35 in Burnett County.

The land near Danbury was let out for homestead as late as 1900, demonstrating that life on the Wisconsin frontier is not so far removed from the minds of Burnett County residents. Donna Nelson, a secretary in the county's tourism office, recalls that her Swedish father-in-law, Johan Nelson, was a tote driver who brought food, mail, and kerosene by horse-drawn wagon to the local folks. It took a whole day to drive the 35 miles from the supply center at Grantsburg to Danbury. Tell that to the teens who want a car to drive 3 blocks to school! When the railroad came through the community in 1912, however, the link to the outside world was solidified.

GANDY DANCER TRAIL (all ages)

Danbury, an unincorporated village on State Highway 77, is the trail-head for the 50-mile Gandy Dancer Trail, which was opened in 1990. Called a "silent trail" because motorized vehicles cannot use it (except for all-terrain vehicles and snowmobiles in winter), the trail will eventually be paved. Now it is primarily a mountain-bike route that travels along an old railroad line track from the Minnesota/Wisconsin border near Danbury southward to St. Croix Falls in Polk County. The rugged route mostly travels through the scenic wilderness, passing close to towns but far enough away to provide a real sense of adventure. As one resident indicated, though, bikers have a tendency to run into trees, so the community has outfitted an ambulance with tracks that can be hauled by truck to the trailhead. The rescue vehicle can then churn its way into the woods. The trail traverses remote areas of the county, so riders are admonished not to ride alone in case of emergencies. This is something to consider when taking smaller children out on the trail.

Webster

Webster is 9 miles south of Danbury on State Highway 35.

For 200 years Wisconsin was one of the prime centers of the frontier fur trade. The state is dotted with old forts and cabins that once served as the economic outposts of the growing nation. Each year, trading companies operated "wintering" posts in the wilderness. Native Americans would bring their prime pelts to these facilities and trade them for supplies. In mid-1802, a contingent of adventurers from the XY Trading Company out of Grand Portage, several hundred miles to the north in pre-Minnesota, launched their canoes and aimed south. Their mission was to service the *folle avoine* (wild rice) region of Wisconsin. At Forts Folle Avoine, they built a trading post near that of another firm, the North West Company, which had found a lucrative market there already.

The traders remained at Forts Folle Avoine for two winters, trading with the Ojibewe Indians who lived in the vicinity. Today, costumed guides depicting typical traders who lived at the fort during its heyday demonstrate the principles of barter and explain life in the forests. Other guides show off Native American craft traditions, from basketry to food preparation.

FORTS FOLLE AVOINE (all ages)

Forts Folle Avoine is reached via State Highway 35, 4 miles north of Webster to County Highway U. Go west on U for 2½ miles through the forest to the site, which is managed by the Burnett County Historical Society.

A stockade and outbuildings at the original site of Forts Folle Avoine can be toured. Plenty of information is available on why things were done the way they were back in the good old days. Questions are encouraged at this hands-on re-creation of *Let's Make a Deal* woodsy-style. Regularly scheduled interpretive programs are held in the evening and on weekends in two outdoor amphitheaters.

HOLE IN THE WALL CASINO (ages 21 and up in the casino)

Intersection of State Highways 35 and 77, Danbury; (715) 656–4333 or (800) BET–UWIN. Thirty-eight rooms in easy-access location. Be aware that this is also a casino, with slots, blackjack tables, and bingo. $. Baby-sitting services are available for younger children.

For a more contemporary adventure, the Hole in the Wall Casino, 8 miles north of Webster, is an easy jaunt from town on State Highway 35. Since early 1995, the hotel has offered a baby-sitting service and supervised kids' play area with slides, swings, and climbing units. Baby-sitting charges are $6.00 per hour. The grownups then can play at any of the 300 slot machines or try a hand at blackjack, bingo, and other games of chance. As they say in Burnett County, "Try us once, and we bet you'll be back." The casino is owned by Chippewas from the St. Croix Reservation.

CREX MEADOWS WILDLIFE AREA (ages 5 and up)

Located ½ mile north of Grantsburg; (715) 463–2896.

The Crex Meadows Wildlife Area has a 2,399-acre bird refuge in its center. Nearly 300 acres have been cultivated to provide feed for the huge flocks of ducks and geese that call the place home. It is estimated that more than 20,000 birds at a time fly in and out of the refuge on any given day. Once-rare sandhill cranes, which zoom in from the horizon like small airplanes, have made a strong comeback within the safety of the preserve. Kids can identify these gangly birds by the high-pitched screeches that sound like a card party of witches. Roads and observation points around the preserve allow good "birding." Bring binoculars for close-up watching.

The lakes and marshes throughout Burnett County are now also home to about one hundred trumpeter swans, reintroduced to the state in 1989 after an absence of more than one hundred years. These are giant birds, with wingspans of 7 or more feet. The trumpeters actually sound as if they are bugling when they communicate, hence the name. Easily identified with their all-white feathers and black bills, each has a yellow neck collar with a black two digit/two letter code, placed there by the state's department of natural resources to help track the birds' movement. The birds feed on aquatic vegetation, and visitors to the county are asked to not give them anything else. Such bird spotting is a good activity for youngsters while biking or driving the back roads.

Loving Lutfisk

Loving Lutfisk Much of Burnett County was settled by tough, yet sauna-loving, Scandinavians who appreciated the rugged country-side that reminded them of home. Many went into the logging industry. Norwegian, Danish, and Swedish influences are still strong throughout the region, with more guys in hunting jackets nicknamed "Swede" than probably anywhere else in Wisconsin. And many of the churches in the Grantsburg area still stage lutfisk suppers as fund-raisers. Vacationing kids will find these fjord feasts much more exotic than a drive-in's standard double Whopper.

Kokt lutfisk is dried cod that has been preserved in lye and soda and softened into a glutinous mass by letting it sit in salt water for about a week. It is then boiled and served with a white sauce *(mjolksds)* along with boiled potatoes. Everything is liberally dosed with salt and white and black pepper. *Lefsa*, a rolled and sugared pancake, is the typical side dish.

For the times and dates of these suppers, check the area's newspapers: the *Inter-County Leader*, which is published in Frederick in adjacent Polk County; and the *Burnett County Sentinel*, published in Grantsburg. The weeklies can be picked up at grocery stores, gas stations, bait shops, and other outlets. Out-of-town vacationers are encouraged to drop by for samples.

WILD RIVER OUTFITTERS (ages 10 and up)

15177 Highway 70; (715) 463–2254.

One good way of spotting birds is to take a canoe trip along the upper St. Croix or the Namekagon Rivers. Wild River Outfitters is one of several companies in the county that can put together jaunts ranging from an afternoon to a week. Owners Marilyn Chesnik and Jerry Dorff say with a laugh that they "won't leave you up a creek without a paddle."

SYTTENDE MAI MARATHON (ages 10 and up)

Starting in Grantsburg; (715) 463–5301.

To find Grantsburg, drive south on State Highway 35 to Siren and turn west on State Highway 70. The village is then about 13 miles away.

The Syttende Mai Marathon is usually run in honor of the May 17 independence day celebrations in Norway. One of the North Country's major sporting events, several thousand runners take off from downtown Grantsburg for a multilength run. The course loops around the rugged Burnett County countryside. The town itself is barely on the Wisconsin side of the Minnesota–Badger State border, about 6 miles in from the St. Croix River. All ages of runners participate, from youngsters to grandparents in their respective age divisions. The historic old logging city is built on a hill overlooking the scenic St. Croix River valley and used to be the county seat. In the early 1980s, however, the old county building needed refurbishing. In a referendum, it was agreed to move the new facility to more centrally located Siren. (Of course, Grantburgians were rather unhappy at losing their county seat status, but they could reconcile themselves with their *lutfisk* crown.)

Places to Eat

Ike Walton Lodge. *Located on north shore of Yellow Lake. Drive 4 miles north of Webster, then turn left on County Highway U; (715) 866–7195.* Family dining with a kids' menu. The Sunday breakfast buffet is as big as the North Woods. $$

Jo MaMa's Cafe. *County Roads A and H; (715) 635–2386.* Irreverent? Yeah, but good food. Take the kids and fill 'em up. $

North View Drive Inn. *Corner of State Highway 35 and County Road FF, Webster; (715) 866–7642.* Yep, they still have car hops here. Root beer, ice cream, and burgers. Just like the old days. $

Oak Grove Supper Club & Lounge. *25851 State Highway 35; (715) 866–7265.* You don't have to be fancily dressed at the Oak Grove, although they do serve a classy spread. Prime rib, steak, and the other North Woods fixin's are tops in these parts. $$

Sunshine Family Restaurant. *Siren; (715) 349–2570.* Owner Sue Winch knows how to take care of kids: Fill 'em up with good hearty food. It's easy. $$

Yellow River Inn. *27043 State Highway 35 North; (715) 866–7375.* Drop by for cocktails and an extensive menu of soups, salads, and regular specials. Kids welcome. $$

Places to Stay

Bed-and-breakfast inns near the Gandy Dancer Trail accept tired, foot-weary youngsters, as do motels and hotels throughout the region. Pets, though, are seldom welcome. Be sure to call ahead to find out who and what is allowed. Here are a few of the many places to stay in the region:

Bashaw Lake Resort. *3215 Lakeview Church Road, Shell Lake; (715) 468–2310.* The resort is the only such facility on Bashaw Lake and offers both cabins and campsites. $$

Forgotten Times Country Inn. *Siren; (715) 349–5837.* Tucked away on 133 acres of prime wilderness land, kids can run and yell to their hearts' content. The ten guest rooms are in century-old log cabins that are handicap accessible. Innkeepers Al and Pat Blume turn out a hearty breakfast, as well. $

Pine Wood Motel. *23862 State Road 35, Siren; (715) 349–5225.* Fourteen rooms; kid- and pet-friendly place. $

Wagner's Port Sand Resort and Campground. *4904 State Highway 70, Webster; (715) 349–2395.* The resort has a bathhouse, lakeshore sites, picnic tables, a fish-cleaning house, laundry facilities, and other amenities. $$

More Things to Do in Burnett County

JANUARY: Golf on snow at Yellow Lake Golf Course, Danbury

FEBRUARY: Wonderland Pancake Breakfast, Webb Lake

MARCH: St. Patrick's Day Parade, Siren

MAY: Forts Folle Avoine Fine Arts Festival, Webster

JUNE: Old-Fashioned Ice Cream Social, Grantsburg

JULY: Fire Department Brat Feed and Waterball Fights, Webster

AUGUST: Central Burnett County Fair, Webster

SEPTEMBER: Muskie Madness Tournament, Webster

OCTOBER: Crex Meadows Wildlife Area open house, Grantsburg

DECEMBER: Christmas at the Fort, Forts Folle Avoine, Webster

St. Croix Falls

Take State Highway 47 about 5 miles south from Grantsburg where it picks up State Highway 87. Continue on 87 to St. Croix Falls.

INTERSTATE PARK (all ages)
P.O. Box 703, St. Croix Falls, WI 54024; (715) 483–3747. State-park vehicle pass required. Open 6:00 A.M. to 11:00 P.M. daily. Interpretive Center is open from 8:00 A.M. to 11:00 P.M.

The 1,400-acre Interstate Park at St. Croix Falls presents some of the best scenic views in Wisconsin, with 100-foot-high cliffs tumbling down to the rampaging St. Croix River. The "dalles" (or gorges) of the the St. Croix were earmarked as the state's first state park at the turn of the twentieth century. Several trails loop through the park near the intersection of State Highways 35 and 8, directly across the river from Minnesota. For the kids, one of the best routes amid the rocks is the Pothole Trail at the base of the cliffs. Numerous holes of varying sizes and depths show where glaciers tumbled stones around and around, making them as smooth as cannonballs and burrowing deep pockets into the bedrock. Regular tours are held in the summer, with the rangers providing plenty of background on geological phenomena.

ST. CROIX NATIONAL SCENIC RIVERWAY (all ages)
National Park Service Interpretive Center, 401 Hamilton Street in downtown St. Croix Falls; (715) 483–3284. Summer hours are 8:30 A.M. to 5:30 P.M. Monday through Friday. From Labor Day to Memorial Day, hours are 8:30 A.M. to 6:00 P.M. Friday, Saturday, and Sunday.

The park is a key hub of the St. Croix National Scenic Riverway, covering 250 miles of the Namekagon and St. Croix Rivers. The system was established in 1968 to keep the flowages in a primitive form. Helpful rangers can answer questions about the Scandinavian emigrants who settled the region, the logging business, and area recreational opportunities.

WILD MOUNTAIN RECREATION PARK
P.O. Box 235, Taylors Falls, MN 55084; (651) 465–6315 or (800) 447–4958.

If vacationing in the area, it's only fair to mention Taylors Falls, directly across the St. Croix River in Minnesota. For more commercial fun, the Wild Mountain Recreation Park has bumper cars, water slides, go-carts, and picnic areas. The facility also has two 1,700-foot-long Alpine slides.

SCENIC BOAT TOURS

P.O. Box 235, Taylors Falls, MN 55084; (651) 465–6315 or (800) 447–4958.

Hop aboard vessels that look like old steamboats. Dinner and picnic cruises are available, with a backdrop of sheer cliffs for ambience. The same company operates both the rec park and the boats; many school groups take charter combo packages that include both adventures.

Top Hiking Paths While meandering the other paths (River Bluffs Trail, Echo Canyon Trail, Meadow Valley Trail, and Eagle Peak Trail), encourage sharp-eyed kids to identify the "Old Man of the Dalles." This craggy formation, which peers out over the river, resembles a man's face. Just don't become so intent on finding the old guy that someone falls over a cliff. There are no handrails over the gorge (unlike on the Minnesota side at Taylors Falls), so keep a close watch on young climbers. Plenty of campsites in the park are available for overnight stays.

FAWN-DOE-ROSA ANIMAL PARK (ages 5 and up)

U.S. Highway 8 East; (715) 483–3772.

Back into Wisconsin, 2 miles east of St. Croix Falls on U.S. Highway 8, is the Fawn-Doe-Rosa Animal Park. A collection of cougars, bears, wolves, and other wild critters are there to observe. Some of the smaller, tamer beasties can be fed and petted.

Places to Eat

Dalles House. *Corner of U.S. Highway 8 and State Highway 35; (715) 483–3246.* After spending a day looking down the river gulch, pause for a kick-back evening at the Dalles House. Comfortable, quiet, and convenient for a night out. $$

St. Croix Valley Golf Course. *2200 U.S. Highway 8; (715) 483–3377.* After hitting all those birdies, plan on reflection time in the supper club at the golf course. $$

Weathering Wisconsin

Weathering Wisconsin Wisconsin has a generally temperate climate, although the joke in the winter is that everyone wants to walk as far south as they can with a snow shovel over their shoulders. They will stop migrating only when someone says, "Hey, what's that you're carrying?" Sandwiched between Lakes Superior and Michigan, the state has cooler summers and milder winters along its shorelines than on the interior. Average January temperatures range from 12°F in the north to 22°F in the south. Average July temperatures vary from 69°F in the north to 73° in the south.

Chetek

Chetek is right off U.S. 53. From Amery drive back north to U.S. 8, turn east on 8 and proceed to U.S. 53. Turn south and go about 8 miles to Chetek.

When it comes to fishing tourneys, plan a trip to Chetek, "the city of lakes," which is tucked into a southeastern corner of the county where there are some 120 miles of shoreline. The lakes—Chetek, Prairie, Pokegma, Moose Ear, Ten Mile, and Ojaski— cover 3,800 surface acres, with depths going to 22 feet. Northern pike, walleye, bass, perch, and dozens more varieties of finny critters have been drawing vacationers to the town for five generations. Prairie Lake is the biggest, covering 1,545 acres, and is rimmed with wilderness land alive with muskrats, Canada geese, and other wildlife.

When It Rains On rainy days, take the family to **Miller Cheese House** (715-234-4144), 1 mile north of Rice Lake on State Highway 48, to watch homemade fudge being made. The **Chetek Lanes** (715-924-3227), with its bowling and racquetball, is another grumpy-weather-day alternative. The lanes are at the south edge of town on County Highway SS.

Chetek has been in the hospitality business for a long time, so numerous resorts and campgrounds border the waterways. The Chetek Resort Association booth downtown can fill in a visitor with all the possibilities, from the cottages at Pop Ward's to the Chetek River Campground with its indoor heated pool and miniature golf. To get an advance copy of a resort guide, contact the association at P.O. Box 172, Chetek, WI 54728; (715) 924-4440.

FISH-O-RAMA (ages 5 and up)
Rod and Gun Shop, 513 Second Street; (715) 924–4181.

With all this water, the community sponsors numerous fishing contests. A kid can hardly keep up catching worms. Each Sunday from May 1 through October 15 offers a full day of fishing competitions. In addition, the community's summerlong Fish-O-Rama offers $50,000 in prizes for lucky anglers of all ages who can bring in one of the tagged trophies. Each of the walleye, bass, or northern pike winners gets $1,000 each. There are also prizes for crappies, perch, and bluegills. The Mariner Open Bass Tournament on the first Sunday in June attracts eager anglers from around the Midwest, who compete for $3,000 in guaranteed first-place prize money.

Amazing Wisconsin Facts There are ten metropolitan areas in Wisconsin that are within the state boundaries, but there are several others that are multistate. The La Crosse area extends into Minnesota, with residents on both sides of the Mississippi traveling between states for jobs and entertainment. Two Minnesota urban communities extend into Wisconsin: Minneapolis–St. Paul, which reaches into the Hudson, Wisconsin, area; and Duluth-Superior, along Lake Superior.

Chippewa Falls

From Chetek, drive south 25 miles on U.S. 53 to Chippewa Falls.

 COOK-RUTLEDGE MANSION (ages 10 and up)
505 West Grand Avenue; (715) 723–7181. Open from Thursday through Sunday, June through August, with tours at 2:00 and 3:00 P.M.

The Cook-Rutledge Mansion is the house that timber built. With its solid redbrick facade, graceful white porch, and high widow's walk atop the main building, the building exudes power, vast riches, and burgher stability. Built in 1873 by attorney and state assemblyman James Monroe Bingham, the home was purchased in 1887 by lumber baron Edward Rutledge, who undertook extensive remodeling. Judge Dayton Cook recognized a good rehab job when he saw one and purchased the home in 1915. Bingham, Rutledge, and Cook are are now gone with the woods that were slashed to feed the demands of America's nineteenth-century building boom. The 1860s-era house, however, is open for tours from June through August, providing a peek at the secrets behind the walls. All the place needs is a ghost or two. Tell that to the youngsters as they dash up the front steps.

A Lot o' Wood Chippewa Falls once had the world's largest sawmill under one roof: **Chippewa Log and Boom Inc.**, which was built by Irvin Weyenhauser and his partner, Edward Rutledge, during the 1870s. Harvested from the surrounding forests, white and red pine with trunks several feet in diameter were sliced, diced, and chawed by the ripping blades to produce tens of thousands of board feet of lumber a year. The old mill is now just a memory in this town, which was once a hub of the state's lumber world.

JACOB LEINENKUGEL BREWING COMPANY (ages 10 and up)

Jefferson Avenue; (715) 723–5557; www.leinie.com. The hospitality center is open 9:00 A.M. to 4:00 P.M. Monday through Friday and 10:00 A.M. to 3:00 P.M. Saturday; summer hours are 9:00 A.M. to 5:00 P.M. and 11:00 A.M. to 3:00 P.M. Saturday.

Fun for the family can be had at the Jacob Leinenkugel Brewing Company, where tours of the brewery and samples in the hospitality center make a rainy vacation day (or any other day) much more pleasant. While parents can tip a brewskie, sodas are available for kids who have just learned the High Trinity of Brewing: malt, mash, and wort. Jake Leinenkugel, the fourth-generation family member in the business, is proud to head the city's oldest business, established in 1867. Jake portrays a down-home type of guy in his company's ads, belying the fact that this fortyish brewmeister is a savvy businessman who eased his firm through a potentially rocky buyout by Miller Brewing Company in the 1980s. Leinenkugel proves that even in the shark-eat-shark world of the international beer industry, small-town street smarts, good management practices, and hard work can be the equal of wunderkind urban suits who only breathe bottom line. The brewing complex features rows of sparkling bronze kettles and stainless-steel drums, inside of which hops and barley perform their fermenting magic. As a longtime Leinie's lover, years before it was discovered by the Miller moguls, I was glad to see the small brewery survive, even as many of its less fortunate cousins fell by the wayside.

IRVINE PARK (all ages)

State Highway 124 and Highway Bridgewater Avenue. For information contact the City Parks and Recreations Department, 109 East Spruce Street; (715) 723–3890. Open 7:00 A.M. to dusk year-round.

After a pleasant pause over a Leinie's, it is now time again to treat the kids. Take the chilluns to Irvine Park on Bridgewater Avenue for a tour of the zoo there, with its excellent and exotic assortment of fangs, hooves, claws, and horns, none of which will be seen on neighboring farms. After admiring the bears, lions, and other critters, a dip in the park's outdoor swimming pool presents an opportunity to cool off. There are also 300 acres of woodland for camping (for a fee) and hiking. In December the city sets up a Christmas Village in the park and drapes upward of 30,000 brightly colored lights over the trees. There are also seventy-five individual Victorian holiday displays around the park, which you can see by driving the roads that wend their way between the firs. With the splash of light playing across the snow—and it always snows in Chippewa Falls in December—the effect is mind-expanding. Then tumble back to a nearby restaurant for hot chocolate.

Wisconsin's precipitation averages about 31 inches a year. That includes rain and melted snow. Ah, that brings back memories of damp campgrounds, wet-all-over kids, sneezing dogs, soggy hot dog buns and a few choice mutterings under the breath. I recall pitching a tent at the base of a hill somewhere in the North Country on one of our first camping trips as a family . . . so we're talkin' toddlers here. Along with the assorted Hintz munchkins was a friend from New York—a tried-and-true city girl on her first "wilderness" adventure away from Manhattan's concrete.

When everyone was tucked into bedrolls, the stars also blinked out and a wind and rain storm hit. Runoff rushed down the hill behind us, sweeping through the tent and almost carrying away the by-now-quite-damp-and-getting-grumpier-by-the-minute friend. It took us two days to dry out. The lesson learned was not to pitch at the base of a ridge. The friend? Oh, she's never gone camping again.

LAKE WISSOTA STATE PARK (all ages)

Drive north of Chippewa Falls on State Highway 178. Pick up County Highway S to County Highway O for a 6-mile run to the park entrance. Open 6:00 A.M. to 11:00 P.M. State-park vehicle pass required; (715) 382–4574.

The park's lake was created in 1918 by a dam built by the Minnesota-Wisconsin Light & Power Company. Lake Wissota has 12 miles of trails poking into the most hidden parts of the woods and prairie land. The lake is one of the best in the North Woods for bass and muskies, so be sure you take plenty of lures and bait.

CABIN RIDGE RIDES (ages 5 and up)

To get to Cabin Ridge, drive County Highway O east to County Highway K, go south until you hit County Highway X. Then turn east to Town Line Road and travel south for 1½ miles; (715) 723–9537.

For another attraction not far from Lake Wissota, take in Cabin Ridge Rides for a leisurely, old-fashioned horse-drawn wagon or sleigh ride along the banks of fast-flowing Painted Creek. Several marked nature trails are in the vicinity, as well.

Places to Eat

Connell's Supper Club. *18525 Fiftieth Avenue; (715) 723–5656.* Connell's serves up leisurely dining experiences, figuring that a night out is well deserved. The supper club offers the usual, and hearty, American fare of steaks, fish, soups, and salads. $$

Medford

Take State Highways 29/73 east to State Highway 13. Turn north on 13 and proceed 14 miles to Medford.

TAYLOR COUNTY RODEO DAYS (ages 5 and up)

The rodeo is held at the county fairgrounds at the intersection of State Highways 13 and 64; (715) 678–2282. Early June.

Taylor County Rodeo Days brings bull riding and calf roping to northern Wisconsin, with real ranch hands trying to maintain their seats in the saddle. The weekend includes horse sales, pony races, and plenty of country-western music after the riding. Open team penning, where quarter horses get to show their training, brings cattle and cowpokes into close contact. The event is sanctioned by the International Professional Rodeo Association and is the richest IPRA rodeo in the United States, with thousands of dollars in purse money for winners.

TOWN AND COUNTRY DAIRY BREAKFAST (all ages)
While in Medford for the rodeo, stop for breakfast at a host farm participating in the annual Town and Country Dairy Breakfast, usually held on the same weekend as the bronc busting. Visitors can drop by for a hearty home-cooked breakfast of eggs, flapjacks, and plenty of other goodies. Folks such as Alvin and Rosie Kloth are proud to show off the dairy operations after guests finish munching. Kids can learn modern milking methods, find eggs, pet rabbits, cuddle kittens, and generally learn about life on a Wisconsin dairy operation. Check the *Medford Star News Shopper,* the local weekly newspaper, for the location of the year's host family. The paper is easily available at outlets throughout the county.

Amazing Wisconsin Facts
The population of Wisconsin is 4,906,745, according to the 1990 census. This places the state sixteenth in population. Of that number, 66 percent is urban and 34 percent is rural. The density is eighty-seven persons per square mile, while the United States average is sixty-nine per square mile. In 1840, the population was only 30,945. By 1850 it had risen to 305,391. Growth has been upward ever since.

But for your reference, there was life in Wisconsin (or what would be Wisconsin) about a half billion years ago. Fossils of early crustaceans, such as crabs, shellfish, and seaworms, are found throughout the state. Remains of ancient sturgeon were uncovered in Milwaukee's Estabrook Park.

Places to Eat

Black River Villa. *One-half mile east of State Highway 13 on County Highway O;* (715) 748–2250. Steaks, chicken, salad, and soups that can't be beat. $$

Earl's Bar. *Five miles west of Medford on State Highway 64;* (715) 785–7431. Beer and good pub grub. $.

Miracle Mile Diner. *Downtown Medford;* (715) 748–2434. Family-style eating. The kids can graze through an extensive menu of sandwiches, soups, and salads. Don't you forget to eat. $

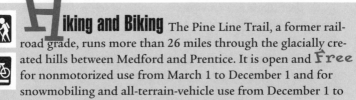

H̲iking and Biking The Pine Line Trail, a former railroad grade, runs more than 26 miles through the glacially created hills between Medford and Prentice. It is open and **Free** for nonmotorized use from March 1 to December 1 and for snowmobiling and all-terrain-vehicle use from December 1 to March 1, when snow conditions permit. In Medford the trailhead is located on Allman Street, about 1 mile west of State Highway 13, and on streets in Prentice, Ogema, Westboro, Chelsea, and Whittlesey. The northern part of the trail runs through heavily wooded areas, while the southern portion travels through dairy farms.

The National Ice Age Trail runs for 70 miles across Taylor County, starting at the State Highway 64/County Highway F intersection near Lublin in the southwest portion of the county. It runs to the Lincoln County line east of Woodlake.

TRAIL ETHICS:

- Leave wildlife alone
- Stay out of private property
- Do not litter
- Do not make fires
- Signal when overtaking
- Use caution at road crossings
- Travel on the right side of the trail

Rib Lake

Drive north 11 miles on State Highway 13 to State Highway 102. Turn east on 102 and drive the 10 miles to Spirit.

ICE AGE DAYS (all ages)

Ice Age Days at Rib Lake is usually held the second weekend in August to commemorate the glaciers that once held the county in its ice-cube grip. The Franzen Brothers Circus is a regular entertainment feature, but no woolly mammoths perform in the center ring, just your stock-in-trade Indian elephants. A mountain-bike race, radio-controlled model airplane demonstration, bed races, parade, bake sale, bingo, and an all-terrain-vehicle mud run are part of the fun. Even the largest family on holiday will fill their tummies at the event's Sunday chicken dinner held in the American Legion Hall. An Ice Age prince and princess are named to host the activities.

The National Ice Age Trail, which follows the rim of the last glaciers that covered Wisconsin, runs north to southwest through Taylor County and is well marked. The trail actually skirts downtown Rib Lake.

For More Information

Rib Lake Commercial Club, *P.O. Box 5, Rib Lake, WI 54470-0005; (715) 427–5761.*

Top Campgrounds

Some of the best camping in the Medford area is at the Mondeaux Flowage in the Chequamegon National Forest. Several campgrounds are within the flowage district, which was created in the 1930s. A section of the National Ice Age Trail runs along the western rim of the flowage, which is great for bass fishing and birdwatching. A concession stand, fishing pier, play area, and paddleboats to rent round out the recreation area. The campgrounds include Eastwood, Spearhead Point, West Point, North Twin Lake, Kathryn Lake, Chippewa, and Picnic Point. Rates range from $10 to $24 a night. For details on amenities, contact the Medford District Ranger, 850 North Eighth, Highway 13, Medford, WI 54451; (715) 748–4875.

Spirit

Spirit is only 13 miles north of Rib Lake on State Highway 102.

TIMM'S HILL COUNTY PARK (all ages)

Drive 6 miles west of Spirit, turn south on Price County C, and drive 1 mile to the park entrance; (715) 339–4505.

There's not much to see in downtown Spirit; it is primarily a wide spot in the road with a few homes spread along State Highway 86. Timm's Hill County Park is the highest point in Wisconsin. Plenty of parking is available near a picnic area and lake in the park near the actual hill. A steep trail through the thick woods leads to an observation tower crowning the 1,951 ½-foot-high peak. Take your time with little kids; stubby legs might have a hard time scrambling upward, particularly if there are slippery leaves and pine needles en route. But they'll love the feeling of accomplishment once they reach the base of the tower, far from the sight of autos and covered picnic shelters far below. It's a real neck-craner looking upward from the bottom of the tower, and it's easy to lose track of the number of steps to what seems to be a cloud-tagging platform. Yet a stalwart climber is rewarded with an awesome view of the surrounding countryside. The view is best in the autumn, when the oaks, maples, and birches burn with the season's Jack Frost fire. Be sure to take a camera to capture the quiltlike visual effect.

Phillips

Go west on State Highway 80 to State Highway 13. Turn north and drive 32 miles to Phillips.

WISCONSIN CONCRETE PARK (all ages)
State Highway 13 South; (715) 339–4505.

Wisconsin Concrete Park is difficult to miss on State Highway 13 South—just look for cement. More than 200 concrete statues of cowboys, Native Americans, and animals were created by the late Fred Smith, a retired logger. Smith spent fifty-six years in the woods, whacking away with his ax and slicing through tree trunks with a massive saw whose teeth rivaled those on any great white shark. When he finally decided to hang up his red flannels and wide suspenders, he said good-bye to the mustachioed shanty-house cookie and his bunkhouse mates and began sculpting to occupy his off-hours. Now considered among America's most famous folk artists, Smith's whimsical creations compose one of the world's largest outdoor collections. Dazzling with bits of broken glass imbedded in the forms, the variety of pieces is mind-boggling. There are plenty of toddler-size dogs, smiling dinosaurs, and happy-go-lucky rodeo riders placed around the grassy grounds.

CHEQUAMEGON NATIONAL FOREST (all ages)
The sprawling treescape of the Chequamegon National Forest is north of Phillips about 14 miles. The Park Falls district headquarters is in Park Falls, at the junction of State Highways 13 and 70.

*S*nowmobiling Snowmobiling is great fun in the national forestland, and clubs help maintain the trail system. The Sno-Drifters, Black River Rock Dodgers, Northwoods Riders Snowmobile Club, Medford Stump Jumpers, Jump River Runners, Pine Creek Riders, Moonlite Sno-Kats, Westboro Sno-Dusters, and the Interwald Wanderers are among the many clubs that ensure quality riding. These are family-based groups, with Mom, Dad, and kids participating.

Entire communities support the tourism effort in these forest areas. For instance, Perkinstown (18 miles west of Medford) is a hub of winter recreation in Taylor County, which sponsors a Winter Sports Area there. The park is complete with a cozy chalet, where folks can find a fireplace and nibble food. Kids will love tubing down the snow-covered hills in the park. There are both rope tows and stairs available for them to get back to the ridge peaks.

SMITH RAPIDS BRIDGE (all ages)

You'll find the bridge near the Round Lake logging dam by driving on U.S. Highway 51 north to Minocqua and turning west on State Highway 70 to Forest Road 148. The bridge is only 1½ miles north on 148.

While most of the forest's 840,000 acres are in neighboring Taylor County, a section extends into Price County, where the only working covered bridge in Wisconsin is located. Built in 1991 and situated in the forest's Smith Rapids Campground, the bridge is over the south fork of the Flambeau River. Its fresh new light-colored pine construction, but traditionally rustic visual appeal, is popular with artists, who prop up their easels and pads in an adjacent picnic area. Get the kids to take photos from all angles for their what-I-did-on-my-vacation scrapbooks. After heavy rains, however, watch for flooding in the area. In September 1994, Price County was hit with 11 inches of rain in three days, which closed many roads. Check with the Price County Tourism Office in Phillips (800–269–4505) for conditions.

For More Information

Park Falls Ranger District, *U.S. Department of Agriculture, 1170 South Fourth Avenue (State Highway 13), Park Falls, WI 54552; (715) 762–2461.*

Manitowish Waters

The next drive through the North Country is toward Manitowish Waters, about 25 miles north and east of Park Falls. Take State Highway 182 east through the lake district to State Highway 47. Drive north 4 miles on 47 to the junction with U.S. 51. Turn east on 51 and proceed another 3 miles through Manitowish and on to Manitowish Waters.

For some reason, in the 1920s and 1930s gangsters from Chicago used to enjoy Wisconsin's North Woods. The rustic lifestyle, woods, and lakes were probably considered great R&R after a day of bank robberies, auto chases, and bootlegging. Sometimes, however, their holidays were interrupted by the guys in the white hats.

LITTLE BOHEMIA (all ages)

Two miles south of Manitowish Waters on U.S. Highway 51; (715) 543–8433. $$
At Little Bohemia, John Dillinger and his buddies were ambushed in 1934 by feds and local police as they were relaxing over a card game. Bullet holes can still be seen in the walls of a cabin beside the restaurant, hidden in the forest along U.S. Highway 51. Some of the gang's memorabilia is on display there. One local man was killed in the shootout, and most of the thugs and their molls escaped into the brush despite the hail of gunfire. Today's restaurant serves thick steaks, home-made soups, and hot bread right out of the oven. Just check out the guys at the next table, though.

Manitowish Waters Skiing Skeeters Manitowish Waters brags that it is the "Barefoot Water Skiing Capital of the Midwest." The fifty members of the Skiing Skeeters have been putting on waterskiing shows since 1961. Participants start as juniors and are slowly moved up in the program. Their ski show bowl is on Rest Lake near the city dam, where programs are presented at 7:00 P.M. on Wednesday and Sunday in July and August. Donations are accepted to help pay for the club's equipment.

POWELL MARSH WILDLIFE AREA (all ages)

This 13,000-acre marshland is a shallow bog that is now a game-management project. It is one of the best sites in the North Country in which to watch migrating waterfowl, especially Canada geese. There is an observation area on Powell Road, opposite Dead Pike Lake, about 1 mile south of the Manitowish Waters airport on U.S. Highway 51. Stay in your car when watching birds to avoid frightening them.

Places to Eat

Ehrich's Bavarian Inn. *Downtown Manitowish Waters; (715) 543–2122.* Lunch is served from 11:30 A.M. to 2:30 P.M., with dinner from 5:00 P.M. Ehrich's specializes in German and American food. $$

Places to Stay

Butler's Four Seasons. *535 Alder Circle; (715) 543–2955.* Swimming, fishing, boating, loafing; all the best elements of a vacation area are here. $$

Fishing Guides For the best results in fishing the Manitowish Waters chain of lakes area, it is good to have a guide who knows the region and where the lunkers lurk. For help finding the big ones, write to R. A. McClellan, P.O. Box 246, Manitowish Waters, WI 54545, or call one of the following guides:

- Bob McClellan: (715) 543-2359
- Rick Bakken: (715) 385-2103
- Bill Eldridge: (715) 356-6437

Hurley

From Manitowish Waters, drive north on U.S. 51 to Hurley, on the Wisconsin-Michigan border.

Hurley still has a reputation as a two-fisted mining and lumbertown, which once had more red lights per square inch in its Tenderloin District than on the Shanghai docks. The stories that come out of its rough-tough era, which ran from the turn of the twentieth century into the 1950s, are enough to make a stevedore blush.

When in Hurley

AUGUST: Paavo Nurmi Marathon

DECEMBER: Red Light Snowmobile Rally

IRON COUNTY HISTORICAL MUSEUM (ages 10 and up)
303 Iron Street; (715) 561–2244. Open 10:00 A.M. to 2:00 P.M. daily. Closed holidays.

The Iron County Historical Museum brings alive the region's rich mining, farming, and logging traditions. The building in which it is housed has a sky-piercing tower with a clock on each side that can be seen for miles. This is handy when telling the time to traveling tykes. The building is on the National Register of Historic Places. Craftworkers inside make rugs on old-fashioned looms, which provides a fascinating peek into the past. A bonus is that the rugs are for sale.

 POTATO RIVER FALLS (all ages)
The area around Hurley is rugged, perfect for deer hunting during the season. The neighborhood has numerous waterfalls, with one of the best on State Highway 169, 3 miles south of Hurley near the village of Gurney. Rowe Farm Road, at the southern end of town, leads west to a picnic area alongside Potato River Falls. If the kids are tired of looking at falls and groan about seeing yet another one, convince them that yes, indeed, there is a falls made of french-fried spuds. Check their reactions when they see the real thing.

Places to Eat

Iron Nugget, *404 Silver Street; (715) 561–9800.* Even though there's "iron" in the name, everything is tender here, from the steaks to the desserts, served—of course—with tender loving care. $

For More Information

Hurley Area Chamber of Commerce, *110-A Second Avenue South, Hurley, WI 54534; (715) 561–4334.*

Glidden

To see more of the Chequamegon National Forest, drive southwest from Hurley on State Highway 77. Pick up State Highway 13 at Mellen, a distance of about 24 miles. Turn south on 13 for the 13-mile drive to Glidden.

CHEQUAMEGON NATIONAL FOREST (all ages)

Glidden District Ranger, U.S. Forest Service; (715) 264–2511.

The sprawling timberland of the Chequamegon National Forest is a prime camping area for anyone between novice and highly motivated, experienced backpacker. Even kids can have an adventure deep inside the thousands of square miles of pine, maple, poplar, and sumac that make up the U.S. Forest Service's Glidden District. Adventure four-wheel driving is part of the fun on old logging trails and gravel roads, where grazing moose can be spotted in foggy predawn hours. And yes, there are bears, too; honest to gosh, hungry bears.

Glidden calls itself the **Black Bear Capital of the World** and offers a reward for anyone bringing in a bigger beast than the 665-pounder that was shot near town in 1963. That bear is now stuffed and displayed in a glass-enclosed case near one of the downtown gas stations. The bear was so big it had to be weighed on the lumberyard scales.

So who would want to take kids into a place where large, toothy animals meander? Anyone who enjoys the outdoors will find the forestland a great place for hiking, camping, fishing, and hunting. And the bears?

Camping Tips Looking for a shaker for outdoor cooking when it comes to scrambled eggs or making muffins? Carry a common shaker (or a container with a screw top) in your camp utensil box, along with a 16-inch length of thin wire, plated chain. Toss dried egg or milk powder, along with water, into your shaker, along with the chain. A vigorous shake and everything is mixed to Julia Child's specifications.

HEALTHY CAMPFIRE SNACKS

Here are a couple of healthy snacks for late nights around the campfire:

- Brush some halved pears with melted butter and place the pieces on a square of heavy-duty foil. Fill the center of the pears with chopped nuts and raisins. Dot the centers with some more butter. Seal the package and place on medium coals for about ten minutes. Ah, delicious!

- Core several apples and fill each cavity with a teaspoon of raisins. Top them off with sugar and cinnamon and dot with butter. Seal each apple in a square of foil and place on medium coals for about forty-five minutes or until the apples are tender. You can also substitute marshmallows, cloves, or other goodies for the raisins. Be creative.

Well, they generally stay out of sight and out of mind. Campers should hang food high in a tree or keep it locked in a car trunk overnight, well out of reach of busy paws. These precautions are no different than what a wise parent does to protect the contents of the home refrigerator when a son's high school football team comes to visit. Bears will leave campers alone who leave them alone.

The district is a maze of waterways with such interesting names as Hell Hole Creek, Dead Horse Slough, and Dingdong Creek. There are plenty of camping opportunities throughout the area, such as at Day Lake, Lake Three, and East Twin Lake. The forest service operates these facilities via a fee system. Most offer developed sites, but primitive camping is allowed in certain areas. *Primitive* means what it says, so any teenagers should know there are no electrical outlets for hair dryers.

ST. PETER'S DOME (all ages)

One of the must-see stops in the district is St. Peter's Dome, a rock overlook on the far northern border of the district. From the top, the blue waters of Lake Superior 22 miles to the north can be spotted on a clear day. Take Forest Service Roads 387 to 198 and 197 to reach 199, the main road leading close to St. Peter's. An old gravel quarry is used as a parking area, with a path to the dome near the entrance to the long-abandoned pits. Anyone in good physical condition can make the climb, and for those with more bounce in their legs, a less-developed trail goes up the mountainside several hundred feet to the south. A lot of family tugging, pushing, and hauling helps get everyone up to the crest, which is a subtle lesson in the whole gang working together.

Bayfield

After Glidden, double back on State Highway 13 for a 30-mile drive north to Ashlands. Take U.S. Highway 2 around the south edge of the beautiful Chequamegon Bay and reconnect with 13 on the other side. Drive north on 13 to Bayfield.

The gateway to the Apostle Islands National Lakeshore, Bayfield seems to be the end of the world. In a way it is, tucked high atop the rim of northern Wisconsin where the freezing green waters of Lake Superior lap at its ankles. Twenty-one of the Apostles are just offshore, including Madeline Island, which is not part of the national lakeshore. They are mere smudges on the horizon when viewed from boat docks at the foot of the hill on which most of the village perches. I recall a gentle August shower that freshened what had been a humid dog-day afternoon. Leaving the dry comfort of a nearby little restaurant, the hamburger-and-apple-pie stuffed kids and I strolled down to the water's edge to sit on a white park bench (never minding the resulting damp behinds). A brilliant rainbow leapt from the lake to seemingly leapfrog from island to island. Everyone agreed the sight was better than a laser show, and

Go Fish Like to fish? Try your hand at Wisconsin's bass, muskie, pike, trout, and crappie in the lakes and inland waterways. Coho salmon, German brown trout, and lake trout are found offshore in the Great Lakes.

the kids wanted to immediately venture forth to find the buried treasure at its source. Being the perfect father, I naturally turned the discussion to the visual treasure just offshore.

Once a commercial fishing village, Bayfield is now home to guest houses and restaurants, with apple orchards and raspberry farms in the surrounding area. The biggest fruit grower in the state, Inar Olson, left Milwaukee's urban rush a number years ago with his family. They took over a farm and began growing berries and harvesting apples. After two decades of love and sweat, he now ships product around the upper Midwest, with his Bayfield Orchards apple jam being a prime lip-smacker. Tours of the orchards are available. In spring, the trees are a blaze of white blossoms, with a sweet fragrance permeating the gentle air.

The village is named after Adm. Henry Bayfield, who surveyed Lake Superior between 1823 and 1825. Its prime location quickly made it a favored harbor for fishing fleets. Summer visitors from the Twin Cities, Milwaukee, and Chicago then added their own flavor over the generations.

OLD RITTENHOUSE INN (all ages)
301 Rittenhouse Avenue, Bayfield, WI 54814; (715) 779–5111. $$
　　　Several of Bayfield's Victorian-era mansions, such as the fabled Old Rittenhouse Inn, have reopened as country inns or bed-and-breakfast facilities. Several of the inns and homes are now listed on the National Register of Historic Places. The Rittenhouse is noted for its table-groaning meals featuring fresh products from the neighborhood. Families are generally welcome, just don't let the toddlers climb up the chintz curtains or swing from the crystal chandeliers.

LAKE SUPERIOR BIG TOP CHAUTAUQUA (ages 10 and up)
State Highway 13; (715) 373–5851.
　　　The Lake Superior Big Top Chautauqua is only 3 miles south of Bayfield at the base of Mount Ashwabay. Performances reminiscent of old-time tent shows are presented nightly from mid-June to Labor Day. Even

youngsters can get into the swing of the ricky-tick music, folk singing, and side-groaning vaudeville jokes. The only things this event lacks are dancing dogs and ball-balancing seals. Dress for the weather, because even summer nights along the lake can be cool. Sometimes bug spray is also required: The show is under billowing blue-and-white striped canvas, but skeeters have no respect for artistic sensibilities.

Lake Superior Sailing There are several excellent charters that offer sailing excursions from the Bayfield harbor and numerous options to consider when choosing a sailing yacht. You can cruise on a captained boat piloted by the owner, or if you have experience, you can try out your own skills on a bareboat charter. (Naturally, bareboat certification is required for insurance purposes.) Sailboats out of Bayfield range from 24 to 44 feet. Yachts can be fully stocked, or you can choose to supply your own bedding and provisions. Here are several companies that offer great packages: Animaashi Sailing Company (888-272-4548 or 715-779-5468; www.animaashi. com); Apostle Islands Cruise Service (800-323-7619 or 715-779-3925; www. apostleisland.com); Bayfield Fishing & Sailing Charters (715-779-7010); Catchun-Sun Charter Company (888-724-5494 or 715-779-3111); Moon Shadow Sailing (612-757-6498); Sailboats, Inc. (800-826-7010; www.sailboats-inc. com); Superior Charters (800-772-5124 or 715-779-5124; www.superiorcharters.com); and Trek & Trail (715-779-3320).

Places to Eat

Greunke's Restaurant. *Downtown Bayfield; (715) 779–5480.* Seafood, steak, and homemade pies have made Greunke's a popular Bayfield restaurant for more than fifty years. $$

Maggie's. *257 Manypenny; (715) 779–5641.* The place brags of its real food, real drinks, real fun, and fake flamingos. Open 6:00 A.M. to 11:00 P.M. $$

Apostle Islands

There are several ways to get to the Apostle Islands: walk on water, swim, canoe or kayak; however, the best option is to hop on the ferryboat in the Bayfield harbor and let the captain do the driving. The trip takes about twenty to thirty minutes.

After exploring Bayfield, take the time to visit the Apostles, with Madeline Island being a prime destination. Sailors love the wind and freshwater action around all the rocky, fir-crowned pinnacles. The Apostles received their name from early settlers who obviously couldn't count but had a Biblical sense of nomenclature. Instead of only twelve, there are actually twenty-two islands in the chain. Sailboats add colorful dashes of color during the season. Several regattas and races are held throughout the summer, with entrants scooting across the lake like waterbugs.

One of the most exciting trips of my several to Madeline Island was a 5:00 A.M. snowmobile expedition across the frozen waters of Lake Superior. The jaunt, part of a 400-mile run along the tip-top of the state, took place on a crisp, thirty-five-degree-below-zero predawn several years ago. Following a trail marked by old Christmas trees, our convoy of sleds scooted the 3 dark miles from Bayfield across the creaking, groaning ice to La Pointe. Everything was in hard relief; the cold seemed to have frozen the world in its tracks. The stars were mere stabs of light overhead. Protected by helmets, leather suits, and gloves, we hit the beach and toured the shuttered town and hibernating island for two hours before heading back to Bayfield for breakfast.

MADELINE ISLAND FERRY LINE (all ages)

P.O. Box 66, Department S, La Pointe, WI 54850; (715) 747–2051.

Generally, when spring brings the thaw, Madeline is most easily reached via a twenty-minute ride aboard one of the vessels belonging to the Madeline Island Ferry Line. The dock is on Washington Avenue. Kids can act as jolly tars, catching the spray from the bow and letting the wind tousle their hair on the ride over. Just watch out for screeching seagulls and their dive-bomb droppings. Bring your bicycle.

MADELINE ISLAND HISTORICAL MUSEUM (ages 5 and up)

La Pointe; (715) 747–2415. Open 10:00 A.M. to 6:00 P.M. August 22 through October 17.

Take the time to wander the streets, poke for shells, and drop by the Madeline Island Historical Museum in La Pointe. Housed in four historic buildings and an information center, the museum traces the community from its pre-European days to the contemporary. La Pointe itself, along with Green Bay and Prairie du Chien, is one of the three of oldest European settlements in Wisconsin, dating to the 1600s and 1700s when the first French *voyageurs* set up their encampments.

Most of the artifacts on display were found on the island or its tinier neighbors and were donated by area residents. Baskets, beadwork, and other items from the Ojibwe Indians are a major feature of the exhibition. The tribe regarded Madeline Island as their spiritual homeland, a fact easily understood when standing quietly alone under the summer's brilliant full-moon skies. Other displays feature hunting, trapping, fur trading, fishing, and the Great Lakes maritime industries, missionaries, and island residents.

The museum was started by Leo Casper and his artist wife, Isabella, two longtime summer visitors to the island whose home was in St. Paul, Minnesota. They opened the facility in 1958 and gave it to the state historical society in 1968.

MADELINE ISLAND BUS TOURS (all ages)

Ferry Dock, La Pointe; (715) 747–2051.

If you don't have a car or bike or prefer not to walk, Madeline Island Bus Tours start from the La Pointe ferry dock. The tours operate from April through December. After that, it's snowshoes, skis, or snowmobiles.

Red Cliff

RED CLIFF INDIAN RESERVATION (ages 5 and up)

Three miles north of Bayfield on State Highway 13 is the Red Cliff Indian Reservation, ancestral home of the Red Cliff band of Lake Superior Chippewa. Red Cliff Bingo on the Bay (715–779–3712) is a nightly feature throughout the year. No one under eighteen is allowed in the bingo hall, however, so plan accordingly. The reservation overlooks a picturesque bend of Lake Superior where Raspberry, Oak, Sand, York, Hermit, and Basswood Islands are easily seen to the east and northeast. The dots of land are part of the Apostle Islands.

Isle Vista Casino Three miles north of Bayfield on State Highway 13; (715) 779–3712 or (800) 226–8478.

The casino is owned and operated by the Red Cliff Band of Lake Superior Chippewa. The casino touts that it is adjacent to more than 600 miles of groomed snowmobile trails.

Cornucopia, Herbster, and Port Wing

From Red Cliff to the communities along the Lake Superior shoreline, drive west along State Highway 13. Cornucopia is 18 miles from Red Cliff, Herbster is 26 miles, and Port Wing is 35.

State Highway 13 skirts the underbelly of frosty Lake Superior, that ship-eating pond laying claim to being the world's largest body of fresh water. The lake is 350 miles long and 160 miles wide, covering 31,820 square miles, 20,620 of which are in the United States. The average depth is 475 feet. That's a lot of H_2O. Even jaded teens will be in awe after gazing at all those green-black waves. The tiny towns of Cornucopia, Herbster, and Port Wing offer lakeshores for strolling and deep-water charter fishing for monster lake salmon and German brown trout. Cornucopia may be Wisconsin's northernmost village, a mere sneeze in size tucked into Siskiwit Bay, but the town does boast a small private airport.

ST. MARY'S GREEK ORTHODOX CHURCH (ages 5 and up)

The onion-shaped dome of Cornucopia's St. Mary's Greek Orthodox Church doesn't seem out of place. It served as a central gathering place several generations ago when a contingent of Greek fisherfolk first moved to the area. A wayside just off the highway in the heart of town is a perfect spot to pull over and picnic. It is usually breezy in these parts, so be sure someone in the family is in charge of retrieving lost napkins. This is a good job for the preschool set when they tire of skipping flat stones across the watery deep.

CRANBERRY RIVER (ages 5 and up)

Just to the west of Cornucopia in nearby Herbster, the fast-flowing Cranberry River offers good fly-fishing potential for trout. A campsite on the shore of the lake presents excellent views of Lake Superior when morning eyes slowly open. Another 7 miles west is Port Wing, home port to a charter-fishing fleet. Day and half-day trips are available, and kids are welcome to try their hand at angling. Everyone on board gets a crack at the fish when their turn comes up. Captains and mates are skilled in dealing with landlubbers of all ages and are ready and willing to offer suggestions and comment about life on the greatest of the Great Lakes.

Amazing Wisconsin Facts

Some ninety-seven out of every one hundred Wisconsinites were born in the United States. When breaking heritage down along ethnic lines, more than half of the state's citizens are of German descent. Other large populations include Polish, Irish, and English. About 5 percent of the population is African-American.

CITY PARK (ages 5 and up)

City Park in Port Wing has replicas of an early school bus and a mail wagon, as well as the bell tower from Wisconsin's first consolidated school building. The kids probably don't want to be reminded of classrooms on a vacation jaunt, so take them down to the sandiest beach along this leg of the lakeshore. Give them a stint at castle-building.

For More Information

Cornucopia Business Association, *P.O. Box 316, Cornucopia, WI 54827; (715) 742–3232.*

Superior

AMNICON FALLS STATE PARK (all ages)

c/o Pattison State Park, U.S. Highway 35, 6294 South State Road 35, Superior, WI 54880; (715) 398–3000 in the summer; (715) 399–8073 in other seasons. Open from May through October. A state-park vehicle sticker is required.

Continue driving westward toward Superior on State Highway 13, crossing the Brule River and on to County Highway U, which enters Amnicon Falls State Park. Three of its four waterfalls are higher than 30 feet, roaring over the ledges to explode with foam and fury into pools at their feet. Line up the kids along the covered bridge in the park for the requisite family portrait.

*B*ong Memorial Just to the east of Amnicon Falls is the small town of Poplar, home of Richard Bong, the Army Air Corps's leading ace of World War II with forty confirmed kills in the Pacific Theater. The Bong Memorial in town includes an authentic P-38 fighter plane.

PATTISON STATE PARK (all ages)

U.S. Highway 35, 6294 South State Road 35, Superior, WI 54880; (715) 399–8073. About 10 miles south of Superior on U.S. Highway 35.

Speaking of waterfalls, if the family hasn't tired of landscapes looking like leaky faucets, they might enjoy a peek at Pattison State Park. The park is home to Big Manitou Falls, the state's highest waterfall at 165 feet.

Places to Eat

Barker's Island Inn. *300 Marina Drive; (715) 392–7152.* Watch the freighters entering the Superior Harbor from the wide windows inside the restaurant. Salads, steaks, sea-faring theme . . . it's all here. $$

Fullers Family Restaurant. *5817 Tower Avenue; (715) 392–7510.* Bring the whole gang to Fullers and fill 'em up. That's a common refrain here in Superior country. $

The Shack Supper Club. *3301 Belknap Street; (715) 392–9836.* There's nothing shacklike about this place, one of the more popular eateries in Superior country. Even Duluth folks from across the nearby Minnesota border are known to frequent the supper club. $$

Cable

After your drive along the southern rim of Lake Superior and a visit to Amnicon Falls, proceed back eastward on U.S. Highway 2 to Brule, about 16 miles. Turn south on State Highway 27 to County Road N, which takes you through Barnes and on to Drummond. At Drummond, turn south on U.S. Highway 63 to Cable.

 CABLE NATURAL HISTORY MUSEUM (ages 10 and up) *County M and Randysek Road; (715) 798–3890. Open year-round from 10:00 A.M. to 4:00 P.M., Tuesday through Saturday.*

Head inside the Cable Natural History Museum for an impressive tour of stuffed-and-mounted regional wildlife and other nature exhibits. The museum also offers hands-on field trips into the surrounding countryside for a special look at all the rich flora and fauna. Lectures and workshops are held throughout the year, many of which are geared to youngsters. It is an important facility to visit so that kids can understand what makes nature tick.

Hayward

From Cable, drive south on U.S. Highway 63 to Hayward.

Hayward is one of the state's best year-round launching points for families on a vacation fun quest. Located on State Highway 77, the city is a getaway hub amidst deep-blue lakes and emerald-green pine forests. Stock up on groceries, wash campfire-smudged jeans, take in a movie after a television-less week in the woods, visit souvenir shops to purchase the requisite T-shirts and postcards, and grab a real restaurant meal following days of beans and burned eggs in the bush.

In Hayward, everyone from the Common Council to the gas station attendant talks fish: perch, trout, walleye, crappie. Who caught what, what bait was used, what about the water temps, who swamped their canoe while netting a monster. After all, the hundreds of bumper stickers seen around town point out that a bad day of fishing is better than a good day at work. In cafes, on street corners, and in the sport shops there's only talk of fish, fish, fish. Speaking about fish stories, what must be the most fabulous dream experienced by any angler can be seen leaping over the oaks on the drive into Hayward. A giant muskie, the sharp-toothed monster fish of a thousand casts, rears high on the horizon with mouth agape and fiberglass scales flashing in the sun.

 ## NATIONAL FRESHWATER FISHING HALL OF FAME
(ages 5 and up)

Hall of Fame Drive; (715) 634–4440. Open 10:00 A.M. to 5:00 P.M., mid-April to November 1.

Landlocked and not real, the four-story muskie is the main feature of the National Freshwater Fishing Hall of Fame. Take the kids into the muskie-shaped museum to show off its mind-boggling displays of homemade and commercial lures, antique outboard motors, and photos of grinning guys and gals posing with their record-setting catches. To reach the mouth of the muskie, you meander up an incline past awards, memorabilia, and trophies marking the biggest this and thats of the finny world. One wonders what a worm would think of all this, but that question probably never crosses the minds of numerous brides who bring their newly landed husbands to the muskie maw for wedding portraits. "Smile. You can go fishing right after we're done," is a common refrain. Giant-size bluegills and bass bound out of the grass in front of the museum. There's even a rowboat anchored in the scene. It's a great place for gag photos, with the children aboard the boat facing the leaping concrete fish.

 ## AMERICAN BIRKEBEINER CROSS-COUNTRY SKI RACE TRACK
(ages 10 and up)

Birkie details can be obtained by calling (800) 872–2753 (national) or (800) 722–3386 (Wisconsin). For registration information write the race headquarters at 110 Main, P.O. Box 911, Hayward, WI 54843.

One section of the 47-kilometer American Birkebeiner cross-country ski race track between Hayward and Cable is used in the summer by hikers and mountain bikers. Later in the year, hundreds of bikers enter the

Chequamegon Fat Tire Bike Race and Festival. No Pee-wee Herman bikers, these hardy souls pound over the rugged landscape to demonstrate that hardy calves and thighs can do wonders in the woods.

Hayward is also the starting point for the American Birkebeiner, the highest-touted cross-county ski race in North America. Held each February, the Birkie hosts 8,000 to 10,000 skiers for the tortuous 47-kilometer course over slopes and flatlands between Hayward and Cable. Norway, Sweden, Finland, Germany, Austria, and France have been among the nations represented, along with a plethora of sleekly attired Canadians and Yankees. There are various legs of the event for skiers of different skill levels, but each section puts physical demands on participants that are unequaled in any other race on the continent. Yet there are heats for kids and oldsters, too. So the Birkie makes a fine, albeit exhausting, winter weekend for any family that loves outdoor challenges.

For racewatchers, the best spot is right in downtown Hayward when the pack takes off along the jammed main street. Bring a stepladder or a periscope to peer over the heads of the watching crowd, and—of course—dress for the weather. Heavy socks and waterproof boots are a necessity for anyone standing around in the below-freezing temperatures. Then there are mittens, scarves, stocking caps, jackets, pants, ski masks, and all the other high-fashion garb that rounds out a winter in the North Woods. It's well worth it, though, especially if you're participating.

Places to Eat

Anglers Bar & Grill. *133 Main Street; (715) 634–4700.* No one would probably mind if you brought in your trophy muskie to show off to the guys at the bar. They'd probably buy a round of drinks. This gang knows fish. Then step over to the tables for supper. Fish sandwich, of course. $

Karibalis Restaurant. *212 Main Street; (715) 634–2462.* Home cookin' at its North Woods finest. $

The Moose Cafe. *106 Dakota Avenue; (715) 634–8449.* We've never eaten a whole moose here, nor a partial one, either. But who is to say one isn't lurking in the kitchen, ready for takeout? Until the antlers peek through the swinging door, I'd suggest going for the burgers. $

For More Information

Hayward Area Chamber of Commerce, *101 West First Street, P.O. Box 726, Hayward, WI 54843-0726; (715) 634–4801.*

Couderay

For another leg of your trip, drive south from Hayward on State Highway 27 to the junction with State Highway 70 near Stone Lake. Take 70 east to Couderay.

Whenever Windy City gangster Al Capone needed a break from breaking the law, he would head to the Wisconsin's Northwoods for a little R&R, leading his convoy of limos and gun-toting pals.

Winter in Rusk County

Winter doesn't mean a vacationer needs to lose perspective in Wisconsin. So the drifts pile up throughout the glacially formed countryside of Rusk County. So what if the weather is frosty. It's the time when snowmobiles and cross-country skis, followed by family games in front of the fireplace, take the edge off Old Man Winter's threats. There are more than 250 miles of snowmobile trails throughout the county, with a wildly wonderful panorama of dazzling snow and ice. Some of the best power sledding is through the Blue Hills, which once were composed of a 20,000-foot-high mountain range but were smushed by the grinding action of glaciers several eons ago. The Five State Corridor Trails lead to every corner of Rusk County.

Even when chilling out on the wind-blown trails, there are opportunities to warm up after a day of riding. The Weyerhauser Snowmobile Club offers use of its warming hut on a lovely overlook on Trail 133, in the northwest part of the county. Six miles north of Weyerhauser, the fully enclosed "snug" has a Franklin stove, picnic tables, and benches. A generator there can be switched on to the run lights if a sledder stops by in the evening.

THE HIDEOUT (ages 10 and up)
The complex is on County CC, a couple of miles north off State Highway 70; (715) 945–2746. $$.

Not that criminal activity is glorified at The Hideout, but the place has a definite place in the state's history. Al Capone and his cronies stayed at the lodge on a regular basis to fish, play cards, tell FBI jokes, and target practice. Stone outbuildings are well settled into the woodsy landscape like squat undersized castles; at least one taller structure is reputed to have been a watchtower. Not that anyone bothered Scarface on his visits—the locals always took a wide berth around the lodge when he arrived. The Hideout is now a steak house, offering some of the best meals and best gangster ghosts this side of Chicago's Michigan Avenue.

The kids should be impressed with the rumors of secret cellars that allegedly hid Prohibition booze. They'll be wide-eyed with the legends of long-deceased dandies in double-breasted suits who carried guitar cases but couldn't play a tune. Just remind the youngsters to pay their taxes, because it was such a little oversight that did in the famed criminal.

For More Information

Rusk County Information Center, *817 West Miner Avenue, NW Ladysmith, WI 54848; (800) 535–7875 or (715) 532–2642.*

Rice Lake

After Couderay, drive south on State Highway 40 to the intersection with State Highway 48. Then follow 48 into Rice Lake, about 40 miles.

RED BARN SUMMER THEATER (ages 10 and up)
State Highway 48 and County Highway M; (715) 234–8301. Open early May through Labor Day.

Rice Lake was founded in 1868 as a logging-camp headquarters and received its name from the numerous wild-rice beds that once fed the resident Chippewa. The community is now noted for its Red Barn Summer Theater, which draws vacationers staying in nearby resorts. The locals go, too, so you know it has to be good.

Places to Eat

Dev's Restaurant. *807 South Main Street; (715) 234–4257.* If you want to hear hunting and fishing stories, come early and tune in one ear to the good ol' boys at breakfast. Pancakes!!! $

Lehman's Supper Club. *2911 South Main Street; (715) 234–2428.* Families are welcome for a quiet, getaway evening in this town that caters to visitors. $$

Barronett

Drive west on State Highway 48 to U.S. 63. Turn north on 63 and drive 7 miles to Barronett.

CAROUSEL CREATIONS (all ages)

The workshop is located on U.S. Highway 63 between Cumberland and Shell Lake. Just look for billboards.

At Carousel Creations, woodcarver Ron Helstern creates delightfully intricate merry-go-round figures for an international clientele. Some of his prancing steeds and fierce dragons weigh more than 250 pounds. One carving features a 9½-foot snake wrapped around a tiger. Operating since 1986 in what used to be an old implement shop, Helstern and his wife, Sue, started making signs and "branched" into carving. In addition to the carousel animals made from patterns and old photos, they also do custom carving and restorations. Helstern, for instance, completed a 7-foot-tall horse weighing 500 pounds for a corporate client. All his pieces are carved from basswood, the traditional wood used by old-time master carvers.

Their showroom displays lions, tigers, and horses inside a small gift shop. Guests can crowd up to a viewing window that opens on Helstern hard at work. If he has time, he often gives lectures on carving. When the shop was totally open to visitors, folks kept looking over Helstern's shoulders, so it was sometimes difficult for him to get his work done. Yet he will often steal a few minutes to put little kids on the back of one of his glamorous horses.

Formerly an insurance investigator, Helstern is a self-taught carver who originally started carving in his home. He and his wife moved into town because of the growth of their sign business.

The traveler with an extra $2,000 to spare can probably take home a small carousel horse. The cost depends on the details of the carving and the length of time it takes to complete the project, which might be up to three or four months.

 ## THE CAROUSEL CAFE (all ages)

2974 U.S. Highway 63; (715) 822–3424. $

The Carousel Cafe, next door to the Carousel Creations workshop, features several of Helstern's creations, along with relief carvings. The cafe is casual family-style, with great hamburger baskets. Originally a grocery store, the Carousel Cafe was built in 1910 and still has the original light fixtures and floor boards. Barronett had a disastrous fire in 1895 that practically leveled the city, so most of its buildings date from the period after the blaze.

BOYER CREEK RANCH (all ages)

Five miles west of Barronett on Boyer Creek Road; (715) 469–3394 or (715) 822–4097.

For live-animal viewing, the Boyer Creek Ranch has the largest herd of European red deer in the United States. Visitors are welcome to visit and poke around the pens.

Shell Lake

Shell Lake is about 8 miles north of Barronett on U.S. Highway 63.

 MUSEUM OF WOODCARVING (ages 5 and up)

U.S. Highway 63 North; (715) 468–7100. Open 9:00 A.M. to 6:00 P.M., May 1 through October 30.

For cut-ups in the family, the Museum of Woodcarving is a slice above the usual museum. There are more than 100 life-size and 400 miniature figures of famous historical characters, including a full complement of apostles gathered for the Last Supper. Local carver Joseph T. Barta spent thirty years chipping away on his hobby.

Wisconsin's Rustic Roads Wisconsin's Rustic Roads program marks stretches of getaway back roads that retain the charm of a slower era. There are fifty-six such designated roadways in the state, ranging from 2½ miles to 10 miles in length. Most are paved but some are gravel. Therefore, the speed limit is often around 45 mph, so beware of slow-moving vehicles. For a pamphlet describing the roads, contact Rustic Roads, Wisconsin Department of Transportation, Box 7913, Madison, WI 53707; (608) 266–0639.

Spooner

Travel north of Shell Lake for 5 miles on U.S. Highway 63 to Spooner.

The Namekgon River near Spooner is one of the best canoeing streams in the state. The river flows into Trego Lake, where a sixteen-pound, eight-ounce walleye was caught. The fish was one of Wisconsin's largest catches. On rainy days, take advantage of the **Badgerland Civic Center,** which has a swimming pool, health club, jogging track, and roller rink open for public use. Located at 301 Walnut Street; (715) 635–6144.

 BULIK'S AMUSEMENT CENTER (ages 5 and up)
U.S. Highway 63 North; (715) 635–7111. Open noon to 7:00 P.M. daily from Memorial Day through Labor Day.

Bulik's Amusement Center, 1 mile north of Spooner on U.S. Highway 63, has enough water slides, go-carts, and mini-golf holes to satisfy the most demanding kid, from teenager to toddler. Turn them loose, sit back and watch, or plunge in.

Places to Stay

American Heritage Inn. *101 Maple Street, Spooner; (715) 635–9774 or (800) 356–8018.* Forty-five rooms, swimming pool. $$

Country House Motel. *717 South River Street, U.S. Highway 63 South, Spooner; (715) 635–8721 or (800) 715–8721.* Twenty-two rooms. $$

Green Acres Motel. *N4809 U.S. Highway 63 South and State Highway 253,* *Spooner; (715) 635–2177 or (800) 373–5293.* Twenty-one rooms. $

Inn Town Motel. *801 River Street, Spooner, WI 54801; (715) 635–3529 or (800) 652–1422.* Twenty rooms. $

Trego Inn Motel. *U.S. Highway 53 and U.S. Highway 63, Trego; (715) 635–3204 or (800) 681–5939.* Twelve rooms. Five miles north of Spooner. $

Central Wisconsin

The state's heartland is fun land. Theme parks, museums, and attractions of all kinds await the traveler. There are cities and small towns to explore, with all their historical and contemporary richness. There are state and county parks with camping and resort opportunities. You can't admit to boredom in central Wisconsin.

This is a branching-out kind of place, where wide, smooth interstates can get you quickly through, or to. The choice is always yours. We usually opt for the "to" part of the equation. Sometimes, we admit, getting there is not necessarily half the fun, especially when you want most of the "fun" to be at your final destination. But if you have the time, central Wisconsin is the dawdler's paradise. Peek into a

Hintz's Top Picks

- Exploring Madison's museums
- Waterskiing or ice fishing on Madison's lakes
- Canoeing the Wisconsin River
- Visiting Frank Lloyd Wright–designed buildings
- Admiring the autumn colors
- Watching a late-afternoon thunderstorm roll over Governor Dodge State Park (from the comfort and safety of a tent)
- Poking around the Mustard Museum in Mount Horeb
- Attending an art fair in a small town near Madison
- Crossing the Wisconsin River aboard the ferry
- Watching the politicians acting up in the state legislature

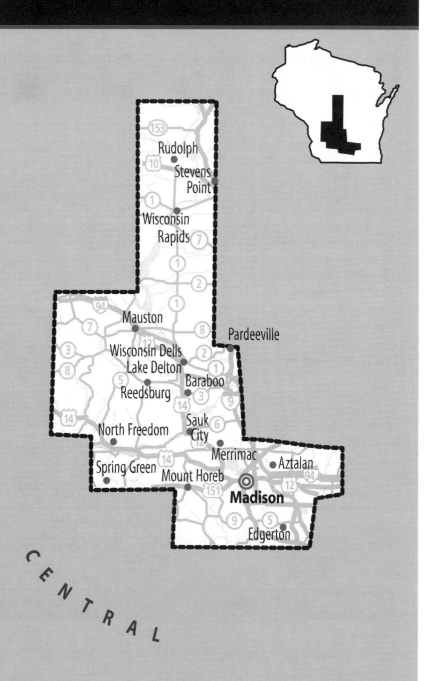

CENTRAL

sooty blacksmith's shop in a re-created pioneer village. Bike the thigh-stretching high ridges above architect Frank Lloyd Wright's home near Spring Green. Count the Holsteins grazing in clover-rich pastures along the lazy Wisconsin River. Sample an explosive, fiery mustard in the Mount Horeb Mustard Museum. Explore caves, wildlife parks, county museums, state forests, arboretums, and crafts shops from the Mississippi River to Madison, the state capital. If the opportunity arises, put the clock aside and simply poke along at a snail's pace. Some of the stops in this part of Wisconsin should be spur-of-the-moment, "hey-let's-pull-over-cuz-that-looks-neat" decisions. Others may take a bit more planning, such as calling ahead to confirm admission times and schedules for tours or dates of programs. Regardless of how a decision is reached, the result should be the same: discovery.

The Wisconsin Division of Tourism, *Wisconsin Trails Magazine,* local tourism offices, weekly newspapers, and such guides as *Fun with the Family in Wisconsin* are invaluable for getting the broad scope of what to see and do. Or just ask any town native on the street corner. "What's going on?" is an easy way to break the ice. Involve the kids as much as possible in planning. Fill in everyone on the wheres and hows of the trip to central Wisconsin. This is important whether it entails a week in the theme-park-rich Wisconsin Dells, a more rustic getaway, or a city experience.

Chambers of commerce and other information centers are happy to provide material in advance. So pick a destination and call or write for what to see and do. You'll be buried in all sorts of good stuff. Visit a local travel/vacation show, if possible. Ask questions of tourism representatives, outfitters, and resort owners. Providing answers is their job.

Central Wisconsin has a great blend of urban and rural experiences. It's as fun to walk the halls of the state capitol and count the carved badger statues there as it is to sit quietly on a log in Governor Dodge State Park and watch white-tailed deer during their evening snack hour. Take the kids to dine in big-city gourmet splendor, picnic in the woods, or grab a crisp, fresh apple on the run in between. Every locale provides a unique experiential culinary niche, whether questing after liver pâté or granola bars.

Central Wisconsin has a travel menu for every palette and budget.

Reedsburg

Reedsburg is a great place to begin a jaunt through central Wisconsin because it is in the heart of this fantastic tourist region. Reedsburg is at the intersection of State Highways 23 and 22 in northern Sauk County.

Amazing Wisconsin Facts The Wisconsin River rises in the Lac Vieux Desert on the Wisconsin-Michigan border. The 430-mile-long stream flows to the south through central Wisconsin, going past Portage and then turning west. The Wisconsin empties into the Mississippi River a couple of miles below Prairie du Chien. Near the Wisconsin Dells, it forms Lake Delton, while cutting through sandstone rock to a depth of about 150 feet.

MUSEUM OF NORMAN ROCKWELL ART (ages 10 and up)

227 South Park Street; (608) 524–2123. Summer hours are 9:00 A.M. to 5:00 P.M.; winter hours vary, so call for details. Norman Rockwell video shown hourly.

Junior and Muffy might not know the name Norman Rockwell, but they can certainly identify with the characters in his paintings. The artist spent his life chronicling the ups and downs of ordinary folks in situations that are so real they seem to leap from the canvas. The youngsters, therefore, will probably enjoy the Museum of Norman Rockwell Art, which showcases some 4,000 pieces of the famed illustrator's work. The collection has been called the largest of its kind in the world, with curators always interested in finding more pieces. So rummage through the attic and garage in search of collector's treasures and bring them with you on a visit. If you find something previously unduplicated in the collection, your family has friends for life.

PIONEER LOG VILLAGE AND MUSEUM (ages 5 and up)

Intersection of State Highways 23 and 33; (608) 524–2807. Open 1:00 to 4:00 P.M. Saturday and Sunday, from Memorial Day through September, Labor Day, and also July 4.

The museum includes a school, store, and other buildings dating from the Civil War era. Visitors can poke around the church and blacksmith shop to get an idea of what life was like during the so-called good old days.

Places to Eat

Greenwoods Cafe. *116 South Walnut Street; (608) 524–6203.* Clean, comfortable, convenient—that's the Greenwoods Cafe. Cookin' like your dreams of Mom's best. $

Longley's Restaurant. *1599 East Main Street; (608) 524–6497.* Every town should be so lucky to have such a Main Street eatery. Drop by and be greeted warmly. They know about families here. $

North Freedom

To find trains, follow the sound of the steam whistle to North Freedom. Take State Highway 23 south from Reedsburg to State Highway 154. Turn east on 154 to County Road PF. Go south on PF to North Freedom.

MID-CONTINENT RAILWAY MUSEUM (all ages)

Take State Highway 136 west to County Highway PF, then south to North Freedom. Walnut Street; (608) 522–4261. Open 9:30 A.M. to 5:00 P.M. daily from mid-May through Labor Day, with rides at 10:30 A.M. and 12:30, 2:00, and 3:30 P.M. Open Saturday and Sunday from early May through mid-October.

Take a ride into the past at the Mid-Continent Railway Museum. While the fifty-minute rides are given four times a day throughout the summer, taking the train in the autumn or winter is the most scenic and nostalgic. (The trains make special snow runs.) Old No. 1385 pulls its string of coaches through the countryside tinged by Jack Frost in the fall, then plows through the snow when Old Man Winter does his thing. The train will stop several times for kids to hop off and scoot out to photo-snapping spots. In the winter the train backs up after unloading the shutterbugs and slips around a scenic bend. Then, with whistle blowing and steam snorting into the frozen air, the engine chugs back around the corner for a fantastic picture opportunity. The ensuing clicking of camera shutters sounds like crickets lost on a frozen lake. Volunteers, dressed as old-time engineers

Amazing Wisconsin Facts

Vinnie Ream of Madison was the first woman sculptor commissioned by Congress to produce a work for display. In 1866, when she was only eighteen years old, Ream began work on a statue of Abraham Lincoln. The piece, which was completed in 1870, can be seen at the U.S. Capitol in Washington, D.C.

and conductors, man the car-repair shops and operate the rides. Several dozen pieces of rolling stock are on the sidings, including several European train cars. Some of the museum members even have their own sleepers, where they can sprawl on holiday visits between tinkering with these giant locomotives.

Spring Green

Trundle south to find Spring Green, home of Frank Lloyd Wright. From North Freedom, take County Road W to State Highway 23. Turn south and go about 17 miles.

While Spring Green may be small (only about 2,000 resident population), it is big in things to see and do. It is a hub for central Wisconsin's canoeing, camping, hiking, biking, golfing, poking around, and lolling under a maple. This is the so-called driftless region of Wisconsin, where glaciers didn't rumble, so the ridges and valleys are worn by erosion, not by ice-age action. This means there are still hills to pedal up and scoot down, rivers cut into deep limestone banks, and hiking trails across high ridges with vistas where on a clear day one can see almost forever or at least 100 square miles.

FRANK LLOYD WRIGHT BUILDINGS (ages 10 and up)

A visitors center (608–588–7900) and restaurant at the corner of State Highway 23 and County Highway C is the starting point for tours. Many Wright-connected buildings are in Jones Valley, 3 miles south of Spring Green on Highway 23. Hillside tours are 10:00 A.M. to 4:00 P.M. daily, May through October.

This natural getaway was at least one reason why famed architect Frank Lloyd Wright loved this area so much. He established his **Taliesin** studio as a "hope and a haven" for creative thinking; it became a complex of buildings that shaped design for generations. At Taliesin, Wright developed plans for the Imperial Hotel in Japan, the Johnson Wax administration building in Racine, and other marvelous structures. Tours of his former home, now a national landmark, are regular components of the tourist scene in the area. Wright designed the elaborate, 300-foot-long visitors center, as well. Tell the kids that the trusses throughout the center were made from the skeleton of the *Ranger,* a World War II aircraft carrier, and they should be impressed. The visitors center is a pleasant place from which to start a day, as it looks over the rolling Wisconsin River. Have morning buns and tea for breakfast. Children are welcome, and nose prints on picture windows can easily be wiped off.

Architects still work and learn at the Taliesin complex across the highway and down the road, which is reached by van from the visitors center. Tours of the complex range from about an hour to half a day or more. Smaller young ones, naturally, might opt for the shorter version, while older kids appreciate the lengthier hour because of the depth of the visit. Regardless of which you choose, the program highlights Wright's philosophy that land, nature, structures, and interior design should be treated as an entity. It is a concept that even youngsters can understand after seeing up close how Wright managed to blend all these forms into a comfortable, user-friendly environment.

AMERICAN PLAYERS THEATER (ages 10 and up)

County Highway C and Golf Course Road; (608) 588–7401. Open June through October.

Across the street from the Springs Golf Club Resort is the American Players Theater. The complex is actually set far back from the road on its private acreage. Its open-air stage is devoted to the classics, primarily Shakespeare, but a bit of Molière or Chekhov might be thrown in for spice during any given season. Guests can picnic, order a box lunch, or even cook on a grill. The theater wants to make everyone feel at home, so it often stages special events, including "skip-out-of-work-early" productions. A shuttle service runs from the House on the Rock Resort, so a guest doesn't need to walk the mile or so from door to door. Tell Junior to bring the bug repellent and Muffy to tote the sweaters or jackets. There is no controlling the bugs or the weather, so be prepared for any eventuality.

Other Wright Structures in Wisconsin Within a two-hour radius of Madison are Frank Lloyd Wright–designed buildings that are open to the public. They cover the seventy-year span of Wright's career. Among them are:

- **A. D. German Warehouse.** 300 South Church Street, Richland Center, WI 53581; (608) 647–2808.

- **Annunciation Greek Orthodox Church.** 9400 West Congress, Milwaukee, WI 53225; (414) 461–9400.

- **S. C. Johnson Wax Administration Building.** Fourteenth and Franklin Streets, Racine, WI 53403; (262) 260–2000.

- **Seth Petterson Cottage.** E9982 Fern Dell Road, Lake Delton, WI 53940; (608) 254–6051. Available for vacation rentals.

- **Unitarian Meeting House.** 900 University Bay Drive, Madison, WI 53705; (608) 233–9774.

HOUSE ON THE ROCK (all ages)

5754 State Highway 23; (608) 935–3639. Open 9:00 A.M. to dusk, late March through October. Special holiday tours run from mid-November to early January. Partial handicap accessible. Call for ticket information.

South of Spring Green on State Highway 23, the House on the Rock boggles the mind. Designed and built by artist Alex Jordan atop a 60-foot chimney of rock in the early 1940s, the house overlooks Wyoming Valley. That's a 450-foot drop, folks. Greatly expanded into a warren of museum space and living areas, the house, outbuildings, and gardens cover more than 200 acres. The kids will know that something special is in the works when entering the long drive to the structure.

Large urns overflowing with flowers as well as dragons, elves, and imps stand sentinel along the highway and on the road leading to the house. Plan on spending at least a half day exploring all the recesses and secret places within the house. Each turn offers something excitingly different and almost overpowering because of the amount of "stuff" that is found. Everything about the House on the Rock has to do with big numbers, starting with the outside. Jordan and his gardeners planted 50,000 trees on his grounds and 100,000 flowers in his rock garden. The latter are augmented by 3,000 flower pots, each with their own brilliant display.

The Infinity Room has 3,246 windows and extends out over the valley floor some 218 feet below. The room narrows at the end, and mirrors give the impression that it continues forever. The Heritage of the Sea Building is home to a 200-foot-long whale fighting with an octopus. The whale is longer than the Statue of Liberty is tall. More than 200 ship models line the ramps that encircle the watery battle in the three-story structure. Off to one side is a diorama of the Battle of Trafalgar, one of the most famous engagements in English naval history.

The house also holds the world's largest carousel, one that has more than 20,000 lights and 269 handmade animals (not one horse) twirling and whirling to bombastic organ accompaniment. The carousel stands 35 feet high, is 80 feet wide, and weighs 35 tons. The best time to show the masterpiece to the kids is at the end of the day, when most of the crowds have gone home. Visitors step into the enormous room from a darkened hallway and are greeted by an explosion of light and sound as the carousel begins moving. Hanging overhead are several hundred mannequins outfitted as angels in various stages of disarray. The effect on a youngster, or any old-timer with a youngster's imagination, is jaw-dropping.

The exhibits go on and on and on. Be prepared for a lot of walking up and down ramps and spiral staircases, underneath waterfalls, and over bridges. Simply follow the arrows and no one will get lost, even when you're in the Hannibal Crossing the Alps diorama, amid the eighty-piece mechanical orchestra in the Circus Room, or in the Organ Building, with its 45-foot-high perpetual-motion clock. There are, however, strategically placed rest rooms and cafeterias.

The Gift of Food

The Wisconsin Restaurant Association offers a booklet of gift certificates to member restaurants around the state. Contact the organization at 125 West Doty Street, Suite 200, Madison, WI 53703 (800-589-3211). The certificates can be ordered in any denomination and are valid at any of the restaurants listed. There is a 75 cent per-certificate charge for shipping and handling.

Highlights of the house? Votes go to the two-level doll merry-go-round with its several hundred bisque dolls. This is a fantastic exhibit, but it's rather disconcerting with all those eyes staring back at you. Then there is a weapons exhibit that includes a derringer pistol concealed in a woman's wooden leg, and the 250 dollhouses, furnished down to the interior lighting and wallpapering.

For the holiday season, which extends from mid-November through early January, the house displays some 6,000 Santa Claus figures, plus a collection of life-size Father Christmas characters. Of any attraction in central Wisconsin, the House on the Rock is a must-see, no matter what the age. Stupendous, simply put.

TOWER HILL STATE PARK (all ages)

Two miles south of Spring Green via State Highway 23, then 1 mile east on County Highway C. Look for the signs on 23 and C. The park is open from 8:00 A.M. to 6:00 P.M. Monday through Thursday and 8:00 A.M. to 11:00 P.M. Friday and Saturday, May through October. Call the park at (608) 588–2116 for more information.

At seventy-seven acres, Tower Hill is one of Wisconsin's smallest state parks. Yet it is one of the prettiest, a perfect layover for many of our picnics as we've meandered from central Wisconsin into the southwestern section of the state. The park is located along the banks of the Wisconsin River, a popular stopover when canoeing. The site was once the nineteenth-century village of Helena, one of the first incorporated towns in the state. An old stone tower in the park was once a site where lead shot for muskets was made. You can climb a flight of steps up the hill to the tower and enter the old building, which now has displays on the old-time musketball-making business. A 120-foot-deep shaft was dug from the base of the tower to the river level. Hot, molten lead would be poured through screens at the top of the tower, solidifying into balls by the time it came to the bottom. A 90-foot horizontal tunnel leading from the shaft to the river was wide enough for a team of mules.

One of the miners who dug the shaft was challenged to a duel by another worker. He was told he could pick his weapons and location for the fight. The first miner selected rocks, taking his position at the top of tower and the shaft. He told his opponent to stand at the bottom. When the other fellow saw those odds, he backed out of the duel.

Pedaling and Paddling There are many opportunities for the family to hop on bikes and explore the area around **Spring Green.** The 20 level miles of **County Highway C** and **Kennedy Road** take cyclists of any age along the **Wisconsin River.** On the other hand, the **Upper Snead and Percussion Rock Roads** are recommended for more serious cyclists, but their steep climbs offer rewarding views.

For **mountain biking,** the unpaved 9 miles of **Lakeview and Snead Creek Roads** are a challenge (and add another 6 miles by starting from the Upper Wyoming Valley). Experienced bikers in the area recommend a loop consisting of a mixture of county and state roads such as Z, ZZ, 130, and C. That 30-mile-long run is probably a bit much for the preadolescent set but good heart pumping exercise for the older gang.

Canoeing along the **Wisconsin River** in the Spring Green area is like dying and going to paddler's heaven. South of Sauk City and on to the west past the State Highway 23 bridge, the riverbank is relatively unspoiled by developers. Put-in points include **Sauk City, Tower Hill State Park, Peck's Landing,** and **Lone Rock.** There are numerous sandbars on which to rest. (Alert! Alert! Some sandbars are enjoyed by sun and nature lovers in the buff.) Once beached, canoers can fix a meal or pitch camp for the night. Be careful, however—don't let the kids swim in the river. Strong currents can pull a beginner, and even a strong swimmer, quickly downstream.

HOUSE ON THE ROCK RESORT (all ages)
County Highway C on Golf Course Road; (800) 822–7774 or (608) 588–7000.
$$$

One of the most comfortable and civilized places to stay in the Spring Green area is the House on the Rock Resort. Comfortable suites are decorated with class. There is plenty of room for golf bags, cross-country skis, or extra urchins. The resort offers fantastic food in both the main restaurant and the smaller cafe. The exercise opportunities in its fitness center also make this resort better than the average getaway. Advisers can help youngsters plan a good workout while the folks go out to play eighteen holes. A 50-kilometer trail system on the ridges behind the resort can be used for hiking or cross-country skiing. The House on the Rock Resort does it up right, with its gourmet nature hike in the autumn (call to check dates), where regular stops on the trail could include pheasant, wine, chocolate-covered strawberries, and other temptations quite unlike the usual granola bar. Now this is a hike the family won't forget, and, yes, children are invited.

Places to Eat

Culver's Spring Green. *E4919 U.S. Highway 14; (608) 588–2305.* Anything you get here—from burgers to steaks—is usually top o' the line. $$.

Round Barn Restaurant and Lodge. *U.S. Highway 14; (608) 588–2568.* The Barn can't be missed at the outskirts of Spring Green on the road to Madison. Long a landmark for the traveler, the barn-shaped restaurant offers a full range of breakfasts, lunches, and dinners. Guests and the public share the dining room just off the swimming pool. This has long been a favorite for the Hintz clan. $$

The Post House. *127 Jefferson Street; (608) 588–2595.* Locals know the Post House as one of the best dinner locales around the area, so there is sometimes a wait. But don't let that put you off; the meals are well worth it. $$

For More Information

Spring Green Chamber of Commerce, *Box 3, Spring Green, WI 53588-0003; (608) 558–2042 or (800) 588–2042.*

Mazomanie

Mazomanie is just 15 miles east of Spring Green on U.S. Highway 14.

HOOFBEAT RIDGE CAMP (ages 7 to 16)
5304 Reeve Road, Mazomanie, WI 53560; (608) 767–2593.

Hoofbeat Ridge Camp is suited for youngsters who love the outdoors, and it may be the best place in Wisconsin to learn to safely ride a horse. Western- and English-saddle riding are emphasized in the programs, which range from weekly sessions to two-week-long getaways. Many kids sign up for a month. The camp is certified by the American Camping Association, which demonstrates its commitment to quality and care. In addition to riding, kids are taken on canoe expeditions down the Wisconsin River, nature hikes, museum explorations, fishing trips, camp-outs, and other such outings. *Fun with the Family in Wisconsin* coauthor Steve Hintz, his brother Dan, and sister Kate spent a number of summers at Hoofbeat.

 M ore Horseback Riding

- **Canyon Creek Riding Stable.** One mile north of I–90 on Hillman Road, Lake Delton; (608) 253–6942. Horsefolk in the family will get a kick out of seeing the Wisconsin Dells' Lost Canyon by horse and carriage via Canyon Creek Riding Stable. The carriages take fifteen persons each trip on the thirty-minute-long ride through the 1-mile-long gulch, hidden away on the south shore of Lake Delton. Assembly point is on Canyon Road, just off I–90/94. Canyon Creek also has trail rides through the woods near Lake Delton. A pony ring is on the grounds to suit the tiniest cowpoke.

- **Eagle Cave Natural Park.** Blue River; (608) 537–2988. Learn to groom and care for horses while practicing riding skills. Pick up lasso skills. Rates vary depending on the hours ridden.

- **Wilderness Pursuit.** N5773 Rosewood Avenue, Neillsville; (715) 743–4484. Riding/camping packages are available for riders of all skill levels, including kids. Packages range from overnight to six days. Great riding opportunities are available through Clark County forest lands. Tours include meals, tack, guides, horses, and equipment.

Places to Eat

The Old Feed Mill. *114 Cramer Street; (608) 795–4909.* Not far from the railroad tracks in downtown Mazomanie, the Mill is easy to spot. Stop for the best sandwiches on the south side of the Wisconsin River. $

Sauk City

Take U.S. 14 from Mazomanie to State Highway 78, which leads directly to Sauk City.

Sauk City is the launch point for canoe trips down the lower Wisconsin River. A number of outfitters in town can supply everything from vessel to life jacket. They will even pick up you and the gang at a predesignated point from a day to a week after you take off. The Wisconsin is the state's longest and mightiest river and is called the "workhorse" because it was used to float logs downstream, carry freight and passengers upstream, and generate power. Camping is allowed on the numerous sandbars that peek up out of the water. Choose one that sits high above the water, and pitch a tent or sleep under the stars.

Amazing Wisconsin Facts

The world's first water-powered electrical plant began operating in Appleton in 1882. The facility was located on the roaring Fox River.

Assign one of the kids to carry the bug repellent, because mosquitoes the size of aircraft carriers seize any and every opportunity for a meal.

NATURAL BRIDGE STATE PARK (all ages)

Junction of U.S. Highway 12 and County Highway C, 16 miles south of Baraboo and 15 miles northwest of Sauk City; (608) 356–8301. Open year-round.

This scenic park offers fishing, hiking, biking, and picnicking. The highlight of the 560-acre park is a sandstone arch that towers 25 feet high and 35 feet wide, which is the result of wind-, water-, and, ice-caused erosion. People used to live in the area 10,000 years ago.

Places to Eat

Green Acres. *Corner of U.S. Highway 12 and State Highway 78; (608) 643–2305.* Just off of the Wisconsin River bridge, Green Acres is in a perfect locale for folks going north and south or east and west. You'll see plenty of canoes atop car carriers during the summer season and skis and poles in the winter. $

For More Information

Sauk-Prairie Chamber of Commerce, *213 Water Street, Sauk City, WI 53583;
(608) 643–4168.*

Mount Horeb

After visiting Sauk City, drive south 20 miles to Mount Horeb on State Highway 78.

Mount Horeb was originally a Scandinavian farming community, and many
touches of the Norwegian and Swedish settlers are still evident here. Several
gift shops feature items from Oslo, Stockholm, Copenhagen, and Helsinki. The
stores are easily identified, not just by the various flying national flags, but by
the trolls peeking out from almost every corner. Several large carvings of the
ugly folk characters are on the street corners downtown.

MOUNT HOREB MUSTARD MUSEUM (ages 5 and up)

*109 East Main Street, Mount Horeb; (608) 437–3986. Open year-round from
10:00 A.M. to 5:00 P.M.*

When a guest says "pass the mustard" at the Mount Horeb Mustard
Museum, the clerks might be a little puzzled. After all, there are several
thousand varieties of mustards on the shelves in this neat little store on
Mount Horeb's main street.

There are fiery types, bland types, wine-based types, down-to-earth
types; there are stacks upon stacks of jars, bottles, bags, and boxes. Try
the Inner Beauty sweet papaya mustard from Costa Rica; the Royal
Bohemian Mustard made by hand by Ed (The Radish King) Pavlik of
Ladysmith, Wisconsin; or the Run for Water Mustard from Mound
Edgecomb, Maine. No hot dog or hamburger will ever taste the same.
Samples are offered, and recipes are given out in profusion. Ever try
mustard on ice cream? Give the kids a taste and check their reactions.

Places to Eat

Mount Horeb Pub & Brewery. *105
South Second Street; (608) 437–4200.*
Typical of the new brewpubs, this
Mount Horeb establishment still has
plenty of charm, lip-smacking brew,
and excellent sandwiches. Spend the
evening. $$

Blue Mounds

Blue Mounds is 2 miles west of Mount Horeb on U.S. Highway 18.

LITTLE NORWAY (ages 5 and up)

3576 County Highway JG North, Blue Mounds. Little Norway is 3 miles west of Mount Horeb, minutes off State Highway 18/151, exiting on Cave of the Mounds Road. Turn right on County Highway JG and drive to the site, following the signs; (608) 437–8211. Open 9:00 A.M. to 5:00 P.M. from May to October.

Signs direct guests to the Little Norway complex, a farm site built in 1856 by a Norwegian settler. A costumed guide can explain how the family lived and worked in those pre–Civil War days. An interesting feature for a photo backdrop is the wooden church, the Stavekirke, which was originally built for the 1893 Columbian Exposition in Chicago.

CAVE OF THE MOUNDS (all ages)

Brigham Farm, Blue Mounds; (608) 437–3038. Open 9:00 A.M. to 5:00 P.M. daily from mid-March through Memorial Day; 9:00 A.M. to 7:00 P.M. daily after Memorial Day through Labor Day; 9:00 A.M. to 5:00 P.M. Monday through Friday and 9:00 A.M. to 5:00 P.M. Saturday and Sunday, mid-November through mid-March.

While in the neighborhood, pause at the Cave of the Mounds on County Highway ID. The cave is a registered National Natural Landmark, located on the Brigham family farm. It was discovered in the late 1930s when the farmer was quarrying limestone and were eventually mapped and opened to tourists. On the grounds is a visitor center, picnic area, snack bar, and a garden. A nature trail winds its way through some nearby woods. The cave is the most interesting feature, though, with its beautiful array of stalagmites and stalactites that seem to glow under the artificial light. The forty-five-minute-long tour is not too involved for little kids, and the older youngsters will get plenty of detail for the required what-I-did-on-my-summer-vacation paper.

Edgerton

To get to Edgerton from Blue Mounds, take State Highway 78 south to State Highway 39. From 39, go east to State Highway 92 at New Glans; turn north on 69 and follow it to State Highway 92. Drive east again on 92 to State Highway 59 and on to Edgerton.

This rock-ribbed town is the boyhood home of author Sterling North, who wrote the children's classics *So Dear to My Heart* and *Rascal*. Both books sold more than 2½ million copies and were made into Walt Disney movies. The city was also the tobacco capital of the world at the turn of the twentieth century, and a few of the original fifty-two drying warehouses still stand. Buyers from around the world came to town to bid on the quality product that was grown on surrounding farms.

A Hintz Adventure by Steve Hintz

My brother and sister and I would all pile onto the travel mattress on the floor of our family's black van. Every summer of my childhood, it seemed, Mom and Dad took the crew to the Wisconsin Dells. From Tommy Bartlett's Water Show, to the walks downtown and into haunted houses, to nature rides on the Ducks, to Native American powwows, we couldn't find a better place to spend a summer vacation.

Exaggerated memories of the wonderful times I had remain ingrained in my childhood experience, but if they weren't exaggerated, they wouldn't be memories. For example, the two-and-a-half-hour trip was like an endless journey through a scorching hell with a brother and sister playing the part of the Devil. Then risking our lives on the Ducks amphibious vehicles, careening down wooded trails into the Wisconsin River, and watching death-defying stunts performed in Tommy Bartlett's Water Show all left lasting memories in a little boy's head as we adventured in Wisconsin.

Those trips, and our many family jaunts throughout our home state and elsewhere, have shown me that there is a fascinating world out there. Now when I travel, whether it is to Nassau, Tel Aviv, Philadelphia, or Chicago, I know that I can find my way around and that people are the same everywhere. It's a good feeling.

(Steve Hintz graduated from the University of Wisconsin-Milwaukee with a degree in sociology, with an emphasis on African-American studies. He and his father have completed books on the Bahamas, North Carolina, and Israel. He has white-water rafted on Israel's Jordan River, fished for salmon in New Brunswick, Canada, and parasailed in the Atlantic Ocean off Freeport-Lucaya in the Bahamas. He is currently the executive director for a mentoring agency in Milwaukee County that works with court-ordered youth.)

TOBACCO HERITAGE DAYS (all ages)

(608) 884–8417.

The Heritage Days are held each July, with activities throughout downtown Edgertown. There are parades, a crafts show, special sales in shops, and street-corner concerts. Look for rummage and garage sales along the side streets. When finished walking through Edgerton's business district and taking in the fun, hop in your car and drive along any of the rural roads around the community. A number of farms in the area still grow tobacco, producing a variety that is used primarily as cigar wrapping. Their drying sheds are packed with the pungent leaf during autumn harvest season. Even from the highways, kids in the backseat can pick out the distinctive sheds because of their building style; they have open sides or alternating slats to allow the wind to circulate and dry the leaves.

Places to Eat

Mario's Pizza. *201 West Fulton Street; (608) 884–9488.* This is one of central Wisconsin's best pizza parlors. Don't miss it. $

Aztalan Area

After visiting Edgerton, drive north on State Highway 73 to U.S. Highway 18. Turn east on 18 and go County Road A. Turn north on A to Lake Mills and Aztalan State Park.

AZTALAN STATE PARK (all ages)

1213 South Main Street, Lake Mills; (920) 648–8774. The main parkland is 2 miles east of I–94. Open 7:00 A.M. to 9:00 P.M. May through October and dawn until dusk in the summer.

This state park is a perfect picnic place atop a site settled by Native Americans who were believed to have ancestral links with the Aztecs in Mexico. A rebuilt stockade, similar to one archaeologists believe stood there from A.D. 1075 to 1175, is a major feature of the 172-acre park. A museum nearby displays artifacts from the area's pioneering days, along with an extensive collection of arrowheads and utensils once used by the tribe that settled here so long ago.

Amazing Wisconsin Facts Wisconsin has a wealth of Indian mounds. At one time, there were more than 12,000 of these earthen panthers, birds, lizards, snakes, eagles, and bears, as well as simpler domes and ridges. The mounds were not always used for burial and served some ceremonial purpose, now lost to history. Prior to the arrival of settlers who leveled most of them, the main concentration of mounds were found in Milwaukee, Madison, Waukesha, Baraboo, Beloit, Lake Mills, Prairie du Chien, around Lakes Winnebago and Koshkonong, and along the Fox and Wisconsin Rivers.

Fort Atkinson

Pick up State Highway 89 in Lake Mills and drive south to Fort Atkinson.

HOARD HISTORICAL MUSEUM AND DAIRY SHRINE (all ages)

407 Merchants Avenue; (920) 563–7769. Open year-round from 9:30 A.M. to 4:30 P.M. Tuesday through Saturday, 1:00 to 5:00 P.M. the first Sunday of the month, and 1:00 to 5:00 P.M. every Sunday, June through August.

This unique museum is a shrine honoring the world's dairy industry; it's where kids can learn the value of milk in health, economics, and politics. Dairy artifacts, including a dog-powered treadmill once used to churn butter, are on display. Exhibits in the building's basement tell the story of milk and its products. The building is named after a former governor of Wisconsin, who was considered the father of the Wisconsin dairy industry because of his support for research to help the dairy farmer.

In addition to the dairy displays, the museum has an extensive collection of artifacts dating to the Black Hawk Indian wars of the 1830s. The running fight between the militia and American army and Chief Black Hawk's Sac and Fox tribe was waged throughout the Fort Atkinson area and on the Mississippi River, where the Native Americans were eventually massacred.

THE FIRESIDE (ages 10 and up)

Business Highway 26 South; (920) 563–9505 or (800) 477–9505; www. firesidetheatre.com. Dinner packages range from $37.95 to $39.95. Nine shows are set each week, from Wednesday through Sunday, with 10:30 A.M. and evening productions.

Feed 'em and then have the kids enjoy a theatrical production. What better way to expose youngsters to music and drama? Take in the Fireside buffet or order off the menu for a leisurely getaway evening, followed by *Fiddler on the Roof* or any of a number of great musical comedies.

Cycling the Glacial Drumlin Bikers can pick up the **Glacial Drumlin Bike Trail**, a 47-mile pathway of crushed rock on a former railroad bed. The trail, which winds through some of the most scenic parts of central Wisconsin, extends from Cottage Grove in the west to Waukesha in the east. It is easily ridden by cyclists of any age and is used by cross-country skiers and snowmobilers in the winter. There are plenty of places to pause along the route for restaurants, rest stops, and ice cream. One unusual sight is the Welsh national flag that flies over the trailside stop in the town of Wales, which is along the route. For more information contact Glacial Drumlin Bike Trail East (262-646-3025), c/o Lapham Peak State Park, W329 N846 Waukesha County Highway C, Delafield, WI 53018; or Glacial Drumlin Bike Trail West (920-648-8774), 1213 South Main Street, Lake Mills, WI 53551.

Watertown

To reach Watertown from Fort Atkinson, drive north on State Highway 26 about 25 miles.

OCTAGON HOUSE & AMERICA'S FIRST KINDERGARTEN (ages 5 and up)

919 Charles Street; (920) 261–2796. Open 11:00 A.M. to 3:00 P.M. daily from May 1 through Memorial Day and after Labor Day through October and 10:00 A.M. to 4:00 P.M. daily from Memorial Day through Labor Day.

Take the kids to see the Octagon House and site of the first kindergarten in the United States. Now operated by the Watertown Historical Society, the kindergarten was founded in 1856 by Margarthe Meyer Schurz, whose husband, Carl, was an American diplomat. From Watertown, the concept of early education spread around the country. The school was moved to the site of the Octagon House in 1956.

Places to Eat

Mullens' Dairy Bar. *212 West Main Street; (920) 261–4278.* This is the place where you can't go wrong: malts, shakes, and ice cream desserts. At Mullens', kids can get a taste of what real ice cream is like. $.

Madison

From Watertown, drive 20 miles west on State Highway 19 to U.S. 151. Turn south on 151 to Madison, the state capital.

City of 194,591: students, professors, politicians, lobbyists, government workers, and a stray real person or two. This is Mad City, Wisconsin's state capital and home of the University of Wisconsin. ("We're the Rose Bowl champs of 1994," some folks still say upon being introduced.) It is a city built on an isthmus between Lakes Mendota and Monona, where bicycling is politically correct and three-piece suits easily mingle with torn shorts and long hair on the eclectic main drag, State Street.

It is a "capitol idea" to visit Madison for a family outing. Go for a picnic atop the Monona Terrace (from a design by noted architect Frank Lloyd Wright), then take in a play at the Madison Repertory Theater, or get an ice cream cone at the Wisconsin Memorial Union and take in the annual World Dairy Expo at the Dane County Expo Center.

Whad'ya Know A surprised guest may find him or herself on the radio during *Whad'ya Know*, a nationally syndicated program on **Wisconsin Public Radio** (608-263-2244). The irreverent hilarious host, Michael Feldman, pulls people into his goofy on-air quizzes and then sends jokes sailing out onto the airwaves. Sitting in the back of the room doesn't hide bashful guests. Feldman often crawls over chairs to get to folks for a comment or two. Yet that is all part of the fun, and a good way to win a silly prize. The program is broadcast on Saturday mornings from the Monona Terrace Convention Hall, with the show starting at 10:00 A.M. In addition to the United States, Feldman's show airs in Berlin, Stockholm, Helsinki, and Geneva.

An inexpensive way to get around town is with the **Madison Metro Visitors Pass,** which allows unlimited fixed-route bus rides for just $3.00 a day. Visitors passes can be purchased at Madison Metro, 1101 East Washington Avenue, Madison (608-266-4904). Many professionals, students, government workers, and other persons use the metro system because of its convenient scheduling and the ease with which it gets you around the city.

 ## CAPITOL BUILDING (all ages)
4 East State Capitol; (608) 266–0382. Tours are set at 9:00, 10:00, and 11:00 A.M. and 1:00, 2:00, and 3:00 P.M. Monday through Saturday. Tours on Sunday are given at 1:00, 2:00, and 3:00 P.M. Tours are also offered at 4:00 P.M. from Memorial Day through Labor Day to ease the summer crunch.

Start with a tour of the capitol building itself, perched high on a hill in the center of the city. The edifice is hard to miss because it seems to hover several feet off the ground. Hot air from politicians does the trick, according to locals. Parking is available in nearby multilevel city garages, which is a safer bet than trying to find an opening on the crowded one-way streets closest to the capitol. The lots offer all-day parking for only a few dollars, which is well worth it since downtown Madison is an easy stroll. Be warned that Madison traffic cops are merciless and have heard every "I'm from out of town" plea ever made, but they do smile when they hand out tickets.

Tours are held daily and on some holidays, with a tour of the governor's mansion sometimes thrown in for good measure. The capitol's marbled hallways are conducive to echoes, so tell the urchins to keep their voices down while they look for the carved stone badgers peeking out from secret recesses. Remember that it is easy to get turned around in the myriad corridors leading from the central rotunda, and dropping bread crumbs to find one's way back to the main doors (there are exits on each side) is frowned upon. If older kids are allowed to quietly tour sans parents (but still using a buddy system, of course), predetermine an assembly point and time. The main floor information booth is a good place. Have the kids go around with a list of questions to be answered. Those with the most correct responses can be treated to a hot-fudge sundae at the university's Babcock Hall. The ice cream, made from the agricultural school's own happy Holsteins, is 12 percent butterfat instead of the standard industry 10 percent.

Some sample questions: What is the name of the toga-draped statue on the capitol dome? (Officially, she is called *Wisconsin,* but the locals call her "Miss Forward.") How many Wisconsin soldiers served in the

Civil War? (About 83,000 men, a figure provided by the exhibits in the Grand Army of the Republic Hall.) When was the capitol built? (Between 1907 and 1917.)

If you are a Wisconsin voter, pop in on your local legislator, speak your mind, ask a question, say thanks, or lodge a complaint. Their doors are always open.

HENRY VILAS ZOO (all ages)

702 South Randall; (608) 266–4732).

The Henry Vilas Zoo has elephants, fuzzy bears, prowling lions, frantic monkeys, and dozens of other creatures from jungle, desert, forest, and mountain. Friendly, well-informed staffers can answer questions from even the smallest visitor. Regular kid programs are held on weekends throughout the year; simply call for details. The zoo is small enough to take in on an afternoon, but still large enough to have plenty of exotic and near-to-home species.

UNIVERSITY OF WISCONSIN-MADISON (all ages)

The main campus number is (608) 262–1234; the operator can direct calls to the appropriate department hosting an event. Most major facilities can be phoned directly. Call the university athletics information number (608–262–1911) for details on sporting events.

The university is a great resource for entertainment, cultural offerings, sports, term-paper research, and just hanging out. The latter is best done inside the Memorial Union or on the veranda in the back, overlooking Lake Mendota. Perching there for a time gives the kids a look at college life. It is also *the* place to look cool. Occasionally, a Hollywood movie is filmed on campus because site locators love the Ivy League look (and low cost) of the Big Red One. Classical, folk, and rock concerts are regularly held in the numerous halls, art galleries explode with color, and lectures are open to the public.

CAPITOL SQUARE (all ages)

More commonly known as **The Concourse,** the square is the site for numerous outdoor activities, from the **Taste of Madison** (608-255-2537), with its sixty-plus restaurants, five music stages, a waiters' race, and a kiddie korner with games and activities, to a celebration of **June Dairy Month** when cows—live cows—are brought to the square. Kids can try their hand at milking as part of the program. Bring a picnic and listen to the classical music concerts presented by the **Wisconsin Chamber Orchestra** the last Wednesday of June, each Wednesday in July, and the first Wednesday in August.

The **farmer's market** is also held on the Concourse. It opens at 6:00 A.M. on Saturday throughout the summer and into the autumn harvest season. Send the kids around to buy fresh beans, apples, tomatoes, and other produce. They can then help carry the agricultural treasures back home or to your hotel. The market is also a good place to stop for munchables on the way through town.

ART ON THE SQUARE (all ages)

The weekend after the Fourth of July brings together thousands of strollers and gawkers interested in art pieces from the traditional to what-the-heck-is-that contemporary. Street performers, stilt walkers, and other entertainers flit through the crowds, too. The kids can watch the Peruvian musicians, the English Morris dancers, the fire eaters, the sword swallowers, and even the governor making their rounds while Mom and Dad look for the perfect painting to adorn the living room wall.

ATHLETICS

Madisonites enjoy the outdoors with a vengeance. Paths ring the lakes for biking, hiking, and cross-country skiing. The area's waters are perfect for sailing, canoeing, waterskiing, and fishing.

Madison Marathon. Madison is a town for active folks, whether they are ice-fishing fans or golfers. For runners, the Madison Marathon at the end of May brings together runners—and walkers—of all ages for an extended loop around the city. The race starts on the south side of Lake Monona, loops up to the north, through downtown and past the capitol building, around the upscale Maple Grove neighborhood where the governor lives, out to the west side of town, and back past Lake Wingra. Not everyone needs to gallop the entire length, especially with kids in tow, and there are varying distances in which to participate. Many families take part as a group, with volunteers assigned to help with family reunions. Call (608) 256-9922 or (800) 373-6376 for all the particulars.

George Vitense Golfland. *5501 West Beltline at Whitney Way; (608) 271-1411.* This golf course challenges everyone to improve their swing. The facility has a double-deck golf range, miniature golf, a par-three course, a golf shop, and PGA lessons for those in need. The range is lighted at night for those late-night practices. The park offers other sports opportunities, as well. Baseball players always edge over to the batting cages for a few quick swats before heading to the links. Golfland's promo folks say it is Madison's place "fore" family fun. It is.

Capitol City Ski Team. *Law Park, 7:00 P.M. on Thursday and Sunday from May through September.* **Free**. Since the 1960s, the Beverly Ski-Billies (actually, the official name is the Capital City Ski Team) have been entertaining audiences with their fantastic aquatic acrobatics each summer. Barefoot skiing, jumping, and many more pro techniques are part of the show, which takes place on the blue-green waters of Lake Monona. Bring a blanket, a cooler, and the kids and stake out a grassy site.

MUSEUMS

ELVEHJEM MUSEUM OF ART (ages 5 and up)

800 University Avenue; (608) 263–2246. Open 9:00 A.M. to 5:00 P.M. Tuesday and Friday and 11:00 A.M. to 5:00 P.M. Saturday and Sunday. Closed Monday, Thanksgiving, Christmas Eve, and Christmas Day. **Free**.

The museum has extensive displays of paintings and sculptures both in its permanent collection and on loan from traveling shows. There are often special kids' programs and tours for the creative-minded young. Tailor-made, foreign language, and special-needs tours are available, too.

STATE HISTORICAL MUSEUM (ages 5 and up)

30 North Carroll Street; (608) 264–6555. Open 10:00 A.M. to 5:00 P.M. Tuesday through Saturday; noon to 5:00 P.M. Sunday. Closed Monday.

Three floors of permanent exhibits explore the state, from its prehistoric origins to contemporary times. Two galleries feature changing exhibits. One popular display focuses on Wisconsin during the dawn of the atomic age in the 1950s. Reaching farther back, though, the museum has a button from the vest of Revolutionary War hero John Paul Jones and similar interesting artifacts.

GEOLOGY MUSEUM (ages 5 and up)

1215 West Dayton Street; (608) 262–1412. Open 8:30 A.M. to 4:30 P.M. Monday through Friday; 9:00 A.M. to 1:00 P.M. Saturday. **Free**.

This university facility has a walk-through cave that is spooky enough to be fun for kids and educational enough to be satisfying for serious-minded grown-ups. The main eye-opening display in the museum is the towering skeleton of a mastodon, a critter that roamed across Wisconsin during the last Ice Age 10,000 years ago.

U.S. FOREST SERVICE PRODUCTS LABORATORY (ages 5 and up)

1 Gifford Pinchot Drive; (608) 231–9200. Tours are held 2:00 to 3:00 P.M. for adults eighteen and older and accompanied children Monday through Thursday. No groups larger than eight persons permitted.

Madison is the home of Wisconsin's state and federal governmental offices and related service agencies, so there are many other to-do opportunities for families on the run. The U.S. Forest Service Products Laboratory is a great place to knock on wood for good luck. All the factors of what makes up wood are studied to determine how it can be used in construction, science, and other possibilities. Plenty of handout material is available for the youngster who needs information for botany class or woodworking.

CREDIT UNION NATIONAL ASSOCIATION (ages 10 and up)

5810 Mineral Point Road; (608) 231–4000.

To learn about money, credit unions, and banking, visit the Credit Union National Association, where an extensive display traces the hows and whys of trade, coinage, and the world's monetary systems. Easily understood exhibits are in the complex's main building in a **Free** museum open during normal business hours. The association is the headquarters for the World Council of Credit Unions, which has more than sixty million members. Flags of several dozen participating nations fly from poles fronting the visitor parking lot; have the youngsters identify as many as possible.

MADISON CHILDREN'S MUSEUM (ages 2 to 12)

100 State Street; (608) 256–6445. Open 10:00 A.M. to 5:00 P.M. Tuesday through Saturday and 1:00 to 5:00 P.M. Sunday.

Amid the bustle of grown-up stuff to see and do in this city is kid-oriented fun. The Madison Children's Museum is a hands-on, jump-right-in facility where even little wallflowers can gain the confidence to try a scientific experiment or a craft of some kind. Eye-level exhibits are all geared to children, toddlers to grade schoolers. Exhibits and activities change regularly.

WISCONSIN VETERANS MUSEUM (ages 5 and up)

30 West Mifflin Street; (608) 267–1799; http://badger.state.wi.us/agencies/ dva/museum/wvmmain.html. Open 9:00 A.M. to 4:30 P.M. Monday through Saturday (year-round) and noon to 4:00 P.M. Sunday (April to September only). Closed holidays.

The museum offers 10,000 square feet of dramatic displays on the state's citizen soldiers from the Civil War to contemporary times. Award-winning lifelike dioramas depict historic military events in which Wisconsin troops participated. A computerized Wisconsin Civil War database helps visitors track relatives and other persons who were in service at the time.

MADISON ART CENTER (ages 5 and up)

211 State Street; (608) 257–0158. Open 11:00 A.M. to 5:00 P.M. Tuesday through Thursday, 11:00 A.M. to 9:00 P.M. Friday, 10:00 A.M. to 9:00 P.M. Saturday, and 1:00 P.M. to 5:00 P.M. Sunday. Closed Monday. Donation of 50 cents for students and $1.00 for adults is suggested.

The museum features modern and contemporary painting, sculpture, photography, works on paper, video, and multimedia work by area, regional, and internationally known artists. Children's programs are regularly scheduled with magicians, jugglers, artists, and mimes.

Places to Eat

Big Mike's Super Subs. *454 West Johnson Avenue (also at 2145 Reget, 449 State, 6702 Memorial Point Road, and 6234 University); (608) 251–8444.* Just what the name says: "sighted sub and ate same." $

Deadman's Chocolate Shoppe Ice Cream. *468 State Street; (608) 255–5454.* Super-premium desserts! $

Ella's Deli & Ice Cream Parlor. *2902 East Washington Avenue; (608) 241–5291.* This is a kid place with puppets, coin-operated machines, and other silly business, with an outside carousel spinning from spring through autumn. $

Essen Haus German Restaurant. *514 East Wilson; (608) 255–4674.* Give the kids a taste of the Old World, with real German food and live oompah music every night. For Dad and Mom there are 250 imported beers. $$

Great Dane Pub & Brewing Co. *23 East Doty Street; (608) 284–0000.* This is the city's number-one brewery/restaurant, with an outdoor beer garden great for summer dining. Kids are welcome to select from a children's menu. Try the handmade pizzas. $

Irish Waters. *702 North Whitney Way; (608) 233–3398.* Sandwiches, soups, and salads are year-round treats, but head here on St. Pat's Day for corned-beef wonders. $$

Places to Stay

Madison's bed-and-breakfast facilities are children-friendly. Most have no problems with youngsters, but check age suggestions while booking.

Annie's Bed & Breakfast. *2117 Sheridan Drive; (608) 244–2224.* The building overlooks a marsh and meadow and has a lake nearby. $$

Arbor House, An Environmental Inn. *3402 Monroe Street; (608) 238–2981.* This inn is across the street from the Madison Arboretum. Native gardens and mature trees landscape the grounds. $$

Canterbury Inn. *315 West Gorham; (608) 258–8899.* This bed-and-breakfast inn is above the Canterbury Bookseller Coffeehouse. It offers six rooms featuring characters from Chaucer's *Canterbury Tales.* The latest novels are on bookshelves in each room, so curl up with the kids and read before bed. $$

Collins House Bed & Breakfast. *704 East Gorham; (608) 255–4230.* This is the restored Prairie School Inn. Home-baked pastries each evening. $$

Mansion Hill Inn. *424 North Pinckney Street; (608) 255–3999 or (800) 798–9070.* This 1858 Romanesque Revival mansion has tall arched windows and hand-carved marble. There is a twenty-four-hour valet service. $$$

Stoney Oaks. *4942 Raymond Road; (608) 278–1646.* Fountains and wooded grounds make this a great getaway place. $$

University Heights Bed & Breakfast. *1812 Van Hise Avenue; (608) 233–3340.* Kids twelve and older are welcome. $$

A Free Ride Cross the Wisconsin River on State Highway 113 via the Free ferryboat, one of the few remaining such state-owned vessels in the country. Leave Madison on U.S. Highway 12 to State Highway 78, which runs along the Wisconsin River. Turn right (northeast) on 78 and drive to the car ferry crossing, which is well marked with signage along the route. Holding twelve cars, or the equivalent number of packed kids, the boat runs twenty-four hours a day from mid-April through early December. Underwater cables pull the vessel from shore to shore, about a ten-minute ride. The *Col-Sac II* (derived from Columbia and Sauk Counties, which the ferry links) is operated by the Wisconsin Department of Transportation. A small ice cream stand is on the north shore, with several dozen exotic flavors including elephant's foot ice cream (it's filled with chocolate swirls and nuts). A rest room is on the south shore. Once positioned in the line of cars waiting to board, it is difficult to pull off to one side if one of the kids is in the bathroom when the boat is ready to load. Mom and Dad can always wave from the deck to the tardy one, who will have to catch the next boat.

For More Information

Madison Convention and Visitors Bureau, *615 East Washington Avenue, Madison, WI 53703; (608) 255–2537 or (800) 373–6376.* The bureau is accessible via e-mail at gmcvb@visitmadison.com and via the World Wide Web at www.visit-madison.com.

Portage

After crossing the Wisconsin River, continue driving north on State Highway 78 for about 24 miles to Portage.

FORT WINNEBAGO SURGEON'S QUARTERS (ages 5 and up)

Agency House Road; (608) 742–2949. Open 10:00 A.M. to 4:00 P.M., May 15 through October 15.

OLD INDIAN AGENCY HOUSE (ages 5 and up)

W8687 State Highway 33 East; (608) 742–6362. Open from 10:00 A.M. to 4:00 P.M. daily, May through October.

Portage is the home of the Old Indian Agency House, built in 1832, and the restored Fort Winnebago surgeon's quarters. The city had long been a central water link between the Wisconsin and Fox Rivers and remains a commercial hub of central Wisconsin. Walk on the banks of what was once the Portage Canal, along the designated 2½-mile National Ice Age Trail segment in the city. (The trail traces the edge of the last glacier, which flattened Wisconsin 10,000 years ago.) The canal was used from the mid-1800s until 1951. This is an easy hike or bike ride along city streets and on the rim of the tired old ditch that once bustled with barges and boats. All the giant locks have been welded shut, but the kids can still see how the system functioned. The water levels would be raised or lowered to allow passage of vessels from one part of the river system to the next.

ZONA GALE HOUSE—THE WOMEN'S CIVIC LEAGUE OF PORTAGE (all ages)

506 West Edgewater Street; (608) 742–7744.

The building is the home of Pulitzer prize–winning playwright Zona Gale. She is best known for her play *Miss Lulu Bett,* for which she won the award in 1921. You can drive past the home and admire the architecture. The building is open for civic functions and receptions, but you can also drop by to say hello during the day on weekdays.

Places to Eat

A&W Portage. *717 East Wisconsin Avenue; (608) 742–5759.* Fast service, good root beer: the perfect blend when the kids are antsy. $

Legends Sports Bar & Grill. *214 West Wisconsin Avenue; (608) 742–2202.* If you can talk sports, you're in like Lombardi here. The long-dead, fabled coach of the Green Bay Packers might just be lurking in the rafters. Have a beer and burger in his memory. $

Amazing Wisconsin Facts The first kindergarten in the United States was opened in 1865 by Mrs. Carl Schurz in Watertown. Mrs. Schurz was a pupil of Friedrich Frobel, a German educator considered the founder of the kindergarten movement in Europe. Frobel started his first kindergarten in 1837.

Baraboo

From Portage, drive west on State Highway 33 to Baraboo.

"Hold yer hosses! The elephants is comin'." The shrill cry announcing the conclusion of a circus parade was always enough to get the blood racing for anyone under thirteen years old. Today's kids don't often have the thrilling chance to get up early and race down to the railhead to watch a show unload, then follow it to the grounds and help put up bleachers. There has always been something magical about the circus world.

CIRCUS WORLD MUSEUM (all ages)

426 Water Street; (608) 356–0800. The visitors center is open year-round.
You can still pass along a touch of that center-ring excitement to your youngsters during a visit to the Circus World Museum, the former

winter quarters of the Ringling Brothers Circus. The sprawling acreage along the sluggish Baraboo River is packed with bright red, orange, and white circus wagons dating back generations. The Ring-lings were here well before they linked up with Barnum and Bailey, turning this central Wisconsin town into a place of spangles and tinsel. Many of the performers and workers lived, retired, died, and were buried here in the 1880s and 1890s. The various administration buildings and barns now house delightfully splendiferous displays of pulchritude, acrobatic skill, and uncaged ferocity. (Rather like talking about your family, right?) Photos, posters, and memorabilia from hundreds of artists, clowns, and roustabouts adorn the walls and exhibition cases. Model circus wagons, intricate in their detail, will capture the attention of kids, who can view them at eye level, to say nothing of looking up at the real wagons around the grounds.

Several times a day, circus crews load and unload wagons from railcars to demonstrate how it used to be done by horses and snorting tractors. The same procedures are used when unloading the wagons in Milwaukee before the Great Circus Parade each summer.

Some of my (Martin Hintz) own photos are displayed here at the museum, depicting a day on a typical show, taken while a photographer for *Amusement Business Magazine*, the bible of the show world. In the museum library, I also researched my *Circus Workin's* and *Tons of Fun*, two books for Franklin Watts Publishing done about the sawdust world. The folks here are always able to answer just about any question, whether it deals with elephants ("they only sweat around their toes") or how to remove clown greasepaint. Kids by the score use the museum as a basis for research papers, art projects, school tours, and plain ordinary fun.

On any given hot summer day, the herd of performing elephants may be wallowing in the river after a show, a clown might be teaching his old dog new tricks, and some young lady could be hanging around—literally—by her hair from a rope attached to a trapeze. Nothing is out of the ordinary at Circus World.

On the way out, snap a photo of the kids in the gorilla cage.

In downtown Baraboo, the fabulous Al Ringling Theater, built by the oldest of the Ringlings, is still in use. Around the town square, everything seems to have a circus motif. Even the designs on the outside of the courthouse depict a circus parade.

INTERNATIONAL CRANE FOUNDATION (ages 10 and up)
E11376 Shady Lane Road; (608) 356–9462. Open daily from May through October.

For a stop in the Baraboo area that is strictly for the birds, drop in at the International Crane Foundation. Experts in bird lore, naturalists, and avian researchers use the foundation's facilities to study these gangly birds from Australia, China, India, and other nations. Some fifteen species are represented. It is most fun when the keepers need to act out mating routines to perk interest in the birds. To see people fluttering, hooting, and hopping on one leg or the other is truly amazing. One wonders what the birds think. Whatever it is, tell the kids that it works.

DEVIL'S LAKE STATE PARK (all ages)
State Highway 123, 20 miles north of Madison via U.S. Highway 12; (608)

356–8301. Exit east on State Highway 159. Go east 1 mile to the intersection with State Highway 123; turn south and follow 123 to the park. Or drive south from Baraboo 3 miles on State Highway 159.

Campsites go quickly each year, so be sure to call early in the spring for summer reservations. The park features 500-foot-high rock walls and a 360-acre lake. Trails meander through the park, with **camping, fishing, hiking, cross-country skiing, nature exhibits, Indian mounds,** and **picnicking** among the attractions. Be sure kids stay on the trail and don't climb where they shouldn't. Stay well away from cliffs and keep an eye on the little ones. The nature center, just inside the main entrance, has a basement kids' room where youngsters can learn to identify animal tracks, leaves, and other outdoorsy items. A display there also relates how people have affected the environment. The Future Wisconsin Explorers program, for grades four and up, is easy to enter. To become a member, youngsters just fill out an activities booklet with games such as Wildlife Bingo, Snake-Opoly, and Deer Detectives and show it to a ranger in the park. The program is administered by the Wisconsin Department of Natural Resources. The Wisconsin Junior Ranger program, similar to the Future Wisconsin Explorers, is geared toward grades kindergarten through third. Kids can earn a patch and certificate by completing certain activities.

Naturalist programs are held daily throughout the summer vacation season, with a Kiddie Walk scheduled monthly. Evening programs at the nature center (bring a chair) focus on snakes of Wisconsin, bats, and glaciers. The lectures start at 8:00 P.M.

Places to Eat

J's Food & Spirits. *841 Wisconsin Dells Parkway South; (608) 253–9292.* Burgers, fries, salads, and sodas make for a fitting end to a day of exploring Circus City. $

Kristina's Family Cafe. *113 Third Street; (608) 356–3430.* If the kids are bottomless pits when it comes to chow, take them to Kristina's for sustenance. You'll be pleased. $

Log Cabin Family Restaurant. *1215 Eighth Street; (608) 356–8245.* You might see frontiersman Daniel Boone eating soup here. Well, you never know. Even if Boone isn't hanging out, you can be assured that helpings here are plentiful, so eat like a bear. $

Pardeeville

From Baraboo, drive east on State Highway 33 through Portage and onto State Highway 22. Drive south to Pardeeville.

LAREAU'S WORLD OF MINIATURE BUILDINGS (ages 5 and up)

State Highway 22; (608) 429–2848. Open from 10:00 A.M. to 5:00 P.M. Memorial Day through October 1.

Lareau's World of Miniature Buildings makes a great family outing. The museum has an intricate assortment of scale models of Mount Rushmore, the Washington Monument, the Statue of Liberty, and dozens of other buildings. All the pieces were made of bits of wood, Styrofoam, and concrete.

Wisconsin Dells/Lake Delton

After clowning around in Baraboo, the Circus City, take U.S. Highway 12 north to the Wisconsin Dells. This is a straight, 9-mile stretch of highway.

The Dells deserve a chapter unto themselves. For years I have been taking my gang to this central Wisconsin community, which has all the trappings of one gigantic, never-ending amusement park. There is enough here for everyone in the family, from thrill shows to balloon rallies to water slides. Historically, the Native Americans appreciated the natural wonder of rock and forest for centuries before the first French sallied down the Wisconsin River to "discover" the region. The Europeans used the French word *dalles* ("gorge") to describe the deep canyons and hidden valleys that ranged along the shore. From that term, the "dells" evolved. Since the Civil War vacationers have found the peace and quiet of the region to their liking. Over the years, an increasing number of attractions were built to accommodate the growing numbers of guests. Today's Dells, therefore, are certainly not as remote as when the Ho-Chunk lived here; however, a cruise on the *Red Cloud* or any of the other excursion boats on the upper or lower river takes guests away from the landbound rush and glitz.

Today, U.S. Highway 12/State Highway 23 is a carnival-like midway linking the neighboring towns of Wisconsin Dells and Lake Delton. The communities are five minutes maximum off I-90/94, with billboards in Illinois, Iowa, and Minnesota directing motorists how to get there. The convention bureau (see For More Information on page 142) can provide tons of fliers, maps, guides, and tips on what to see and do.

 River Boat Rides The authentic Dells is actually a strip of some 15 miles of protected river frontage, with sandstone cliffs and landings at such exotic-sounding locales as Witches Gulch and Stand Rock, where visitors can enjoy nature trails. Kiosks strategically placed throughout the Dells area sell tickets for river trips. There is hardly anything better to do than to sit back on a deck chair, put your feet high on a railing, lean back, and enjoy the sunshine. Boat docks are in downtown Wisconsin Dells and at the junction of U.S. Highway 12 and State Highways 13, 16, and 23. Tours are given daily from early April through October. For times and other details, contact Dells Boat Tours—Upper & Lower Dells, P.O. Box 208, Wisconsin Dells, WI 53965.

- **Dells Boat Tours,** (608) 254–8555

- **Olson Boat Company,** (608) 254–8500

- **Riverview Boat Line,** (608) 254–8336

ORIGINAL WISCONSIN DUCKS (ages 5 and up)

1890 Wisconsin Dells Parkway; (608) 254–8751. Open from April 23 to mid-October. Hours are 8:00 A.M. to 7:00 P.M. daily from Memorial Day to Labor Day. Hours vary in early spring and autumn; call for details.

For a more challenging and bouncy way to capture the spirit of the waterway, the Original Wisconsin Ducks present an hour-long, 8-mile tour on the river, Dell Creek, and Lake Delton. Four miles of the trip ramble through Hop-Along Hill and Red Bird Gorge, among other aptly named landmarks, plunging in and out of the water, careening along slopes, and defying death at every sharp turn. At least that's what it seems like, so hang on tight and enjoy the ride. Be prepared, too, for an occasional dampening. Often water will splash over the gunwales of these green-and-white World War II amphibious crafts, which were rescued from the cutters' torch years ago and refurbished. Once back on land, guests can stagger off to a fudge shop or souvenir stand to load up on goodies for the ride home. Actually, the rides are not dangerous at all, but the funny patter of the drivers and the apparent danger gives kids a real thrill.

TOMMY BARTLETT'S SKI, SKY AND STAGE SHOW (ages 5 and up)

560 Wisconsin Dells Parkway; (608) 254–2525. Open Memorial Day through Labor Day. Daily shows are held at 1:00, 4:30, and 8:30 P.M.

For real thrills, this atmospheric collage has jugglers twirling flaming batons and spinning cutlasses; contortionists who can tie themselves into double knots (and free themselves); speeding stunt boats that top 100 mph as they perform tail stands and ramp jumps; skyflier daredevils dangling from hovering helicopters; and, of course, the ski show itself. Three performances are held daily, rain or shine, with a regular 8:30 P.M. laser explosion to top off an evening of lovely ladies and hunky guys doing amazing things on water skis.

ROBOT WORLD & EXPLORATORY (ages 5 and up)

560 Wisconsin Dells Parkway; (608) 254–2525. Hours are 8:00 A.M. to 11:00 P.M. April through October.

Impresario Tommy Bartlett, who looks like a beaming Santa Claus with his white beard and jovial grin, has been at this for what seems to be centuries. His promotional bumper stickers have appeared around the world in the oddest places. Always thinking of new ways to entertain guests, Bartlett also devised the Robot World & Exploratory. The computerized touch-screen games, gravity experiments, and robotic house are guaranteed to grab attention. Much to the delight of the kids, hair literally stands on end during some of the electrical energy experiments.

WONDER SPOT (ages 5 and up)

Near the bridge on U.S. Highway 12; (608) 254–4224.

After a long day of exploring, wiping spilled malts off the rear seat, driving, and more driving, it is natural that Mom and Dad can't stand up straight. This is true, especially when visiting the Wonder Spot, where "you have to see it to believe it." This is one of these puzzling places where everything is off-kilter and kids seem to roll uphill. The building, where even sitting down is a challenge, is a real photographer's holiday.

RIPLEY'S BELIEVE IT OR NOT MUSEUM (ages 5 and up)

105 Broadway; (608) 253–7556. Open May through mid-October.

Another "amazing" look-see is Ripley's Believe It Or Not Museum. Based on the syndicated newspaper column, the museum has plenty of the unusual and odd for kids to laugh at or groan about.

WISCONSIN DEER PARK (all ages)

583 Wisconsin Dells Parkway; (608) 253–2041. Open May through October.

On a more recognizable level, little kids will enjoy Wisconsin Deer Park, a twenty-eight-acre wildlife exhibit set back in the forest away from U.S. Highway 12. Some of the deer can be petted, while the big bucks are best viewed from afar.

STORYBOOK GARDENS (ages 5 and up)

1500 Wisconsin Dells Parkway; (608) 253–2391. Open Memorial Day through Labor Day.

For more landlocked adventure (around a reflecting pool, of course) bring the little ones over to Storybook Gardens, where costumed fairy-tale characters wander the grounds. A fairy princess has a magic wand with which to bestow wishes, and Little Bo-Peep is always looking for her sheep. Youngsters are invited to participate in a daily parade around the site at 12:30 P.M. from mid-June through the end of August. Musical instruments, flags, and signs are provided.

NOAH'S ARK (ages 5 and up)

Wisconsin Dells Parkway; mail to S897 Clara Avenue, Wisconsin Dells, WI 53965; (608) 254–6351. Open Memorial Day through Labor Day.

While the Wisconsin River is okay as far as water adventure goes in the mind of a kid, youngsters really yearn for the slides and bumper cars at all the Dells' water parks. Some fifty different splash-type activities are at Noah's Ark, where the water-logged gang from the backseat can spend days getting wrinkled and pink. Noah's Ark calls itself the largest such theme park in the United States, a claim that is certainly hard to dispute. Bermuda Triangle, Thunder Rapids, Kowabunga, the Wave, Slidewinders (one of twenty-seven slides)—the list goes on and on. Twelve restaurants are on the grounds in case the hungries hit between dives down the Chute Shooters. All-day passes are honored until 8:00 P.M.

RIVERVIEW PARK & WATERWORLD (ages 5 and up)
Located near the boat docks on U.S. Highway 12; (608) 254–2608. Open 9:00 A.M. to 11:00 P.M. daily from Memorial Day through Labor Day.

This park adds a lot of whoop and holler to a hot summer afternoon. Picnic pavilions and **Free** observation areas (for the nonwaterlogged) are available at the Wave Pool and elsewhere on the grounds. The Giant Log Walk and Kiddie Tube Run are the most fun, but the Oceans of Waves pool rates right up there on the heart-in-the-mouth scale, as well. A kids' ticket allows all-day unlimited use of the pools, go-cart tracks, petting zoo, bumper boats, inner-tube rides, fun house, and other activities.

BLACK WOLF LODGE (all ages)
I–90/94 and U.S. Highway 12; (608) 253–2222 or (800) 559–9653; e-mail: blackwlf@dellsnet.com; www.dells.com/blackwlf.html. Open year-round. $$.

Twenty-thousand square feet of indoor water activities are offered at the Black Wolf, including a log-jam ride; kiddie, tube, and speed slides; and bubbling geysers. The kids can tumble out of their room and head for the pool, regardless of the weather. Then they come back clean! The Black Wolf opened in the summer of 1997 with 130 guest rooms, fitness room, gift shop, game room, bar, and grill.

Other Watery Attractions
Several other Wisconsin Dells attractions combine water with . . .

MINI GOLF:
Shipwreck Lagoon; (608) 253-7772
Pirate's Cove; (608) 254-8336

FISHING:
Beaver Springs Fishing Park; (608) 253-7100

SKI BOATS, PARASAILING, PADDLEBOATS, AND CANOES:
Lake Delton Water Sports; (608) 254-8702

Obviously, the Wisconsin Dells area has a thing about H_2O.

FAMILY LAND (all ages)

U.S. Highway 12; (608) 254–7766. Open 9:00 A.M. to 8:00 P.M. from mid-May through Labor Day.

The Tidal Wave at Family Land is another rip-roaring surfing adventure, almost as good as the Australian coast. The Double Tubes, Blue Magnum, Fountain of Youth, Raging River, Demon Drop, and Double Rampage also ensure a vacation without need of a bathtub. What better way to keep a kid clean?

TIMBER FALLS (ages 5 and up)

State Highway 23 and Stand Rock Road; (608) 254–8414. Open Memorial Day through Labor Day.

Try a scrubdown aboard the Timber Mountain log flume ride at Timber Falls, near the Wisconsin River Bridge and Stand Rock Road. A bunch of folks can get wet together as their log ride plunges into a pool with the appropriate drenching.

 WINNEBAGO INDIAN MUSEUM (ages 10 and up)

3889 River Road, 2 miles north of Wisconsin Dells on a spur road just off State Highways 12 and 16. Look for the signs. Hours are 9:00 A.M. to 6:00 P.M. daily in summer.

The Winnebago Indian Museum showcases the heritage of this major Wisconsin tribe, with artifacts, photographs, and memorabilia.

WISCONSIN DELLS FLAKE OUT FESTIVAL (all ages)

Skyline Ski Area, 1900 Thirteenth Court, Friendship, WI 53934; (800) SKI–3811 or (608) 339–3426.

While the amusement parks close in the winter, the Dells area stays open and ready for skiers and snowmobilers. Each January thousands of persons attend the annual Wisconsin Dells Flake Out Festival, which includes internationally sanctioned ice-sculpting and ice skating competitions, horse-drawn sleigh rides, and musical entertainment. On the weekend before the festival, the **Child's Play Doll, Toy Show and Sale** (608-254-4200) is held in the Holiday Inn on State Highway 13, just off I-90/94. Anyone can come to check out the newest and the oldest in toys. This is like Santa's workshop being opened to the public.

Places to Eat

The Wisconsin Dells promises that no one need get the hungries during a vacation. There are pizza parlors, fine-dining locales, quick-and-ready spots, romantic getaways, and nightclubs. Take your pick.

Big Country Colossal Buffet. *1541 Wisconsin Dells Parkway; (608) 254–2480.* This is a food line fit for a king and a heavy eater, at that. The kids can load their plates. $

BJ's Restaurant. *1201 Wisconsin Dells Parkway; (608) 254–6278.* An excellent family-style eatery, BJ's caters to the vacation crowd. This is a casual place with good soups, burgers, and full entrees. A large covered deck provides a great summertime eating spot. There is a kid's menu and a grand breakfast selection. Homemade cheese soup is something to try. $$

Dells Duck Snack Bar. *1550 Wisconsin Dells Parkway; (608) 254–6080.* If you need a quick sandwich, this snack bar is conveniently located in the heart of Dells Country. $

Monk's Bar. *220 Broadway; (608) 254–2955.* Marvelous burgers to keep the family tummies full. $$

Paul Bunyan Meals. *Take the State Highway 13 exit off 1–90/94; (608) 254–8717.* With all this Dells activity, a family gets as hungry as a lumberjack. Paul Bunyan Meals has been a staple eatery in the Dells for generations. Featuring an all-you-can-eat chicken and fish fry on Friday along with spaghetti and potato pancakes, the restaurant looks like a cook shanty in the woods. Long wooden benches, checked tablecloths, and logging artifacts make for North Woods ambience. Parents will appreciate the huge pots of coffee placed on every table, as well as the special kid's prices. $

Pizza Pub. *1455 Wisconsin Dells Parkway, across from Noah's Ark; 739 Superior Street, downtown Wisconsin Dells; 218 Broadway, also downtown; (608) 254–7877.* Don't worry about being too far away from civilization, because Pizza Pub delivers shrimp fettucine, chicken cacciatore, Italian sandwiches, and pizza (yes, with anchovies if requested) to your campsite. The Pub has a kids' menu with mouse-size portions. Just ask.

Places to Stay

STATE PARK CAMPGROUNDS
Even with the dozens of motels and hotels in the area, most of which have waterfalls, swimming pools, play areas, and other amenities, camping is still popular. The two Dells-area state parks are prime locales far enough away from the neon and wax museums to offer all-important solitude. In February the state parks' cross-country ski trails are lighted by thousands of candles for nighttime ambience.

Mirror Lake State Park, *3 miles south of Wisconsin Dells off U.S. Highway 12; (608) 254–2333.* $

Rocky Arbor State Park, *2 miles north of Wisconsin Dells off U.S. Highway 12 and State Highway 16; (608) 254–8001.* $

PRIVATE CAMPGROUNDS

It is always a good idea to ask about on-site facilities, location, and amenities, because some camping areas are resort-oriented while others offer a more "primitive" style of outdoor adventure. The Dells convention bureau (see For More Information, p.142) can provide listings. Among the parks in the Dells area are:

Bonanza Campground RV Resort, *1770 Wisconsin Dells Parkway, Wisconsin Dells; (608) 254–8124 or (800) 438–8139;* $$

Dells Timberland Camping Resort, *N18005 Highways 12 and 16, Lyndon Station (4 miles west of Wisconsin Dells); (608) 254–2429 or (800) 774–0535;* $$

Sherwood Forest, *S352 Highways 12 and 16, Wisconsin Dells; (608) 254–7080;* $

Tepee Park, *E100096 Trout Road, Wisconsin Dells; (608) 253–3122;* $

RESORTS

Dells-area resorts are in a geographic league by themselves. Don't be confused to find:

Aloha Beach, *1370 Hiawatha Drive, Wisconsin Dells; (608) 253–4741;* $$

Caribbean Club Resort, *1093 Canyon Road, Wisconsin Dells; (608) 254–4777 or (800) 800–6981;* $$

Copa Cabana Resort Hotel and Suites, *611 Wisconsin Dells Parkway, Wisconsin Dells; (608) 253–1511 or (800) 364–2672;* $$

Monte Carlo, *350 Hiawatha Drive, Lake Denton; (608) 254–8661;* $$

Polynesian, *857 North Frontage Road, Wisconsin Dells; (800) 27–ALOHA;* $$

Regardless of the names, this is still the delightful Dells.

 Skiing, Skiing, Skiing If your family has any skiing fans, be sure to check out these options:

- **Cascade Mountain,** W10441 Cascade Mountain Road, Portage, WI 53901; (608) 742-5588. Open late November through March.

- **Christmas Mountain Village,** 5944 Christmas Mountain Road, Wisconsin Dells, WI 53965; (608) 253-1000 or (608) 254-3971. Cross-country packages, ski lessons for kids, and sleigh rides are also available. Christmas Mountain sponsors a Winter Carnival in February, with a chili cook-off, live music, and sled-dog races. Get the details from the Wisconsin Dells Convention and Visitors Bureau, which can send you a package outlining all the winter family activities and events.

- **Skyline Ski Area,** 1900 Thirteenth Court, Friendship, WI 53934; (800) SKI-3811. Open early December through March 11.

For More Information

Wisconsin Dells Visitor and Convention Bureau, *701 Superior Street, Wisconsin Dells, WI 53965-0390; (800) 22–DELLS or (608) 254–4636.*

Stevens Point

From the Dells, drive east on State Highway 23 to U.S. 51, then go north on 51 to Stevens Point.

THE GREEN CIRCLE (all ages)

This 24-mile-long nature trail around Stevens Point is a fine way to see the wild side of the city—wild in the sense that it brings nature home to the urban folk. Hikers can also secure a map of the trail system at the **Schmeeckle Reserve Nature Center** (715-346-4992) on North Point Drive. The reserve itself is part of the trail system; wood chips and boardwalks underfoot make for easy trekking. The center is the home of the **Wisconsin Conservation Hall of Fame,** where noted state residents are honored for their work in preserving the environment. Numerous natural-history programs are offered at the reserve; many are geared to youngsters.

PACELLI PANACEA (all ages)

The Pacelli Panacea, a fund-raising drive for Pacelli High School, is held annually in early September with a **polka mass, carnival, arts-and-crafts show,** and **loads of food.** The school cooks spend weeks preparing a roast chicken feast, with parents and community residents donating baked goods for a massive sale geared to the sweet-tooth set. This is a true family festival in the good, old-time sense of the term. Guests are welcome to join in the festivities. Call the high school (715-341-2442) for dates.

UNIVERSITY OF WISCONSIN–STEVENS POINT (all ages)

On the college level, the University of Wisconsin–Stevens Point celebrates each year with its **Spud Bowl football game,** battling top-ranked teams from around the Midwest. Held in early autumn, the game is preceded by a **parade, massive cookout, games,** and **music.** Stevens Point is in the heart of Wisconsin's potato-growing country, so there are always plenty of spuds (hence the game name) in all varieties, from baked to french fried. Kids watch in amazement as the elder college crowd goes through its **Spud Olympics.** Diving for bubble gum in bowls of mashed potatoes, potato sack races, and similarly silly events bring the community together for a laugh. Who says college always has to be serious business? Call the tourism bureau for times and places.

Amazing Wisconsin Facts The Wisconsin state flag was adopted in 1913. In addition to the state seal, the flag design incorporates the name *Wisconsin* and the date *1848*, the year Wisconsin became a state, both added in 1981. The state seal, which was adopted in 1881, incorporates a sailor and a miner supporting a shield that has symbols representing manufacturing, agriculture, navigation, and mining. A small United States coat of arms symbolizes allegiance to the United States. The badger above the shield represents the state animal and Wisconsin's nickname, the Badger State.

Places to Eat

Anthony's Supper Club. *1511 North Second Drive, Stevens Point; (715) 344–5624.* Show your hotel key for a 10 percent discount from the meal bill. The club is only 2 miles from the Holiday Inn, making it convenient for travelers. For hollow-legged teens who never seem to get enough to eat, challenge their appetites with the fifty-ounce sirloins served here. $$$

Belts Softserve. *2140 Division Street, Stevens Point; (715) 344–0049.* This is the home of the genuine "large" cone. Be prepared for sticky chins and fingers. Try the homemade brownies, peanut butter cups, and cherry or apple crisp made each day. In season, fresh berries are mixed in with the sundaes and shakes. $

Blake's Restaurant and Lounge. *Plover Mall, 1501–2 Plover Road, Plover; (715) 345–1477.* For family-style dining, Blake's takes care of any size munchkin crowd. Open daily from 7:00 A.M. to 9:00 P.M., it has great fish fry, prime rib, and a Sunday breakfast buffet. $$

Blueberry Muffin Restaurant. *2801 Stanley Street, Stevens Point; (715) 341–1993.* A good family-style eatery, the Muffin emphasizes that all its food is made from scratch. Thursday is steak night, so take note. $$

Ella's. *616 Division Street, Stevens Point; (715) 341–1871.* Famous for its bagels and hot sandwiches, Ella's also has daily specials. There is a big-screen television, too. $

King Cone. *113 U.S. Highway 10, Amherst; (715) 824–5464.* This popular neighborhood spot offers subs, pizza, and other fast foods. Open seven days a week from May through November. $

Uncle Wally's Burgers. *Center Point Drive (downtown), Stevens Point; (715) 341–7875.* Some of the best burgers in the Wisconsin heartland are served here. Beats the fast-food chains by miles. $

Places to Stay

Americinn. *1501 American Drive, Plover, WI 54467; (715) 342–1244.* Rooms with Jacuzzis keep the kids wrinkled and clean. There is also a decent exercise room. AAA approved. The inn is across the street from the Rainbow Falls Water Park and has plenty of restaurants nearby. $$

Blue Top Motel. *3425 Church Street, Stevens Point, WI 54481; (715) 344–3434.* Blue Top has the usual amenities, with the location a plus for those just passing through town. $$

Holiday Inn. *U.S. Highways 39/51, exit 161, Stevens Point, WI 54481;* *(800) 922–7880.* Kids go nuts in the Holidome pool. $$

Marcyanna's Bed & Breakfast. *440 North Old Wausau Road, Stevens Point, WI 54481; (715) 341–9922.* Kids are welcome here, with plenty of room on the sixty-five-acre grounds to run and jump. Nature trails meander through the woods near the Wisconsin River. $$

A Victorian Swan on Water. *1716 Water Street, Stevens Point, WI 54481; (715) 345–0595.* This 1889 home has huge beds, along with fireplaces, a whirlpool, and antiques. Kids are still welcome, but ask first. $$

For More Information

Stevens Point Area Convention and Visitors Bureau, *23 Park Ridge Drive, Stevens Point, WI 54481; (715) 344–2556.*

Rudolph

To get to Rudolph from Stevens Point, drive west about 4 miles on County Road C.

GROTTO GARDENS AND WONDER CAVE (ages 5 and up)
6975 Grotto Avenue; (715) 435–3120.

The Grotto Gardens and Wonder Cave might seem a slow place to take the kids for a visit, located as it is behind St. Philip's parish school. Maybe that's okay, though. The memorials to veterans and victims of

World Wars I and II are impressive, as are the gardens, with their explosive variety of well-tended annuals and perennials. The kids, however, will probably just enjoy roaming the grounds, peeking into secret recesses, and exploring the cave (which can take up to a half hour). Inside are lighted shrines to saints and other religious exhibits, and the dark tunnel has plenty of spooky, jump-out-and-scare-you possibilities for those who aren't spiritually inclined at the time. While the cave and gift shop are open only from Memorial Day to Labor Day, the grounds are always open for strolling. The grotto was built by Father Phillip J. Wagner and Edmund Rybicki in the 1920s.

Kellner

From Rudolph, aim south on State Highway 34 and drive through Wisconsin Rapids to pick up easterly County Highway Z.

LITTLE BRITCHES RODEO (all ages)

Lazy B Ranch, Kellner. Contact the Wisconsin Rapids Chamber of Commerce at (715) 423–1830 for more details.

The finals of the Little Britches Rodeo are held at the beginning of September each year in Kellner, a Wisconsin Rapids rural suburb. Age groups between six and eleven, eleven and fifteen, and fifteen through high school compete in **bull riding, saddle and bareback bronc riding, goat tying, calf roping, team roping, pole bending,** and **barrel racing.** For a weekend of jumping, flopping, flipping, yahooing, and hanging on tight, the rodeo can't be beat. The entrants are serious about their riding and roping, and many move on to college teams, with some competitors eventually turning pro. The bulls and horses are big, really big, so there is nothing childish about the competition. A sheep-riding contest for little kids, however, is always a funny sight, with the tots trying to mount the mutton and ride off into the sunset. Events are held simultaneously in two large arenas, so viewers sometimes have to move from bleacher to bleacher in order to catch all the action. Several thousand people, mostly families, turn out to yell encouragement and help dust off the jeans after a tumble. Tell the youngsters to watch out for the rear end of horses and be careful where they step if they go out for a stroll.

Trails for All Tastes

GOVERNOR DODGE STATE PARK. U.S. Highway 18, 40 miles west of Madison. Drive to Dodgeville and turn south on State Highway 23. The park is 10 miles farther south. Wisconsin park passes required at $15.00 per year or $4.00 daily.

- **Pine Cliff Nature Trail.** Two miles. This self-guided loop begins and ends at the Enee Point picnic area. Signs along the way tell of the animal and plant life in the area.

- **Lost Canyon Ski-Hiking Trail.** Approximately 8 miles. The tough trail starts at the Cox Hollow Campground. Watch out for steep grades. This is an advanced trek, with heavy boots required. Bring plenty of water or juice to drink.

- **Gold Mine Ski/Hike/Bike Trail.** Two-and-one-half miles. This is an easy walk, accessed ⁴/₁₀ mile west of the Twin Valley Campgrounds. The trail is along a grassy path, looping through timber and over meadows.

- **White Oak Trail.** Four-and-one-half miles. Start at the Cox Hollow Campground. There are rocks and slippery grades (be careful), but the trek is worth the two to three hours it takes.

- **Mill Creek Ski/Hiking/Bike Trail.** Approximately 3³/₁₀ miles. Cox Hollow is the kickoff point for this two-hour trek. The path is wide and easy and provides a comfortable stroll.

BLUE MOUND STATE PARK. U.S. Highway 18, 25 miles west of Madison. The park entrance is on Mounds Park Road, taken from the west side of Blue Mounds. State-park passes required.

- **Pleasure Valley Trail.** Two miles. This is a rolling loop that runs through fields of flowers. Remember that cyclists use the trail, as well.

- **Willow Spring Trail.** Approximately 1½ miles. This is a great trail for bird-watching: look for ruffed grouse.

- **Ridgeview Trail.** Two miles. This takes hikers through the most scenic hills and valleys of the park.

(continued on next page)

- **Flint Rock Nature Trail.** Almost 2 miles. Enjoy the up-and-down run of this path, but be aware it can be slippery after a rain.

- **Indian Marker Tree Trail.** Just over 1 mile. This can be picked up at several points in the park. The two most accessible points are near the grassy picnic area at the west end and the east end near the swimming pool.

For More Information

Wisconsin Rapids Chamber of Commerce, *1120 Lincoln Street, Wisconsin Rapids, WI 54495-0996; (715) 423–1830.*

South and Southwest Wisconsin

I t is easy to fall in love with the full moon in this far corner of Wisconsin. Passion comes whether on an October bluff overlooking the rolling, ink-deep waters of a Mississippi River midnight or in August's steamiest evenings. The moon pulls up the purple trillium from their secret recesses each mud-dampened April night. It caresses December's fluffed snowbanks and brings an Ice Palace glitter to the wee hours. The moon's spotlight sharpens our inner eyes and brings our dim caveperson past partially back to life. The full moon—like Diana the Huntress and Goddess of the Moon—chases away the nighttime fears and keeps the things that go bump in the night far beyond the campfire circle. Forego the flashlight and walk the moon's path. It will lead your family into wondrous places.

But the busy sun has its place, as well. Just bring the sunscreen. Flop on your backs in a pasqueflower meadow at Nelson Dewey State Park

Hintz's Top Picks

- Eating freshly caught catfish
- Admiring the full moon from the Mississippi River bluffs
- Visiting a historical site in Prairie du Chien
- Talking to an old trapper
- Getting lost in the hills of Grant County and eventually finding the way
- Eating freshly made cheese
- Watching snapping turtles on river logs
- Looking for the best ice cream
- Discovering a new bike path
- Buying fresh corn-on-the-cob on the way home at the end of a long weekend

S O U T H and S O U T H W E S T

and have each kid count his or her personal clouds. The midday sun makes the stone and glass particles in the Dickeyville Grotto explode in pinpoints of light. They dazzle the soul of today's young and old visitors. The early July sun clears off the shoreline mists for the Cassville ferry's first morning run across the Mississippi River. The mid-afternoon sun warms the rocks at Magnolia Bluff Park, making for a comfortable, snug perch from which to watch circling hawks. Its late-day rays soften the dim past at Blackhawk Memorial Park, a reflective place where Sac and Fox Indians were killed trying to escape pursuing militia more than a century ago.

Every one of these experiences under the sun or moon can lead to discussions with your kids about life, love, our place in nature, and where the world is going. So be forewarned and be ready. There are more rewards in all of this than you've ever dreamed.

Southwestern Wisconsin is primarily farm country, without the vast tracks of woodlands and rugged, glacially carved landscapes of the north. As such, it is a place for tours of cheese factories; stops at farmers' markets; strolls through church bazaars seeking out the best homemade jams; and jaunts through pick-your-own strawberry patches. Be sure to carry a basket or bag in which to collect the bountiful goodies. Whether biking, hiking, or driving, be prepared to come home loaded down with more than you expected.

Will it be pumpkins, gourds, or freshly picked apples in the fall? Sharp or mild cheddar cheese (ah, go for both!) in the spring? Corn-on-the-cob, tomatoes, herbs, cucumbers, onions, beans, or eggplant in the summer? Hot chocolate and cookies in the winter? Take the list from the glove compartment, place it on the front seat, and have the eagle-eyes from the backseat crowd scan the landscape for potential stops.

Riding through southwestern Wisconsin is a roller coaster of low hills and shallow valleys, much like the European homeland of many of its settlers. The Swiss, Germans, Irish, Poles, Italians, and Scandinavians found a familiar atmosphere in this country. Their Old World tidiness can be seen on the farms and in small towns encountered along the way. Be sure the kids experience the Swiss atmosphere of New Glarus and the German influences in Beloit. Festivals, fairs, and historic sites are great ways to sample this ethnic richness. Check the state tourism calendars and listings in this book for suggestions. Wisconsin loves to showcase its diversity. Pride, in this case, never goes before a fall.

Maiden Rock

Begin your south and southwest Wisconsin trek at Maiden Rock on State Highway 35, the Great River Road.

 HARRISBURG BED AND BREAKFAST (ages 16 and up)
W3334 State Highway 35; (715) 448–4500.

One of the best places to stay in the Lake Pepin area is Harrisburg Bed and Breakfast. With only four rooms, privacy is assured by owners Bern Paddock and Carol Crisp Paddock. The century-old home overlooks the Mississippi River, and a screened-in porch provides a nice spot for summertime breakfasts.

Stockholm

Stockholm is 4 miles south of Maiden Rock on State Highway 35.

The Great River Road (State Highway 35) leads through Stockholm, the oldest Swedish settlement in southwestern Wisconsin. It was founded in 1851 by a group of immigrants from Kalskoga, Sweden. The town abounds in historic buildings, many of which are now occupied by artists and craftworkers. The Stockholm Village Park allows camping, and there is a sand beach for swimming and a boat launch into Lake Pepin.

 AMISH COUNTRY QUILTS AND FURNITURE (ages 10 and up)
199 Spring Street; (715) 442–2015 or (800) 247–7657.

Mom and Dad may wish to stop at this shop, which features comforters and quilts made by Amish women who live nearby. The elaborately stitched covers range from small to king size to accommodate tots, teens, and parents. Also sold is simple Amish-style furniture, which is made by artisans in northern Indiana.

Neillsville

Digress from the beauty of the Mississippi River for a drive inland to Neillsville. From Stockholm, take State Highway 35 south 6 miles to State Highway 25; turn north on 25 to U.S. Highway 10. Turn east on 10 and proceed 40 miles to Neillsville.

Three miles west of Neillsville on U.S. Highway 10 is a picturesque ridge overlooking three counties of south/southwestern Wisconsin. It is quiet here, with only the breeze making any noise as it tinkles the dog tags on a memorial dedicated to the Wisconsin dead of Vietnam.

THE HIGHGROUND (ages 5 and up)

P.O. Box 457, Neillsville, WI 54456-0457; (715) 743–4224.

The Highground, the Vietnam Veterans' Memorial Park, is visited by thousands of vets each year seeking to heal themselves. It is a hushed place, where even the most bubbly youngsters will feel the presence of something bigger than themselves. The focal point of the memorial is a life-size bronze sculpture depicting three soldiers and a sheltering nurse, made by Wisconsin artist Robert A. Kanyusik. There is also a wind chime comprised of 1,215 tags marking each of the state's dead and the thirty-seven still missing in action. An earthen mound in the shape of a dove of peace is at the base of the bluff, commemorating all prisoners of war and those missing in action. In the center of the dove is soil from each of Wisconsin's seventy-two counties.

1897 CLARK COUNTY JAIL MUSEUM (ages 5 and up)

215 East Fifth Street; (715) 743–3655. Open 1:00 to 4:00 P.M. Saturday and Sunday from Mother's Day through Labor Day.

The kids will sober up when they see the 1897 Clark County Jail Museum. The fortresslike building is listed on the National Register of Historic Places. Thick walls, turrets, and guard stations demonstrate that this was certainly not a country club. Tours include a peek in the sheriff's office and cell blocks. The last live-in sheriff and his family departed the premises in 1974, but the cells continued to be used until 1978, when a more modern structure was built. Tours start in the sheriff's old residence, which boasts a parlor, sitting room, and other homey accommodations. An open stairway leads upstairs, where the children of the family stayed and played. The jail portion of the structure is totally different, however. The massive cells doors, peek holes for viewing prisoners, an exercise area, and commodes in the corner of each tiny cell testify to the security-conscious nature of the place. The sections that held women and juveniles now hold a bright display of flags, a sewing room, an antique telephone office, and an old-time barber shop, all of which soften the edges.

Places to Eat

Becker's A&W. *501 East Division Street;* *(715) 743–7900.* Drop in for a root beer float and a burger with fries. $

White Horse Inn. *100 East Division Street;* *(715) 743–2212.* This is one of the best places in town for a full menu. $$

Pepin

After seeing Neillsville, come back toward the Mississippi River via U.S. Highway 10 to Durand, where you can pick up State Highway 25. Take 25 to State Highway 35 to spend more time in Pepin.

The lake community of Pepin is the birthplace of Laura Ingalls Wilder, author of the popular Little House series of children's books. Pepin has named its city park in her honor, and a memorial has been erected there, as well.

Lake Pepin, a widening of the Mississippi River between Wisconsin and Minnesota, is also perfect for fishing, sailing, and motorboating. Numerous cabins and resorts line the Wisconsin shore. To expand and capitalize on all the recreational opportunities, the city of Pepin has joined forces in a united tourism program with towns on both sides of the river. Their effort is called the Mississippi Valley Partners. They host a 12 Days of Christmas extravaganza, where each community hosts a concert, pageant, or some other holiday fun. The towns also sponsor a giant rummage/antiques sale in the summer. Included in the effort are neighboring Bay City, Maiden Rock, Stockholm, and Nelson on the Wisconsin side and Frontenac, Lake City, Camp LaCupolis, Reads Landing, Wabasha, and Kellogg on the Minnesota side.

 PEPIN HISTORICAL MUSEUM (ages 5 and up)
306 Third Street; (715) 442–3161. Open 10:00 A.M. to 5:00 P.M. from May 15 to mid-October.

This museum highlights Laura Ingall Wilder's prodigious literary legacy. Seven miles northwest of town, on County Highway CC, the Little House Wayside sits on a three-acre site that includes a replica of the cabin she wrote about in *Little House in the Big Woods.* Suggest to the gang that they turn their minds inward and imagine Pa and Ma coming out of the tiny house, along with all the other characters made famous in Wilder's delightful stories.

For More Information

Mississippi Valley Partners, *c/o Village Clerk, 508 Second Street, Pepin, WI 54759; (715) 442–2461.*

Trempealeau

Continue south on the Great River Road (State Highway 35) for about 30 miles or so to Trempealeau.

PERROT STATE PARK
West of Trempealeau; (608) 534–6409.

This park was named after a French explorer who wandered through the neighborhood in 1665. The park is atop 500-foot-high bluffs overlooking the confluence of the Mississippi and Trempealeau Rivers. Considered a sacred area by Native Americans, early explorers used the peaks as landmarks on their journeys westward. Several burial and ceremonial mounds built by prehistoric Native Americans can be found around the park. Get the kids to look over the mounds and discuss what type of people must have made them and why.

TREMPEALEAU NATIONAL WILDLIFE REFUGE (all ages)

Four miles north of the park is the Trempealeau National Wildlife Refuge (608–539–2311), managed by the U.S. Fish and Wildlife Service. There is no way that anyone could see the entire 6,000 acres of the refuge in a weekend or even a week, but take the kids along the 5-mile, self-guided auto tour around the park, which skirts the edge of the Mississippi River. There is also a well-marked, ½-mile nature trail and a marsh to explore. White-tailed deer, bald eagles, ducks, geese, and other creatures can readily be seen.

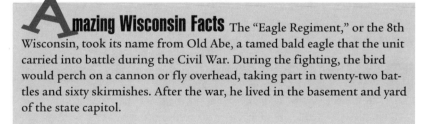

Amazing Wisconsin Facts The "Eagle Regiment," or the 8th Wisconsin, took its name from Old Abe, a tamed bald eagle that the unit carried into battle during the Civil War. During the fighting, the bird would perch on a cannon or fly overhead, taking part in twenty-two battles and sixty skirmishes. After the war, he lived in the basement and yard of the state capitol.

Onalaska

Onalaska is 10 miles south of Trempealeau on State Highway 35.

FUN 'N THE SUN HOUSEBOAT RENTAL (all ages)

1312 Herman Court; (608) 783–7326.

Vacationing aboard a houseboat on the Mississippi River is the ulti-mate in fun and not hard at all. Fun 'n the Sun Houseboat Rental offers three-day weekends, four-day midweek trips, and weeklong options for families wishing to do a Huck Finn experience. The firm is only one of several in the area that put fully equipped boats on the river. Just bring the burgers for those onboard gourmet meals. Kids can also dangle their fishlines over the rail to augment the burgers, beans, and noodles. Houseboating excursions can head either upriver or down, depending on the captain's whim.

La Crosse

La Crosse is 1 mile south of Onalaska on State Highway 35 and U.S. Highway 53.

This city is a geological oddity, escaping the crush of the glaciers that flat-tened most of Wisconsin several eons ago. The pancake effect of all that mile-high ice missed the La Crosse vicinity, so cliffs, gullies, ridges, and valleys abound. The 600-foot-high **Grandad Bluff** overlooks the city and provides a peek at three states: Minnesota, Iowa, and Wisconsin. Contributing to the beauty of the area, three major rivers converge on La Crosse: the **La Crosse,** the **Black,** and the **Mississippi.**

Native Americans appreciated the watery connection, as did early Euro-pean explorers. In 1680 a canoe load of Frenchmen led by Father Louis Hen-nepin marked the location of what eventually would become the city of La Crosse. Permanent European settlement started in 1841 when Nathan Myrick built the first cabin there. The site is now in the city's Pettibone Park. The town received its name from the Native American game of lacrosse, in which long racquets resembling a cross are used to bat a ball back and forth across a playing field.

RIVERSIDE PARK (all ages)

Intersection of State Street and the Mississippi River.

Tell the kids to keep a look out for the giant carved eagle that stands in Riverside Park, site of many of the festivals and events sponsored by the city. Carved by local artist Elmer Peterson, the bald eagle with its out-stretched wings is atop a 35-foot-high pillar. It is a tribute to Old Abe, a mascot of the state's famous Iron Brigade, which fought in the Civil War. Real bald eagles, though, are often spotted from the vantage point of Riverside Park, drifting on the wind high above the Mississippi River.

MYRICK PARK ZOO (ages 5 and up)

2200 La Crosse Street (State Highway 16), directly across the street from the University of Wisconsin–La Crosse athletic field; (608) 789–7190.

Myrick Park Zoo specializes in North American species rather than the exotic. Kids, however, love the antics of the spider monkeys on Monkey Island, a constant reminder of a kindergarten class at full steam. The ten-acre park is bordered by La Crosse Street and the southern edge of the La Crosse River Marsh and its nature trails.

LA CROSSE CLOCK COMPANY (ages 10 and up)

125 South Second Street; (608) 782–8200

While in La Crosse, there is always time to stop at the La Crosse Clock Company, where there are more than 1,000 timepieces in stock. Cuckoo, alarm, grandfather, wall, and mantle clocks all tick-tock their merry way in the shop across from the Radisson Hotel and the Civic Center in downtown La Crosse. This is just the place to stock up for everybody in the family who is late with homework, runs overtime in the bathroom, or habitually misses the school bus because "the alarm didn't work."

ISLAND GIRL CRUISELINER (ages 5 and up)

621 Park Plaza Drive; (608) 784–0556. Cruises depart from the Holiday Inn adjacent to American Marine. Tours run May through October, with trips daily and moonlight and breakfast jaunts on weekends.

With all the new timepieces in the car trunk after visiting the La Crosse Clock Company, there's no excuse to miss the departure of the *Island Girl* dinner cruise at 7:30 P.M., which leaves nightly from the dock on U.S. Highways 14/61. There is also a daily cocktail cruise, which offers **Free** beer, soda, and pizza.

LA CROSSE QUEEN (ages 5 and up)

Riverside Park, on the west end of State Street in downtown La Crosse; (608) 784–8523.

This paddle wheeler has a variety of sightseeing expeditions and dinner cruises up and down the Mississippi.

La Crosse Events

APRIL

Party Line Craft Show. Pick out all you and the family will ever need for crafting on those rainy days. Artisans show and sell these wares, so you can pick up plenty of tips. Call (515) 421-0416 to learn more.

MAY

Reggae Sunsplash. A bit of the Caribbean comes to Wisconsin to dazzle with lively music and Jamaican food at the Trempealeau Hotel. Call (608) 534-6898.

JUNE

June Dairy Days. The state celebrates June Dairy Month, and La Crosse follows suit for the celebration. Events are held at the Village Park in West Salem. On tap are softball tournaments, a crafts fair, a tractor pull, a parade, and music.

Seafood Fest. Sample seafood delicacies from area restaurants, as well as enjoy live music and kids' games. Call (608) 784-4600, ext. 216. The fest is held in conjunction with the American Bass Classic.

American Bass Classic. More than 140 fishermen try for prizes. Call (608) 784-4600, ext. 216.

JULY

La Crosse Interstate Fair. Auto races, livestock sales, and arts and crafts are a few of the things to enjoy at the fairgrounds in West Salem. Call (608) 786-0428.

Riverfest. Top-name entertainers come to the city's Riverside Park. There is also a Venetian parade on the river. Call (608) 782-6000.

AUGUST

Art Fair on the Green. Artists from around the country exhibit their work on the campus of the University of Wisconsin–La Crosse. Call (800) 658-9424.

Festival of Lanterns. Lighted lanterns are floated down the Mississippi in the name of peace after a day of speeches and displays. Call (608) 782-4842.

Great River Festival of Traditional Jazz. The festival is held in the parks along the Mississippi. Great music, food, and fun for the family. Call (800) 658-9424.

(continued on next page)

AUGUST (continued)

Great River Traditional Music and Crafts Festival. Musicians, artists, and craftworkers from around the Midwest show their stuff. Call (800) 658-9424.

NOVEMBER

Holiday Folk Fair. More than 130 exhibitors come to the La Crosse Center with wares geared specifically to the holidays. Call (608) 782-4500.

LA CROSSE OUTDOORS

Outdoor recreation opportunities are plentiful in the La Crosse area. Use the city as a jumping-off point for **biking, hiking, skiing, canoeing,** and other fun.

The **Black and La Crosse Rivers** are popular with paddlers, who have also discovered **Coon Creek** and the **Mississippi River** and its backwaters. The latter might be difficult for beginning canoeists, especially for kids because of the current and underwater obstructions. So start on the rivers and graduate to the more difficult waterways as family members gain experience. There are dozens of rental and sales outlets throughout the region, supplying everything from anchors to bug spray to life preservers. Check the La Crosse yellow pages for the most up-to-date listing of suppliers.

The La Crosse area is a cyclist's image of dying and going to heaven. The **major state bike trails** meander through the region to combine urban and rural rides geared to the interests of all ages. The **Great River State Trail** begins in Onalaska near La Crosse's far north side and rolls about 22 miles along the Mississippi River.

The **La Crosse River Bicycle Trail** is a 21½-mile expedition paralleling the La Crosse River. The route cuts along farm pastures, streams, and maple groves. This trail connects with the **Elroy-Sparta Trail** and the **Great River State Trail.** There is plenty of camping along the routes, most of which are on hard-surface crushed rock along old railroad beds.

Approximately 100 miles of **snowmobile trails** crisscross La Crosse County, eventually hooking up with another 650 miles of trails in the surrounding region. Seven local snowmobile clubs ensure that the trails are groomed to what seem to be interstate-highway specifications. To receive maps call or write the La Crosse CVB, 410 East Veterans Memorial Drive, Riverside Park, La Crosse, WI 54602-1895; (608) 782-2366.

Amazing Wisconsin Facts The nickname Badger State came from the term applied to the "Badgers," lead miners in the western part of Wisconsin in the 1820s. Some of the miners lived in caves they had dug out of the hillsides near Potosi. The protective burrows reminded passersby of badger dens.

Skiing is also a great outdoor recreation opportunity in La Crosse County. **Bluebird Springs Recreation Area,** N2833 Smith Valley Road (608-781-2267), has 25 miles of groomed cross-country trails open during daylight hours. **Goose Island Park** (608-788-7018) near downtown also has excellent groomed paths. **Hixon Forest Nature Center,** 2702 Quarry Road (608-784-0303), presents about 5 miles of trail through heavy woods and along high ridges. **La Crosse County Forest Preserve** (608-785-9007) and **Mount La Crosse** (608-788- 0044; 800-426-3665 outside Wisconsin) also have cross-country opportunities. The latter also has downhill skiing, with instructions and rentals.

Want to take a break? How about a **sleigh ride?** Bundle up the tykes and take them to the **Sunset Riding Stables,** Route 2, W4803 Meyer Road, La Crosse (608-788-6629). During the snow season, rides for two to eighty persons can be reserved each evening of the week. So bring all the cousins, grandparents, great-uncles, and Aunt Matilda for some frosty, extended-family fun. Long johns and heavy mittens are necessary. To keep their patrons from turning into icicles, a warming house is located en route to take off some of the chill. Bonfires for late-night fun are also possible.

Places to Eat

Freighthouse Restaurant. *107 Vine; (608) 784-6211.* This old building, with its walls adorned with railroad memorabilia, is on the National Register of Historic Places. Blues, folk, and jazz music are regular staples, which make a great background for the steaks and crab legs. $$

Haberdashery Restaurant. *200 Harborview Plaza; (608) 784-6680.* The pub-like restaurant, located in the Radisson Hotel, offers burgers that are among the best along the river. $$

Places to Stay

Days Inn Hotel. *101 Sky Harbour Drive; (608) 783–1000.* One hundred forty-eight rooms. The lobby is linked to the second floor with broad sweeping staircases. The kids will enjoy the pool. $$$

The Martindale Bed & Breakfast. *237 South Tenth Street; (608) 782–4224.* Innkeepers Anita and Tim Philbrook have four rooms in the main house and one room in the carriage house of this 1850s home. The building is on the National Register of Historic Places. Kids are welcome, but call first. $$

Radisson Hotel. *200 Harborview Plaza; (608) 784–6680.* One hundred seventy rooms. Babysitting services are available. $$$

For More Information

La Crosse Convention and Visitors Bureau, *Box 1895, Riverside Park, La Crosse, WI 54602; (800) 658–9424.*

Coon Valley

Finding Coon Valley is easy. Simply travel U.S. Highways 14/61 southeast from La Crosse for about 16 miles.

NORSKEDALEN (ages 5 and up)
County Highway PI; (608) 452–3424. Open year-round from 9:00 A.M. to 4:00 P.M. Monday through Saturday.
     Norskedalen ("The Norwegian Valley") is home to the University of Wisconsin–La Crosse Foundation's 400-acre arboretum. Maple-dappled hills, rushing trout streams (the city calls itself The Trout Capital of the Midwest), native plantings, and sculpture make up the grounds, with trails open year-round for seasonal hiking and cross-country skiing.

BEKKUM HOMESTEAD (ages 5 and up)
Thrune Visitor Center; (608) 452–3424. Open 9:00 A.M. to 4:30 P.M. Monday through Saturday; noon to 4:30 P.M. Sunday.
     Bekkum Homestead, a pioneer farm at Norskedalen, brings back memories of early Scandinavian settlers and is also open for touring. Classes and programs on Scandinavian heritage are regularly held.

The town sponsors an **old-fashioned threshing bee** each September at the Bekkum Homestead. Kids can watch the huffing, puffing ancient steam threshers, eat a farmer's picnic outside, and watch how grain was harvested one hundred years ago. For Halloween there is the Ghoulees in the Goulees haunted hike through some of the darkest country this side of Count Dracula's estate. This can be *preeetttty* scary, so kids have to take care of moms and dads who tend to be frightened at all sorts of silly stuff like this.

A Hintz Adventure by Dan Hintz

There is a hole that exists in family vacations. It is that dreaded space between point A and point B. It is a chaotic realm of hot and cranky kids, never-ending demands for bathroom breaks, and car rides that seem to last forever. However, that space has an alternative universe, one filled with odd assortments of small towns boasting the most delicious pies, bizarre mustard museums, fish farms, cheese factories, fascinating burial grounds, grueling hiking trails, gangster hideouts, and quaint, cozy artisan shops that would blow away any big-city collector.

It is here, in this openness, that the real family vacation begins. Or you could always put the kids in a box and ship them special delivery to your destination, but think of what would be missed.

The cool, northern Wisconsin forests and lakes have always been my favorite places. Being such a hard-core city kid, large trees and blue waters were fascinating to me. It was a giant change from the rolling gray water of the Milwaukee River near where we lived. On those remotely wonderful lakes, my family fished. But each person had his/her own style. My little brother and sister often skipped the bait-and-cast routine to go after frogs waiting to be caught along the shores. My dad was content to lie back in a rowboat with a string and hook dangling from his big toe, ready to sleep or read.

However, my mother and I geared up as if going to war. We rented a motorboat, bought all the fishing tackle and lake-related topographical stuff we could carry, made our sandwiches, and then trudged down to the lakefront at some unnatural predawn hour. Our minds were set to catch the Mother of All Wisconsin Fish, that finny monster of a thousand casts: the elusive musky.

During one particular vacation, we were staying at Hintz's North Star Lodge (managed by no relation to us) on Star Lake. We brought in

(continued on next page)

the occasional northern pike and bass. Yet under the water, the musky were laughing at us. You could hear them, even after being on the water for about ten hours. One memorable evening as it was getting dark, I had been the lucky one that day, pulling in four large pike and a fat bass. My mom had not caught a thing. As we trolled back to shore, my mom's pole was almost yanked out of her hand, and the line became taut. When we stopped the motor, all that could be heard were a few bird whistles and the buzz of an occasional cow-size mosquito whizzing past our ears.

Mom started to reel in the line, with the tip of the pole nearly broken from the strain. As she pulled up what she thought was a large clump of guck, there was a large sucking noise. The weeds had jaws, eyes, and scales, with the mass about as large as me. Needless to say, we freaked . . . and so did the fish. As it bit through the twenty-five pound test line, it seemed to smile and say, "Perhaps next time."

With that, the fish arrogantly splashed us both and disappeared into the deep, dark water. My shaking mother and I sat there in the boat, listening to the far-off chatter of a few hikers coming to the resort grounds through the night fog. We knew that that old musky was laughing again. But this time we laughed with him, and everything seemed perfect.

(Dan Hintz has a degree in fine-art film from the University of Colorado-Boulder. He lived and worked in Russia, Venezuela, and Ireland and has traveled extensively throughout the United States, Canada, and Great Britain. He is also an accomplished chef and worked in noted restaurants in Boulder, Milwaukee, and other cities. In addition, he helped his father with several cultural geographies and coauthored an award-winning book on Wisconsin in Globe Pequot's Off the Beaten Path series. Dan also manages his own theater training workshop program, Beanstalk Productions.)

Genoa

Genoa is 10 miles south of La Crosse on State Highway 35. From Coon Valley, however, take State Highway 162 west to the Mississippi River and pick up 35. Then turn south.

GENOA NATIONAL FISH HATCHERY (ages 5 and up)

Fifteen miles south of La Crosse; (608) 689–2605. Visitors can tour the facility from 7:30 A.M. to 4:00 P.M. Monday through Friday.

The Genoa National Fish Hatchery raises both cold- and warm-water species. Bass, walleye, trout, and sauger are among the two million fish produced annually and shipped to state and federal release points around the country. Lock and Dam Number Eight on State Highway 35 (the Great River Road) has several viewing areas from which to watch barges and boats navigate up and down the Mississippi River.

Westby

From Genoa, take State Highway 56 east 20 miles to U.S. Highway 61, turn north, and go about 7 miles to Westby.

SYTTENDE MAI FESTIVAL (all ages)

On the weekend closest to May 17, Westby holds a three-day celebration of Norway's Constitution Day. Called Syttende Mai, the activities include a troll hunt for kids, a huge quilt auction, arts-and-crafts exhibits, music, and dancing. A Sunday-afternoon parade showcases the Scandinavian heritage of the community. For details call (608) 634– 4193.

SNOWFLAKE ANNUAL SKI JUMPING TOURNAMENT (all ages)

Westby is also an outdoors town, with the Snowflake Annual Ski Jumping Tournament (608-634-2002) in February, held at the Westby Ski Club's Nordic Center (north of town off State Highway 27 on Vernon County Highway P). The 65-meter run's landing zone converts to a nine-hole, par-three golf course in the summer. This is not something for the little kids to try off the roof of the house into a snowbank, but they'll get a thrill out of watching the international pros sailing through the air.

Places to Stay

Central Express Inn. *State Highway 27 and U.S. Highway 14; (608) 634–2950.* Twenty-one rooms.

Old Towne Motel. *U.S. Highways 14/61 and State Highway 27 South; (608) 634–2111 or (800) 605–0276.* Twenty-six rooms.

Westby House. *200 West State Street; (608) 634–4112.* Kids are welcome, but call first. This is a nifty, restored 1890s house.

De Soto

After visiting Westby, take U.S. Highway 61 south to State Highway 27. Turn east and pick up State Highway 82, which leads to State Highway 35 along the Mississippi River. De Soto is right there along the river.

De Soto, located on the Bad Axe River, which flows into the Mississippi, was the site of a massacre during the Black Hawk War in the 1830s. Several hundred Sac and Fox women, children, and warriors were killed there as they tried to flee American troops on the Wisconsin side. Many who escaped the soldiers' gunfire drowned in the fast-flowing river. Others were killed when they reached the Iowa banks, where their longtime enemies, the Sioux, were waiting for them with hatchets and knives. A memorial is near the community.

This hamlet hosts **Fish Fly Days** on the third weekend in August. It features a kids' fishing contest that lets the youngsters show old-timers how to bring in the "big ones." There is also a carnival, chicken barbecue, steak dinner, and parades. Call (608) 648–2137 for all the latest information, plus sign-up details for young anglers.

Places to Eat

Great River Roadhouse. *1006 State Highway 35; (608) 648–2045.* Sandwiches, pies, and soups. $

Prairie du Chien

Prairie du Chien is 30 miles south of De Soto on State Highway 35.

Anyone who guesses the meaning of this town's name wins an ice cream cone at the St. Feriole Island Railroad, an assortment of shops in a string of old railroad cars parked along the Mississippi River. Some historians say the city was named after a local Native American leader during frontier days. Others indicate it simply meant "field of dogs," referring to the hundreds of prairie dogs that were seen by the first French visitors in the 1600s. The meaning is unclear, so everyone should probably slurp a cone. Stand on the veranda behind the train cars and watch the river roll by while you lap up the vanilla or chocolate.

The Wisconsin Information Center (see For More Information, p. 168), on U.S. Highway 18 at the Mississippi River Bridge, has oodles of information on what to see and do in the area, as well as elsewhere around the state. Perhaps more important to know is that there are rest-room facilities in the center. On a pedestal overlooking the river is a statue of Père Jacques Marquette, one of the first explorers of the region, who made a journey down the Mississippi his life's mission. Always the guide and teacher, Marquette's upraised arms seem to beckon visitors to the information center.

There are several commercial fishermen in town who offer snapping turtles, catfish, and carp fresh from the Mississippi. Hunks of smoked catfish, along with crackers, are especially great for munching while trekking overland. Be sure to also pick up some squeaky cheese curds (yes, they sound squeaky when you chew them), Wisconsin's favorite snack, to go along with the catfish for a true gourmet picnic. Load up on napkins before heading out of town, because sticky fingers are generally the result.

 ### PRAIRIE DU CHIEN MEDICAL MUSEUM AT FORT CRAWFORD (ages 5 and up)

 717 Beaumount Street; (608) 326–6960. Open 10:00 A.M. to 5:00 P.M. May through October.

The Prairie du Chien Medical Museum at Fort Crawford was a major health-care center in the rugged days before the Civil War. The fort was built in 1816 and was the center of frontier military activity during the Black Hawk War. Dr. William Beaumont, a medical pioneer and surgeon, performed a famous experiment on a trapper who was injured in the stomach: He covered the wound with a flap of skin so he was still able to watch the digestive process. Now a museum of medical history, Praire du Chien's rudimentary tools and drugs used by frontier doctors will amaze the kids. It makes one appreciate the quick med stops, emergency clinics, and CAT-scans available everywhere in contemporary life.

STOVALL HALL OF HEALTH

Take the kids into the fort's Stovall Hall of Health to learn about their bodies from the Transparent Twins, life-size plastic female models. One shows the twenty-five organs of the body, and the other highlights the 200 bones in the skeletal system. Tape-recorded messages describe the function of each organ.

VILLA LOUIS (ages 5 and up)

521 Villa Louis Road; (608) 326–2721. Open 9:00 A.M. to 5:00 P.M. May through October. The day's last tour is given at 7:00 P.M.

The Villa Louis mansion, a state historical site, shows how a wealthy frontier family used to live.

FUR TRADERS RENDEZVOUS (ages 5 and up)

Call the Prairie du Chien Chamber of Commerce and Tourism Council at (608) 326–8555.

Prairie du Chien annually hosts a fur-traders' rendezvous on St. Feriole Island near the Villa Louis on the third weekend in June. Grizzled mountain men, Native American trappers, and appropriately garbed military men from the era fill the grounds with their tents and tepees. They display trade goods, talk shop, cook over open fires, scratch, and look at guests from the twenty-first century with amusement. Of course, when the weekend is over, they all go back to being bank presidents, mechanics, nurses, shop owners, and lawyers. The kids can barter for knickknacks and come away with pelts, muskets, tomahawks, and flint—if it will all fit in the car.

Places to Eat

Culver's Prairie du Chien. *1915 South Marquette Road; (608) 326–5360.* Better butter burgers (burgers with a buttered bun—a Wisconsin tradition) . . . and don't forget the fries and shakes. $

For More Information

Prairie du Chien Chamber of Commerce and Tourism Council, *211 South Main Street, Prairie du Chien, WI 53821-0326; (608) 326–8555.*

Wisconsin Information Center, *Prairie du Chien, WI 53821; (608) 326–2241.*

$\mathcal{S}$entinel Side Trip

Sentinel Side Trip Numerous Indian mounds dot both sides of the Sentinel Ridge Trail, in Wyalusing State Park along the Mississippi River and 2 miles south of Prairie du Chien. After studying the mounds, we like perching on the rocks high above the river and looking over the sprawling river valley below. This vista is especially great during October, when the oaks and maples are in full glory. You can also take this trail from the top of the bluffs at Point Lookout to a boat landing on the Mississippi. The area here is part of the **Upper Mississippi Wildlife and Fish Refuge.** Stay on the trail because the adjoining ground is marshy. Yet despite the mushiness, the bird-watching opportunities make this side trip worthwhile.

Bagley

Take County Road P east from Wyalusing State Park. Follow P along the rough ridges of Glass Hollow to Bagley.

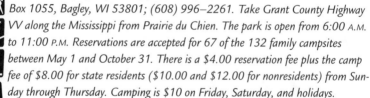

WYALUSING STATE PARK (all ages)

Box 1055, Bagley, WI 53801; (608) 996–2261. Take Grant County Highway VV along the Mississippi from Prairie du Chien. The park is open from 6:00 A.M. to 11:00 P.M. Reservations are accepted for 67 of the 132 family campsites between May 1 and October 31. There is a $4.00 reservation fee plus the camp fee of $8.00 for state residents ($10.00 and $12.00 for nonresidents) from Sunday through Thursday. Camping is $10 on Friday, Saturday, and holidays.

Visit Wyalusing State Park for its camping, hiking trails, and picnic sites. Indian mounds dating back a thousand years can be found on the bluff overlooking the river on the Sentinel Ridge Walk. On one marked overlook, show the youngsters the confluence of the Mississippi and Wisconsin Rivers. The park, sprawling over 2,700 acres, is a veritable wildlife resort. White-tailed deer, bald eagles, Canada geese, muskrats, raccoons, wild turkeys, turkey vultures, and opossums can sometimes be spotted.

In the winter, Wyalusing has excellent groomed and tracked cross-country ski trails, making it a treat for all classes of skiers. The terrain ranges from flat to hilly and from wooded to open, which keeps up the interest of even the littlest skier. Toilets and water are on-site.

WYALUSING HIKING TRAILS (all ages)

- **Bluff, Indian, and Flint Ledge Trails.** Take the 2-mile walk down the bluff side for great views of the Mississippi. These paths are not recommended for toddlers.

- **Old Immigrant, Old Wagon Road, and Sand Cave Trails.** These trails meander for more than 3 miles through heavy oak and maple groves and have some steep slopes, so watch your step. As the names imply, these tracks were used by early settlers moving overland into the river valley.

- **Walnut Springs Trail.** This 2⁹⁄₁₀-mile grassy pathway is a two-hour-long walk.

- **Mississippi Ridge Trail.** Hikers do not have any difficulty getting across this 3½-mile trail, which overlooks the river.

- **Sentinel Ridge Trail.** This 1⁶⁄₁₀-mile trail runs south from the park's main campground along the high ridge. It offers some of the best views of the river.

Cassville

Cassville is on the southern edge of the Nelson Dewey State Park, along State Highway 81.

 STONEFIELD VILLAGE (ages 5 and up)
County Highway VV; (608) 725–5210. Open 9:00 A.M. to 4:00 P.M. from late May through October and 10:00 A.M. to 5:00 P.M. in July and August.

Stonefield Village, a state historical society property, is a replica of an 1890s village. Craftworkers and interpreters show guests around the village. Buildings include a railroad depot, shops, a firehouse, homes, and a school. In mid-June Stonefield Children's Days present a hands-on adventure for kids by showing them how to process honey, cook on a wood-fired stove, and bake bread from scratch.

The best time to visit is on an early summer morning when the Mississippi River fog still hugs the maples and oaks, when it seems as if life has paused long enough to offer a visit to another time. This area is called Wisconsin's Hidden Valleys country because of all the secret spots and hideaways found along the backcountry roads. The name is apt—all sorts of magic can occur here.

NELSON DEWEY STATE PARK (all ages)

12190 County VV; (608) 725–5210. State-park vehicle sticker required.

Across County Highway VV from Stonefield Village is Nelson Dewey State Park, named after the state's first governor. Camping is available in the park, where a predawn visitor to a tent site might be a fox, skunk, or raccoon. Be sure to get the family out along the trail through the park's ten-acre prairie, with its hundreds of varieties of plants ranging from the bluish pasqueflower to June grass. The prairie grows in height as the season advances through the summer, with spring plants only about 1 foot tall and summer/fall plants reaching from 5 to 7 feet high. Remember not to pick any of the flowers in the prairie. As they say: Be sure to take only photographs and leave only footprints.

Five original buildings from the Dewey homestead can also be explored as well as several ancient Indian mounds. One group of twenty mounds is spread along the ridgetop at the highest point in the park. A group of five mounds is found south of Dewey Creek. Archaeologists estimate that they date from the late Woodland period, between A.D. 600 and 1300. Remains of one of their encampments has been found near Stonefield Village. As with the flora and fauna in the park, visitors are asked to treat the mounds with respect and refrain from disturbing them. They are sacred to the many tribes that are still in Wisconsin.

CASSVILLE CAR FERRY (all ages)

100 West Amelia Street; (608) 725–5180. The ferry, which holds six to eight cars and trucks, operates from 9:00 A.M. to almost 9:00 P.M. on Friday, Saturday and Sunday from the first weekend in May until Memorial Day. Between Memorial Day and Labor Day, it runs seven days a week. After Labor Day it returns to its weekend schedule until October 31. Whatever the season, the last trip from Cassville departs at 8:20 P.M., and the last trip from Iowa departs at 8:40 P.M.

Take the Cassville car ferry across the river into Iowa. For a small fee, the little boat plugs back and forth across the Mississippi, keeping up a tradition that dates back several generations. It beats crossing via the modern highway bridges to the north in Prairie du Chien or to the south at Dubuque. The boat links State Highways 133/81 with U.S. Highway 52 at Millville, Iowa (just south of Guttenberg).

Potosi

From Cassville, take State Highway 133 to Potosi.

Potosi is the Catfish Capital of Wisconsin. A **catfish festival** is held each July to celebrate the wonderfully nutritious—but ugly as day-old sin—fish that plops around in the nearby Mississippi River. Potosi was once larger than Chicago and Milwaukee. Lead was discovered in the bluffs overlooking the rolling river in the late 1820s, and thousands of miners flocked to the hills, setting up camps all along a deep valley that cut into the heart of lead country.

Only the village of Potosi remains of what were once several communities stretching along the valley floor, each named for its respective ethnic group (such as British Hollow). The town was originally called Snake Hollow, and *Ripley's Believe It or Not* claimed that in its heyday, the 5-mile-long main road was the longest street in the United States without an intersection. A few ruined building foundations, shadows of the past, can still be seen, but that is all.

THE ST. JOHN LEAD MINE (ages 5 and up)

State Highway 133, 129 South Main Street; (608) 763–2121. Open 9:00 A.M. to 5:00 P.M. May through October.

St. John was one of the deepest and most profitable lead mines. Park near the A-frame (the home of Mr. and Mrs. Harry Henderson) and climb up the steep stairs to enter the dim, cool interior. Lights along the way show the pick and chisel marks made by men working for hours on their backs or hands and knees to recover the precious lead. When the miners first arrived, they burrowed into the hills to seek shelter from the rain and cold. Their refuges reminded one visitor of badger holes, and the nickname of Wisconsin, the Badger State, was born.

Canoe rentals are also available at the St. John Mine for trips along the Grant and Big Platte Rivers; trips can be as short as a couple of hours or as long as three days. Either flowage is adequate for even young canoers. Primitive camping is possible along the way, but be sure to take out everything that is carried in. The folks at the mine can arrange drop-offs and pick-ups at either river. Reservations, however, are recommended.

GRANT RIVER RECREATION AREA AND PARK (all ages)
River Lane; (608) 763–2140. Two miles south of Potosi.

The recreation area and park has camping and a concrete boat ramp into the Mississippi.

Places to Eat

Friedman's Supper Club. *7540 State Highway 133; (608) 763–2526.* Overlooking the Mississippi River, the supper club affords magnificent views. Add that to the menu spread, and you have a dining-plus place. $$

Dickeyville

Dickeyville is 8 miles south of Potosi on State Highway 61.

DICKEYVILLE GROTTO (ages 10 and up)

305 West Main Street; (608) 568–3119. The grotto and shrine are open 8:00 A.M. to 5:00 P.M. daily year-round. Donations are suggested.

Across the river from Dubuque, Iowa, where U.S. Highways 151 and 61 intersect, is the Dickeyville Grotto. The park was constructed by Father Mathias Wernerus out of stone, pieces of glass, and shells that he had collected from around the world. Have the kids identify as many types of rock as possible in the sprawling collection of folk art.

Places to Eat

Muller's Restaurant & Lounge. *108 South Main Street; (608) 568–3161.* This is a good hideaway, with a full menu. Go for the catfish. $$

Mineral Point

Mineral Point is easily reached from Dickeyville. Drive north 25 miles on U.S. Highway 151.

One of several cities in southwestern Wisconsin that owes its birth to the mining industry, Mineral Point is the third oldest community in the state.

PENDARVIS (ages 10 and up)

114 Shake Rag Street; (608) 987–2122. Open 9:00 A.M. to 5:00 P.M. from May through October. Admission for adults is $7.00; children five to twelve, $3.00; seniors age sixty-five and older, $6.30.

Founded by Cornish miners in 1827, Pendarvis is now home to another state historical society complex of refurbished buildings. The name came from an estate in Cornwall near where many of the original settlers emigrated. Called "Cousin Jacks" and "Cousin Jennies," they brought valuable hard-rock skills with them as the tin mines in Cornwall petered out. They were also expert stonemasons and built homes like those they had back in Cornwall, many of which were constructed in a valley near the mouth of the mines. This cluster of houses now forms the bulk of the Pendarvis complex.

After 1847 lead prices and mining declined, and Mineral Point declined. Much of its population was lost as the settlers turned to farming or headed west to join the great Gold Rush. Within several generations, most of the buildings had deteriorated. In 1935, however, Robert Neal and Edgar Hellum purchased one old cottage and restored it. Over the years, they secured more properties

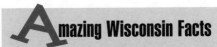

Amazing Wisconsin Facts

Cornish miners in Mineral Point were nicknamed "Cousin Jacks."

and gradually expanded the restorations. The state historical society took over the site in 1971.

Here's a tip for parents tired of yelling for kids at suppertime—do what the folks here used to do more than one hundred years ago: Along Shake Rag Street, wives of the miners used to flap a dishtowel or apron out an upper window or doorway so their families could see that the meal was ready. The family would come running to catch a bit of Cornish pasty, a traditional meat pie, before returning to work.

The community has become a center for the crafts industry, with numerous potters, weavers, and other artisans happy to demonstrate how they work. Among them are Jean Bohlin, a self-taught needlepointer; Solveig Nielsen, whose contemporary wool rugs and wall hangings touch on her Danish heritage; Kathleen Nutter, who specializes in handwoven chenille scarves; porcelain artists Diana and Tom Johnston; and photographer Mary North Allen.

Places to Eat

Redwood Point. *615 Dodge Street;*
(608) 987–2242. Visiting here opens the
door to fine dining opportunities. $$

Pendarvis Activities Several special events throughout the year should be fun for the family; these range from **Pendarvis Founder's Day** (May) to the **Flavours of Old Cornwall** (June), a food fest that features traditional favorites such as saffron cake and clotted cream. Held on several weekends in August and September, the **Drolls of Old Cornwall,** where storytellers relate "drolls," or Cornish folk tales, is sure to please the youngsters. The sessions, held in the Kiddleywink Pub, are free. Have the kids ask if there are still any "tommyknockers" down in the mines. These were Cornish fairies who supposedly caused all sorts of trouble underground if an occasional offering from a miner's lunch wasn't made.

Belmont

After Mineral Point, return on U.S. Highway 151 to Belmont, about 13 miles south.

Trek to the top of the observation tower atop the Belmont Mound, nearly 400 feet above the city. From the 64-foot-high tower, visitors can see three states. The name of Belmont, in fact, comes from the French words *belle mont,* which mean "beautiful mountain." The mound is covered with oak and walnut trees and raspberry and blackberry bushes. Morel-mushroom hunters love poking around in the forest for these special treats.

Take the kids on a walking expedition to see the **Devil's Dining Table,** a flat rock about 40 feet across perched on a pedestal of stone. A few feet away is the **Devil's Chair,** an appropriately shaped seat. Also nearby is **The Cave,** a dark passageway through a giant rock, which is perfect for scrambling youngsters.

Amazing Wisconsin Facts

Wisconsin's state capitol has been in several locations since its earliest days. The three territorial sites were Belmont (1836); Burlington, Iowa (1837–38); and Madison (1838–48). Madison retained the title when Wisconsin became a state in 1848.

FIRST STATE CAPITOL HISTORICAL SITE (all ages)

Route 2, 3 miles northwest of Belmont on County Highway G. The site is 1 mile west of Belmont Mound Park and its observation tower. For information call Yellowstone Lake State Park in Blanchardville at (608) 523–4427. First Capitol is open 10:00 A.M. to 4:00 P.M. from Memorial Day to Labor Day.

First Capitol marks the site of the Wisconsin Territorial Capitol of 1836. At that time, the Wisconsin Territory sprawled over Wisconsin, Iowa, Minnesota, and North and South Dakota, as far west at the Missouri River. Buildings on the site are sometimes closed, so call the Pendarvis historic site (608–987–2122) for details. But you can walk around the Council House (legislature) and the Supreme Court any time. The renovated buildings were also once used as barns, after serving their time in history. There is a certain good-old-days charm to the tidy complex, which sits quietly along the busy roadway.

Pecatonica Trail "Take a hike" on the Pecatonica Trail, which follows a Milwaukee railroad line for almost 10 miles between Belmont and Calamine. The gravel- and cinder-surfaced trail travels along the Bonner Branch of the Pecatonica River. Walkers and bikers are welcome in nonwinter months, and when the snow flies, snowmobilers and cross-country skiers can utilize the pathway. Bonner Branch is a swift-moving little creek that swings back and forth under the trail, making it necessary to have twenty-four bridges on the stretch between the two towns. That totals 1,306 feet of planking. The trail corridor is perfect for spotting quail, pheasant, squirrel, woodchuck, and the occasional deer.

Platteville

To get to Platteville from Blanchardville, drive south 8 miles on State Highway 81. Go west on State Highway 11 about 25 miles to Platteville.

THE MINING MUSEUM (ages 5 and up)

405 East Main Street; (608) 348–3301. Daily tours are given between 9:00 A.M. and 5:00 P.M. from May through October; 9:00 A.M. to 4:00 P.M. from November through April.

This museum traces the development of the area's zinc and lead production. Kids should enjoy a ride in the real ore cars pulled by a refurbished mining locomotive. Then descend the ninety steps it takes to get into the old Bevins Lead Mine. Youngsters might be startled at first, because the lantern lights illuminate mannequins depicting toiling miners. The Rollo Jameson Museum is part of the mine complex and has a wonderfully oddball collection of tools, kids games, and antiques.

Bear Watching When not rummaging through lead mines under Platteville, kids would enjoy the chance to go bear watching. To be more specific, they'd be looking for the Chicago Bears football team, which holds its summer training at the University of Wisconsin-Platteville starting in July. Practice sessions are usually open to the public, so check with the chamber of commerce for times and dates.

Places to Eat

Gamehenge Pub. 70 North Second Street; (608) 348–4212. This college town goes for pub grub. Follow the students; they know the score. $

Steve's Pizza Palace. 15 South Fourth Street; (608) 348–3136. Take out or eat in. Don't forget the anchovies. $

The Timbers Supper Club. 670 Ellen Street; (608) 348–2406. You might run into some of the football players who are in Platteville using the university's practice fields. They eat a lot, so give 'em room. It's fun to see who's who, however. $$

For More Information

Platteville Chamber of Commerce, 97 East Main Street, Platteville, WI; (608) 348–8888.

Shullsburg

To see Shullsburg, go south from Platteville on State Highway 81 and turn east on State Highway 11. The town is about 11 miles to the east.

Shullsburg is named after Jesse Shull, an early lead miner in Wisconsin. By the way, three streets in town are named Faith, Hope, and Charity, so it is almost impossible to become lost here.

BADGER MINE AND MUSEUM (ages 5 and up)

279 Estey Street; (608) 965–4860. Open June through August; call (608) 965–4401 for information when the museum is closed for the season.

Visitors descend through the mine's ore drifts to see how old-time miners hacked away at the rock to reach the lead treasure. The attached museum is packed with mining tools and farm implements dating back a hundred years.

Darlington

Darlington is about 11 miles north of Shullsburg. Take State Highway 11 east to State Highway 23 and turn north.

Darlington is the seat of Lafayette County and has sponsored a museum at its old depot building. Exhibits outline the history of the railroads in the vicinity and their impact on the town.

All-terrain-vehicle riders can also take advantage of the 51⁴⁄₁₀ miles of rough-and-rugged marked trails in the Darlington area. Be sure all riders have helmets and that no one exceeds the 30 mph speed limit. For an idea as to the terrain, consider that one link whoops over Roller Coast Road just south of the city.

CANOE RACES (ages 10 and up)

For information call the fire department organizers (608–776–3773, in the evening) or the University of Wisconsin extension office—Lafayette County branch, 627 Washington Street (608–776–4820). June.

The Darlington Fire Department sponsors annual canoe races along the winding Pecatonica River, starting at the Calamine Bridge on Lafayette County Trunk G. The finish line is 1 block past City Bridge in Darlington itself. Trophies are awarded to the canoe that finishes first in each division, with medallions given to second- and third-place finishers. This can be a total family affair, with classes for girls seventeen and under, high school boys, grade school boys, men, women, Boy Scouts, racing canoes, and men/women, parent/children (kids need to be thirteen and under), and Cub Scout/parents teams. Due to the width of the river, canoes are launched in groups of up to three at a time, at two- to three-minute intervals. Starting times are then radioed to the finish line, with winners declared on a comparative time basis.

During the weekend of the official canoe sprints, the community also has **inner tube races** on the river, **softball tournaments, pony rides, coed volleyball, 5- and 2-mile runs (plus a kids' 1-mile run), talent shows, an**

arts-and-crafts fair, Native American dancers, fireworks, a princess pageant, and many other family-oriented events.

A dairy breakfast on a nearby farm is also part of the fun. All the neighbors get together at a friends' home for omelets, cheese, sundaes, apple sauce, ham, muffins, and lots of milk and coffee. Of course, everyone is invited for the great food, conversation, and a chance to check out the cows. The breakfast is held rain or shine, usually from 6:30 to 10:30 A.M., when everyone rushes back to town to get ready for one of the race events.

CHEESE COUNTRY RECREATIONAL TRAIL (ages 5 and up)

Located in the heart of dairy country, the trail links Monroe, Browntown, South Wayne Gratiot, and Mineral Point. The trail system accommodates horseback riders, hikers, snowmobilers, bikers, all-terrain vehicles, and skiers. There are at least thirty cheese factories in the three counties—Green, Lafayette, and Iowa—that make up the trail system. Some sections of the Cheese Country Trail have incorporated elements of the Pecatonica Trail. Links are marked for the appropriate use (ATVs, for example, aren't allowed where horses can be ridden), so be alert for signage. A $6.00 trail-user fee is required and can be purchased at most gas stations near the trail and at other businesses.

Places to Eat

Bob & Anne's Country Club. *17098 Country Club Road; (608) 776–3377.* Drop on in after cycling through the countryside. $

Towne House Restaurant. *232 Main Street; (608) 776–3373.* Home-style cooking. Go for it. $

Places to Stay

Towne Motel. *245 West Harriet Street; (608) 776–2661.* Eight rooms.

Highland

Take State Highway 23 north from Darlington, pick up State Highway 80 at Mineral Point, and drive north to Highland.

SPURGEON VINEYARDS AND WINERY (ages 10 and up)

Pine Tree Road; (608) 929–7692. Open 10:00 A.M. to 5:00 P.M. daily from April through October and 10:00 A.M. to 5:00 P.M. Saturday and Sunday from November through March.

Pause for gas and a kid/pet pit stop, then take County Q west to the Spurgeon Vineyards and Winery on Pine Tree Road. The winery began growing grapes in 1977 and was able to make wine from its own crop in 1983. Award-winning reds and whites are now available, with winery tours and **Free** tastings. Mom and Dad could even give the kids a teeny sample sip if feeling very European.

Fennimore

To find Fennimore, take State Highway 80 back to U.S. Highway 18, turn west, and go 17 miles.

 ### FENNIMORE DOLL AND TOY MUSEUM (ages 5 and up)

1140 Lincoln Avenue; (608) 822–4100. Open 9:00 A.M. to 5:00 P.M. year-round.

The Fennimore Doll and Toy Museum attracts kids of all ages. Even guys can get a kick out of all the Star Wars and action-figure characters on display. More than 5,000 dolls from varying eras peer out from their glass display cases, and these include some ancient dolls discovered in Mexico. Many of the toys have smiles, while others are serious. They are made of wood, glass, stone, pewter, precious metals, and plain plastic. A local farm lady began collecting the dolls some twenty years ago and decided to donate them to her hometown, so that local kids could enjoy something without having to travel for hours to a big-city museum. Even if a visitor isn't that interested in the entire collection, the magnitude of the thousand-figure Barbie display is awesome. Almost every Barbie is there, as well as all the buxom bombshell's friends from over the years. They are displayed along with their toy cars, houses, tea sets, medical bags, shoes, capes, jet skis, glitter, and consumer gloss.

RAILROAD HISTORICAL SOCIETY MUSEUM (ages 5 and up)

610 Lincoln Street; (608) 822–6319.

Fennimore is also home to the Railroad Historical Society Museum. Exhibits of the town's railroad history are found in the society's headquarters, located near a track that holds the small narrow-gauge locomotive (dating from 1907), which once ran between Fennimore and towns along the Wisconsin River to the north. The museum is far from complete; new artifacts are added each season.

Places to Eat

Frederick Family Restaurant. *430 Lincoln Avenue; (608) 822–7070.* Clean-plate-club rules apply here, but the food is so good, that's no chore. $

Silent Woman/Fenway House. *1096 Lincoln Avenue; (608) 822–3782.*

You can't miss the Silent Woman: The sign in the parking lot across the street has a painting of a headless woman. It's not politically correct, but the food is topflight. The Fenway House is an old, renovated hotel occupying the same block as the restaurant.

Boscobel

From Fennimore, drive north on U.S. 61 for 11 miles.

Several farms in the area have shops featuring homemade crafts or foods, and some are occasionally open for home visits and overnights. To secure a map and other information, call or write "Farm Trails in Southwest Wisconsin," 4478 Riley Road, Boscobel, WI 53805; (608) 375–5798.

EAGLE CAVE NATURAL PARK (ages 5 and up)

Located in Blue River near Boscobel. Follow State Highway 133 northeast to Eagle Cave Road; (608) 537–2988. Open year-round, with guided cave tours between 10:00 A.M. and 6:00 P.M. Memorial Day to Labor Day.

Eagle Cave Natural Park boasts the state's largest onyx cave. The brave and hardy can even camp there during the winter. Bats? Not many! The park has a tiny lake available for swimming and fishing.

Festival Fun Located on the Lower Wisconsin State Riverway, the town of Muscoda is adjacent to thousands of acres of public land open for hunting, fishing, hiking, bird-watching, and just hanging out. The name comes from a Native American term, *mash-ko-deng*, meaning "meadow." These days, visitors know the Muscoda is the morel-mushroom capital of Wisconsin, because the delicious mushrooms are found in abundance in the forestland around town. The **Morel Mushroom Festival** is sponsored by the local chamber of commerce each May, which offers prizes for the largest, heaviest, tallest, and most-on-a-stem morels.

In mid-August, **Muscoda's Harvest Festival** offers an arts-and-crafts fair. There is also a tractor pull, which any kid worth his or her salt will love for the thundering engines and smoke; a 4-H Junior Fair; and a carnival. For more information write or call the Chamber of Commerce, 633 North Wisconsin Avenue, Muscoda, WI 53573-0578; (608) 739-3639.

Wauzeka

From Fennimore, drive west on U.S. Highway 18 to the junction with State Highway 133, which parallels the curving Wisconsin River. Take 133 to Wauzeka.

KICKAPOO CAVERNS (age 5 and up)

W200 Rhein Hollow Road; (608) 875–7723. Open 9:00 A.M. to 5:00 P.M. from May 15 through Labor Day and 10:00 A.M. to 5:00 P.M. Monday through Friday from after Labor Day through October.

Kickapoo Caverns, the largest caves in Wisconsin, are 2 miles west of town. Native Americans used the deep caverns as shelters from the wind and cold, and for some reason they abandoned the site well before the first white lead miners came into the area in the early 1800s. Be sure to bring a sweater or jacket and bundle up the kids, because dim recesses of the cave can be mighty cool on an hour-long tour. The last tour of the day usually departs at 4:00 P.M.

Viroqua

From Wauzeka, drive north on State Highway 133 to State Highway 61. Turn north on 61 to Viroqua.

HERITAGE FEST (all ages)

Viroqua Chamber of Commerce, (608) 637–8727.

Viroqua's Double Daze Twin Contest, held during its Heritage Fest each June, brings twins from around the Midwest to participate in the fun that includes a parade, classic-car show, and gem show. Entrants are judged in different age divisions from toddler to old-timers. Rules are simple: Whoever looks most alike or most unalike wins. Small plaques are then handed out to the victors. Contest participants also get a **Free** breakfast and a ride in the parade.

VERNON COUNTY FAIR (all ages)

North side of town on Main Street; (608) 637–3165. September.

The Vernon County Fair is the final county fair of the season in Wisconsin. Harness racing is the big event, with top horses from throughout the Midwest thundering around the turns. Take the kids back by the stables to watch the grooming and other preparations for the events. Sometimes a driver will let a youngster sit atop a sulky to get a feel for the cart's size and light weight. Then stroll through the exhibit buildings to watch the slicer-dicer-chopper salesmen, talk with implement dealers, stare at the county's largest pigs, admire the 4-H birdhouses and aprons, and eat, eat, eat. Corn-on-the-cob, hamburgers, chili dogs, cotton candy, homemade pie, roast beef dinners—ah, that's the country fair.

For More Information

Viroqua Chamber of Commerce, *Box 348, Viroqua, WI 54665-0348; (608) 637–8727.*

Woodford

After visiting Viroqua, return south to Woodford via U.S. Highway 14 to State Highway 130. Cross the Wisconsin River and angle back to State Highway 130. Follow 130 south to State Highway 78 and then on to State Highway 81 and Woodford.

BLACKHAWK MEMORIAL PARK (all ages)

The park is along Sand Road and Lafayette County Highway Y near Woodford; (608) 465–3390.

Although kids can have a wonderful time visiting Blackhawk Memorial Park, they should know its history to appreciate a little bit more of Wisconsin's story. The park, with its hook-shaped Bloody Lake, was the site of a 1832 battle in which outnumbered Sac and Fox Indians under Chief Blackhawk fought frontier militia and regular army troops. Later that year, the Sac were slaughtered while trying to surrender to U.S. cavalry at Bad Axe, in Vernon County along the Mississippi River. In 1990, Governor Tommy Thompson formally apologized to the descendants of the Sac Nation for what had happened in that long-ago time. The governor's statements marked the first time that any governmental representative apologized to Native Americans for war crimes committed against their ancestors.

Tree-shaded Blackhawk Memorial Park is quiet now, although a rendezvous with trapper and trader reenactors is held the first weekend of each May, complete with black-powder musket shoots and tomahawk throwing. A boat ramp leads into the slow-moving east branch of the Pecatonica River, where bass, catfish, and trout lurk. Primitive camping is allowed, but there are no sewer, water, or electric hookups available. Kids love it.

Browntown

Take County Road M south from Woodford to Browntown.

FOUR SEASONS HOME (ages 10 and up)

For information write P.O. Box 73, Browntown, WI 53522. Tours are possible from 1:00 to 6:00 P.M. Sunday and holidays or by appointment from April through October.

Do you have a teen with a room-decorating dilemma? Take him or her to the Four Seasons Home, a 5,300-square-foot residence that features 320 square feet of oil murals depicting summer, fall, winter, and spring. The wall paintings took thirteen months to complete. Antiques, coin collections, stamps, and newspapers are also used as part of the decor. The builder also included a water fountain and a 2,300-square-foot living room lit by a chandelier with 3,000 Austrian crystals. Buggy rides around the grounds are often given in the summer, too.

Monroe

Monroe is 8 miles east of Browntown on State Highway 11.

CHEESE DAYS (all ages)

P.O. Box 606, Monroe, WI 53566. Held on the third weekend in September in even numbered years.

Wilkommen to Cheese Days in Monroe. The festival has been a tradition here since 1914, although the cheese industry got its kick-start in 1868. The limestone underlying the soil was perfect for pastures and provided the right grasses for happy Holsteins and Brown Swiss cows. Paying tribute to the major industry in Green County, Cheese Day activities bring together farmers, dairy workers, big-city folk, college students, and everyone else. It is a big family reunion, and there's nothing cheesy about this party, with its **Cheesemaker's Ball, children's parade, street dancing, concessions** and **carnival, arts-and-crafts show, cheesemaking demonstrations,** and—of course—**tons of cheese sandwiches.** A cheese sale tent offers up a range of dairy goodies from Swiss to Muenster. Cheese-factory and farm tours aboard buses depart every hour from the northeast corner of the town square (kids eight or under ride **Free**). Harkening back to the country's Swiss heritage, there is plenty of yodeling and alpine music. The Cheese Days Chase consists of 10,000-, 20,000-, and 5,000-meter runs for different age categories.

BROWNTOWN–CADIZ SPRINGS STATE RECREATION AREA (all ages)

Travel 7 miles west of Monroe on State Highway 11 to the Allen Road exit, then go south a hilly ⁷/₁₀ mile to Cadiz Springs Road, turn west, and drive 1¹/₂ miles to the recreation area entrance. For details on the site, call the Department of Natural

Resources in Monroe (608–966–3777 in the summer and 608–325–4844 in the winter).

I like to fish at the Browntown-Cadiz Springs State Recreation Area. The placid waters of Lakes Beckman and Zander within the recreation area boundaries are divided by an earthen dike. Zander, the smallest of the two, was used for raising bullfrogs commercially in the 1930s. Now the kids can catch largemouth bass, crappies, and bluegills from several fishing piers overlooking the water.

Browntown-Cadiz Springs sprawls over 723 acres, with topography ranging from marsh to grassland. Walk quietly down to the end of the dike and watch the Canada geese feeding in the sloughs. Be aware that hunting is allowed in the area during the autumn, so don't go wandering off into the woods without protective colored clothing. Better yet, stick to the picnic and fishing areas.

BIKING THE SUGAR RIVER (all ages)

State Convention and Visitors Bureau, (800) 372–2737.

The 23-mile-long Sugar River State Trail follows the abandoned Chicago, Milwaukee, and St. Paul railroad bed, about 12 miles east of Monroe on State Highways 11/81. Brodhead is the easternmost access point to the trail and is the halfway mark between the Mississippi River and Lake Michigan. Biking is great along the limestone path, which has trestle bridges and a tunnel along the route. I've often spun off from the main trail on marked side routes to explore more of the surrounding farm country.

Top Cheese Companies in Monroe

If the kids weren't sated by Cheese Days, take them on a cheese hunt around the Monroe area. Here are a few of the licensed cheese factories open to tours: **Zimmerman Cheese Co.** (608–968- 3414), Wiota; **Valley View Cheese Co-op** (608–439–5569) and **Wood-Andrews Cheese Co-op** (no listed phone number), South Wayne; **Chula Vista Cheese Co.** (608–439–5211), **Davis Cheese** (608–966–3361), and **Curran Cheese Inc.** (608–966–3452), Browntown; and **Whitehead Cheese Co-op** (608–325–3522), **Deppeler Cheese Factory** (608–325–6311), **Franklin Cheese Co-op** (608–325- 3725), **Prairie Hill Cheese Co-op** (608–325–2918), and the **Green County Cheese Co-op** (608–328–8610), all in Monroe. For a more complete list, write the Cheese Day folks at P.O. Box 606, Monroe, WI 53566.

Milk, Anyone?

Milk, Anyone? South and southwestern Wisconsin have some of the state's prime dairy herd acreage, obvious to anyone driving past pasture after pasture of grazing Guernseys, Jerseys, and Holsteins. "Speak to a cow as you would a lady," said William D. Hoard, publisher of *Dairyman* magazine and experimental farmer who settled in Fort Atkinson.

Encouraged by Hoard, the Wisconsin's dairy industry grew enormously. By 1899, 90 percent of the state's farms had dairy cattle. By the 1930s, the state could boast of having two million dairy cattle, which was 400,000 more than second-place New York. In the 1950s, dairying contributed 53 percent of the state's farm output. Today, there are approximately 1.5 million dairy cows munching contentedly across the Wisconsin landscape.

Dairymen from around the county gathered in 1922 for the dedication of a bronze statue of Hoard, which stands outside the Wisconsin College of Agriculture's main building in Madison. "Cow College" or "Moo U" remains internationally known for its studies in dairy science.

Places to Eat

Bakers Maple Grove Inn. *W5836 Old Argyle Road; (608) 325–5254.* After all the touring of cheese plants in the Monroe area, it feels good to sit down and relax. Bakers caters to the tired-feet set with its fine service and large portions. $$

Hometown Cafe USA. *1713 Eleventh Street; (608) 328–4373.* Put your finger on the pulse of this typical Wisconsin community by listening to the background chatter. Politicians should make a habit of dropping by to hear the Real Story from the Heartland. $

Evansville

From Monroe, drive northeast on State Highway 93 to State Highway 105, then State Highway 59, and finally onto State Highway 20 to Evansville.

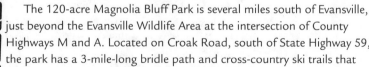

MAGNOLIA BLUFF PARK (all ages)

Rock County Parks Department; (608) 757–5450.

The 120-acre Magnolia Bluff Park is several miles south of Evansville, just beyond the Evansville Wildlife Area at the intersection of County Highways M and A. Located on Croak Road, south of State Highway 59, the park has a 3-mile-long bridle path and cross-country ski trails that challenge both novices and experts. Several picnic areas, with toilets, drinking water, and fireplaces, are scattered around the park. Scenic overlooks provide vistas of the surrounding countryside.

Beloit

From Evansville, drive south 20 miles on State Highway 20 to Beloit.

HANCHETT-BARTLETT HOMESTEAD (ages 10 and up)

2149 St. Lawrence Avenue; (608) 365–7835. Open 1:00 to 4:00 P.M. Wednesday through Sunday from June through August.

Pause at the Hanchett-Bartlett Homestead on the west side of Beloit to tour the old—but restored—Victorian farmhouse. Dating from 1857, the site consists of the main home, the original stone barn, and a smokehouse. An old school has been moved to the property, as well.

HANSON'S TAVERN (all ages)

615 Cranston Street; (608) 362–8559. $.

As a reward for their patience at Hanchett-Barlett Homestead, take the kids to Hanson's Tavern, where they can dive into monster hamburgers that have been voted the best in town. The pub also points out that "hohm maid zoops" are served daily, with a Friday "fisch fry." But hey, no one is there for the spelling anyway.

ROCK RIVER

The Rock River's passage through Beloit lent itself to the development of Riverside Park, between Henry and Grand Avenues. Check out the Heritage Walkway, which tells about the city's history. At the end of the walk is the Turtle Island Playground, an amazing, delightful display of equipment designed with the physically challenged kid in mind. A marina and open areas for outdoor concerts are central to the city's Riverfest, held here each July.

AVON BOTTOMS (ages 10 and up)

There are 1,600 primitive acres of Wisconsin Department of Natural Resources' land along the Sugar River in the town of Avon. The site is between Beloit and Janesville on County Highway D. Walk through oak savannah and across rich prairie land. For information about the area, call or write the DNR, P.O. Box 7921, Madison, WI 53707; (608) 266–2181.

Places to Eat

Liberty Inn. *1901 Liberty Street; (608) 362–2262.* Feel free to order anything from the menu. Ah, that's a joke, folks. $

Mouse Tavern. *1420 Madison Road; (608) 362–1196.* Great fish fry. $

Pitcher's Mound Ltd. *2754 Prairie Road; (608) 365–7022.* Live music. $

Janesville

Janesville is 8 miles north of Beloit on I–90.

ICE AGE TRAIL (ages 5 and up)

Janesville is a city best visited by bicycle and on foot. In fact, a major section of the National Ice Age Trail meanders along the Rock River in the city, making a hiking/biking visit part of the fun. The trail will eventually be a 1,000-mile course from northern to southern Wisconsin, tracing the outline of the last glaciers to steamroll the state. Pick up the trail at the north end of town at Riverside Golf Course on U.S. Highway 14, then follow the signage along the river, through downtown, past many of the city's architectural sights, and around to the following attractions.

ROTARY GARDENS PARK (ages 10 and up)

1455 Palmer Drive (on the south side of Janesville); (608) 752–3885.

This park boasts intricate displays of sculpture and landscaping. There are nine separate gardens as well as a wildlife sanctuary and a visitors center for nature and flower programs.

KIWANIS POND (ages 5 and up)

The "pond," formerly a gravel pit, is northeast of Rotary Gardens Park. Bring plenty of worms and tackle: The pit has been transformed into a fishing hole for kids and is well-stocked with bass and other denizens of the watery deep.

Festivals

FEBRUARY
Annual Chelonia Dance Concert, Beloit College, Beloit; (608) 363-2755.

MARCH
Pioneer Dinner, Milton; (608) 868-7772.

APRIL
Rock Valley Quilt Show, Janesville; (608) 756-4509.

MAY
Drums Along the Rock PowWow, 4-H Fairgrounds, Janesville; (608) 752-2224.

JUNE
Concert in the Park, Edgerton; (608) 884-3731.

JULY
Riverfest Music Festival, Riverside Park, Beloit; (608) 365-4838.

AUGUST
Tallman Arts Festival, Tallman House, Janesville; (608) 752-4519.

SEPTEMBER
Beloit Heritage Days Festival, Beloit; (608) 365-8835.

OCTOBER
Harvest Rendezvous, Milton House, Milton; (608) 868-7772.

NOVEMBER
Holiday Parade and Tree Lighting, Beloit; (608) 365-0150.

DECEMBER
Snowflake Festival and Craft Show, Edgerton Middle School, Edgerton; (608) 884-3731.

ROCK AQUA JAYS (ages 5 and up)

(800) 48–PARKS. Performances are held at 7:00 P.M. on Wednesday and Sunday from June through Labor Day. Shows in August begin at 6:30 P.M.

The family will love the Rock Aqua Jays water-ski team, with their squad of muscular guys and shapely girls. Bleachers overlooking the river in Traxler Park are available.

CAMDEN PLAYGROUND (all ages)

Camden Playground, located in Palmer Park on the city's south side, is the first fully accessible park for kids who are physically and mentally challenged. The playground has a castle where stage shows are presented in the summer, plus swings, slides, and a games area. Volunteers keep the facility in tip-top shape.

WISCONSIN WAGON COMPANY (ages 5 and up)

507 Laurel Avenue (the corner of Laurel and North Academy); (608) 754–0026.

Youngsters will love walking through the Wisconsin Wagon Company, which makes wagons and other toys for tykes. The plant is open to visitors from February through October. Test rides on scooters are usually allowed.

JANESVILLE FAMILY YMCA HALF MARATHON {ages 5 and up)

Usually held in the city's Palmer Park, along Palmer Drive near the intersection of State Highway 11. For specific routes call (608) 754–6654.

If your gang would rather run than walk, enter the Janesville Family YMCA Half Marathon. The event, held for more than twenty years, includes a 10-kilometer road race, a 2-mile run/walk, and ½-mile run/walk for kids. Awards are given for the first through sixth places in each event, and all kids entering the race receive some sort of prize. Following the race is a magic show and comedy act, along with a fire-truck demonstration where the little ones can climb on the rescue vehicles and talk with firefighters. McGruff, the Take-a-Bite-Out-of-Crime dog, also usually makes an appearance to good naturedly warn the kids to stay on the straight and narrow.

LINCOLN-TALLMAN RESTORATIONS (ages 5 and up)

440 North Jackson Street; (608) 752–4519. Open 9:00 A.M. to 4:00 P.M. from June through October. Holiday tours (from Thanksgiving through New Year's Eve) are held at 11:00 A.M. and 4:00 P.M. from Tuesday through Sunday.

Generally kids wouldn't be much interested in the Lincoln-Tallman Restorations, although the rambling brick home was once the home of a major Janesville businessman and friend of Abraham Lincoln. The former president actually did sleep there several times; honest. "So what," say youngsters who might have seen one too many old mansions. Wait until Halloween, though, when creepy (albeit friendly) things crawl about. During the haunting season, the house is decorated with plenty of spooky stuff. A full-blown Victorian funeral is presented in the parlor. One year, the place hosted a production of *Murder & Mayhem in Rock County*, where, in appropriately darkened rooms, performers told true crime stories.

Here is an extra detail on the Tallman place for the trivia file and school reports: The home was one of the first in the country to have indoor plumbing and central heating.

Places to Eat

Oasis Restaurant. *3401 Milton Avenue; (608) 754–5730.* Can't recall ever seeing any camels parked outside near the Fords and Toyotas, yet the Oasis is still a great place to stop when traveling through town. $$

Prime Quarter Steak House. *1900 Humes Road; (608) 752–1881.* If you like meat and lots of it, the Prime Quarter is heaven. Just skip the sour cream on the baked potatoes if you need to consider waistlines. Otherwise, dig in. $$

Wedges. *2006 North Washington Avenue; (608) 757–1444.* Sit back and take your time. This is a relaxing, getaway spot for casual dining. $$

Places to Stay

Baymont. *616 Midland; (608) 758–4545.* One hundred seven rooms; swimming pool. $$

Best Western Janesville. *3900 Milton Avenue; (608) 756–4511 or (800) 334–4271.* One hundred eight rooms; swimming pool. $

Hampton Inn. *2400 Fulton Street; (608) 754–4900.* Ninety-nine rooms; swimming pool. $$

For More Information

Forward Janesville, *20 South Main Street, Janesville, WI 53547-8008; (608) 757–3160.*

New Glarus

After seeing Janesville, drive west to New Glarus via U.S. Highway 14 to State Highway 20. Turn north on 20 to State Highway 92. Take that to State Highway 69. Turn south to New Glarus.

Another of the Swiss-founded communities in southern Wisconsin, New Glarus looks as if it was cut from a picture postcard of the home country. In a way it was, because the settlers found the wonderful rolling green hills reminiscent of their original cantons. Their outbuildings, farms, and residences, too, all have the look of the alpine world from which they came in 1845. The Swiss and United States flags fly proudly next to each other everywhere in town. Be sure the kids know that the design of the Red Cross flag was adapted from that of the traditionally neutral Swiss, with their red banner and its white cross leading to the social service organization's white banner and crimson cross.

The community is proud of its Swiss heritage and sponsors numerous festivals and ethnic events. Announcing the start of many of the programs is a local musician blowing into his sonorous alpine horn, formerly used in the mountains to call the cowherds. The horn is so long that its mouth rests on the ground. The sound is as meaningful to the Swiss as the skirl of bagpipes is to the Scots, and just as distinctive.

 SWISS HISTORICAL VILLAGE MUSEUM (ages 5 and up)
612 Seventh Avenue; (608) 527–2317. Open 9:00 A.M. to 4:30 P.M. May through October.

New Glarus's heritage is preserved in the Swiss Historical Village Museum, where twelve pioneer buildings have been refurbished and are now open for visits. Youngsters can touch the early farming implements, learn how cheese was made, and talk with guides about Wisconsin pioneer life.

 CHALET OF THE GOLDEN FLEECE MUSEUM (ages 5 and up)
618 Second Street; (608) 527–2614. Open 10:00 A.M. to 4:30 P.M. May through October.

A stop at the Chalet of the Golden Fleece Museum will put New Glarus's history into perspective for kids who want to do more research on the ethnic history of the community. Carved wooden craft items, early table settings, and similar homey artifacts are preserved in a building constructed in typical Bernese style: It has wooden shutters and fountains of red and white carnations overflowing from its window boxes.

SUGAR RIVER STATE TRAIL (ages 5 and up)

418 Railroad Street; (608) 527–2334.

When the kids get antsy, it is time to take them out to the Sugar River State Trail. The trail is a 23-mile-long biking/hiking pathway guaranteed to build up calves and get the youngsters busy pumping pedals. Built on an abandoned railroad bed, it even goes through a covered bridge. There are easy grades and long, flat distances, so little kids can do well if nobody rushes. If a family hasn't brought bikes along on their vacation, cycles can be rented at the trailhead offices.

NEW GLARUS WOODS STATE PARK (all ages)

c/o Wisconsin Department of Natural Resources, Pleasant View Annex, Monroe, WI 53593 (call 608–527–2335 in summer and 608–325–4844 in winter). From New Glarus, take Highway 69 south for 4 miles.

New Glarus Woods comprises 350 acres of woods, farmland, and prairie and is a favorite picnic spot for area families. Get the family ready for a hike and check out the following trails located in the park:

Basswood Nature Trail. This short trail is less than ½ mile long, running from the picnic area near the park office to the north of County Highway NN.

Chattermark Trail. This trail loops from the campgrounds through an oak and maple grove.

Great Oak Trail. Pick up this short walk at the north end of the park by the end of the primitive camping area.

Havenridge Nature Trail. Comprised of loops north and south of County NN, this trail leads through heavy groves of oak and maple and past extensive prairie plantings.

Walnut Trail. This proceeds south from the west end of the campground and links with the Havenridge Nature Trail.

HEIDI DRAMA (ages 5 and up)

P.O. Box 861, Department N, New Glarus, WI 53574; call (800) 527–6838 or the New Glarus Tourism and Chamber of Commerce at (608) 527–2095. Performances are held in June; admission is $6.00 for auditorium seats and $5.00 for general admission.

Volunteer amateur actors and actresses star in the *Heidi* drama each June, bringing to life the popular children's story about the little girl of the mountains. These productions are especially geared toward eager, attentive youngsters in the audience.

WILHELM TELL FESTIVAL (ages 10 and up)

Wilhelm Tell Community Guild, P.O. Box 456, New Glarus, WI 53574, or New Glarus Tourism and Chamber of Commerce, (608) 527–2095. Held on Labor Day weekend; tickets are from $1.00 to $6.00.

In 1937 New Glarus residents decided to stage the drama that celebrates the independence of Switzerland. The play touches on the well-known story of Wilhelm Tell, who was forced to shoot an apple from his son's head by means of a bow and arrow. Naturally Tell does well, the uninjured young son is freed, and the nasty despot sheriff is eventually deposed. The Friday and Sunday productions are performed in English, while the Saturday show is staged in German. Alpenhorn blowing, dancing, and yodeling demonstrations are held in the air-conditioned high school auditorium. The village park hosts an outdoor art fair.

Top Events in New Glarus

Among events that the entire family will like are the **New Glarus Swiss Polkafest** and **New Glarus Community Festival** in May and the **Little Switzerland Festival** and **Heidi Craft and Art Fair** in June. In early August New Glarus celebrates **Volkfest**, the **Swiss Independence Day.** The New Glarus **Octoberfest** and the annual **Chamber Antique Show & Sale** in October also attract visitors from around Wisconsin and northern Illinois.

Places to Eat

Flannery's Wilhelm Tell Club. *114 Second Street; (608) 527–2618.* The restaurant looks like a Swiss chalet and offers schnitzels, cheese fondue, and Swiss-style sausages. $$

New Glarus Bakery and Tea Room. *534 First Street; (608) 527–2916.* Fresh breakfast pastries,

soups, salads, sandwiches, and other tasty fare are served. $$

New Glarus Hotel. *100 Sixth Avenue; (608) 527–5244.* For a fancy fondue, take in the hotel's Chalet Landhaus Restaurant. For another taste treat, there's the Ticino Pizzeria on the hotel balcony. $$

Places to Stay

Chalet Landhaus Inn. *State Highway 69, P.O. Box 878, New Glarus, WI 53574; (608) 527–5234 or (800) 944–1716.* Sixty-seven rooms. $$

New Glarus Hotel. *100 Sixth Avenue, New Glarus, WI 53574; (608) 527–5244 or (800) 727–9477.* Seven rooms. $$

Swiss Aire Motel. *1200 State Highway 69, New Glarus, WI 53574; (608) 527–2138 or (800) 798–4391.* Twenty-six rooms. $$

For More Information

New Glarus Visitor and Convention Bureau, *P.O. Box 713, New Glarus, WI 53574-0713; (608) 527–2095.*

Wisconsin Department of Natural Resources, *Pleasant View Annex, Monroe, WI 53593; (608–527–2335 in summer; 608–325–4844 in winter).*

For Even More Information Free Wisconsin travel guides can be ordered from the state's division of tourism. Among them are the 88-page event and recreation guide; the 32-page adventure vacations guide; a 64-page biking guide; the 32-page guide to Wisconsin's African-American heritage; and a 20-page guide to the attractions, events, and history of the six Native American nations occupying 11 reservations in the state.

Other directories include the 80-page arts and crafts fairs directory; a pocket-size attractions guide and highway map; the 64-page innkeeper's guide; a 112-page bed-and-breakfast directory; a 66-page guide to the state's private campgrounds; a pocket-size state park's visitors' guide to the 79 state parks, forests, and trails. Don't forget the 50-page guide to the 300 Wisconsin golf courses and the 32-page *Go-To-It Guide,* highlighting 20 Wisconsin destinations. State snowmobile and bike maps can also be ordered. Call the Wisconsin Department of Tourism at (800) 432–8747 or log onto its Web site at www.travelwisconsin.com.

Blanchardville

To get to Blanchardville, follow State Highway 35 west from New Glarus to State Highway 76. Turn south on 76 and drive to State Highway 81. Turn west and go to County Road G. Follow the signs.

The undulating Blue Mounds of southwestern Wisconsin are the highest ridges in this part of the state, which is generally level farmland. Opportunities to hike, fish, canoe, bird-watch, snowmobile, hunt, and cross-country ski are numerous.

YELLOWSTONE LAKE STATE PARK (all ages)

Route 2; (608) 523–4427. State-park vehicle sticker required.

Yellowstone Lake State Park, where the Yellowstone River was dammed to make a 455-acre lake, offers great crappie and bass fishing for the serious angler, plus swimming for kids who just want to get wet and wild. Boat rentals and camping (150 campsites) are also available. Winter visitors enjoy the heavily wooded, hilly, groomed, and tracked cross-country skiing trails in the winter.

Greater Milwaukee and Southeast Wisconsin

For experiencing the bright lights of urban invigoration, you needn't go any farther than southeastern Wisconsin. Milwaukee, the state's largest city, as well as Kenosha, Racine, and all of their suburban communities, make this the most heavily populated part of Wisconsin.

But that doesn't mean that a family will get lost in the crowd—far from it. Children's museums, lakefront music festivals, concerts, theater, sporting events, magic shows, balloon rides, drag racing, street parties, airplane rides, Lake Michigan charter fishing, dining, natural-food outposts, lighthouses, waterside cafes, trolley tours, dinosaurs, paddleboats, kite flying, bike paths, art gallery tours, bakeries, movie theaters . . . whew! The list of what to see and do is endless.

Each major community has a convention and visitors bureau whose mission in life is to please, so use these services; ask the tough questions. It's the best way to see the most of what each community has to offer. *Laverne and Shirley* television reruns don't provide much about the real Milwaukee.

Then, armed with all the appropriate print matter, huddle around the kitchen table and map out what you want to do and see. Giant-screen IMAX movies? No problem. Where to find kung pao chicken? No sweat. An Irish guest house? Look no more. Reggae bands on your mind? Easy. Mexican fiestas, Puerto Rican celebrations? They are all laid out for you.

Amazing Wisconsin Facts

Wisconsin's shoreline extends 381 miles along Lake Michigan. For metric fans, that translates to 613 kilometers. The shore along Lake Superior is 292 miles (470 kilometers). The two vary greatly in appearance: There are high bluffs and sandy beaches along Lake Michigan, while Lake Superior offers more low-lying hills and pebbled beaches.

Beaver
Dam

West Bend

Hartford

Cedarburg

Port
Washington

Menomonee Falls

Ashippun

Milwaukee

Eagle

East Troy

Union
Grove

Racine

Elkhorn

Burlington

Delavan

Lake Geneva

Bristol

Kenosha

GREATER MILWAUKEE
and
SOUTHEAST

You also have an excellent range of accommodations, from grand hotels such as the one-hundred-plus-year-old Pfister in Milwaukee to nifty bed-and-breakfasts in any of the small towns rimming this side of Lake Michigan. There are rates for any budget—a range that might be harder to find in more rural reaches of the state.

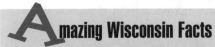

Amazing Wisconsin Facts

According to the 1990 census, the largest cities in Wisconsin are Milwaukee (628,088 residents), Madison (191,262), Green Bay (96,466), Racine (84,298), Kenosha (80,352), and Appleton (65,695).

There is a vibrancy about a big-town atmosphere. The roar of fans at a Milwaukee Admirals hockey match and the virtuosity of the Kenosha Pops Band might seem different, yet in reality, they exemplify only the tip of the iceberg of what to see and do in southeastern Wisconsin.

Getting around is no problem; just substitute the appropriate street maps in lieu of highway maps. You can also bundle the gang aboard the local transit system buses for tours. Or contract with a local step-on guide such as Mary Gilardi and her Mary's Personalized Tours (414–871–9783) to see the ins and outs of Milwaukee. Entrepreneurs in other cities also offer such services.

Southeastern Wisconsin brings the past alive, from the Milwaukee Public Museum's *Streets of Old Milwaukee* to the re-created farmsites at Old World Wisconsin in Eagle. Kids can watch sheep shearing, see a Civil War reenactment, try on a top hat, and learn how to thresh wheat the old-time way.

Every family has its own flock of culture vultures with a variety of sites in mind: youth orchestras, kids' theaters, library programs, film series. You name the highbrow fun, and this part of Wisconsin is bound to please. Again, the local convention and visitors bureaus are the respective Founts of All Knowledge. They can provide phone numbers and other contacts for last-minute clarification of prices and times at whatever appropriate facility strikes your fancy.

Now get out there and have fun.

Milwaukee

The greater Milwaukee area is the largest urban concentration in the state, with almost a million people tucked between Lake Michigan and the outer suburbs. It is a party town—particularly in the summer—where something seems to be going on every minute. This sometimes poses problems because of the subsequent scarcity of convenient hotel rooms. Never fear, though; there is always a place nearby in which to tuck in the kids. Obviously, by the end of the year, everyone in town is ready to curl up and doze.

For walking (or driving) just to see the sights, secure the series of pamphlets on historic building tours prepared by the Department of City Development, 809 North Broadway, Milwaukee, WI 53202 (414–286–5900). Each piece describes what to see and do in various neighborhoods around the city, from Juneautown to Bay View. This gives Milwaukee visitors the chance to talk with locals, peek into tempting out-of-the-way restaurants, investigate mom-and-pop stores, and generally meet the community face-to-face.

GREATER MILWAUKEE CONVENTION AND VISITORS BUREAU

510 West Kilbourn Street, Milwaukee; (414) 273–7222 or (800) 231–0903.

The Greater Milwaukee Convention and Visitors Bureau, located across the street from the convention complex called MECCA and kitty-corner from the Hyatt Hotel (just on the other side of the old Milwaukee Arena), is an excellent starting place to find out what is going on at any given moment, whether by phone or a drop-in visit.

MILWAUKEE'S TOP FESTIVALS

Perhaps the city's greatest claim to fame is its rightfully earned image as the City of Festivals. Check with the Greater Milwaukee Convention and Visitors Bureau (GMCVB) for times, dates, and entertainment lineups. No matter the age, everyone in a family can find something exciting at Winterfest, Summerfest, or any of the ethnic festivals.

Even in winter's frosty temperatures, Milwaukee celebrates the season with ice skating in Cathedral Square downtown. An international snow-carving competition is held on the Performing Arts Center grounds. Area restaurants offer meal specials. Musical entertainment around the community ties in with the winter theme. (Despite the claims that everyone in Milwaukee loves winter, no one complains when June finally rolls around.)

SCOTTISH HIGHLAND GAMES (ages 5 and up)

Old Heidleberg Park behind the Bavarian Inn, 700 West Lexington Boulevard, Glendale; (414) 796–0807. Early June.

There are sheepherding demonstrations by border collies and bagpiping by the kilt-clad set. Caber tossing, akin to throwing telephone poles end over end, is one of the Highland games that will amaze the kids. Then there's sheaf tossing, the farmer's stone carry, and a host of other muscle stretchers.

LAKEFRONT FESTIVAL OF THE ARTS (all ages)

750 North Lincoln Memorial Drive, Veterans Park, Milwaukee; (414) 224–3850. Early June.

The best fun for the little ones is the festival's kids' art corner. The artsy wine and sculpture parties are also a bang. The juried show attracts international attention, with its wide range of pottery, oils, sculpture, and other high-end fine arts. This is not, repeat *not*, a crafts show. Come with credit cards or a stuffed wallet. It usually rains sometime during the weekend, so be prepared.

ASIAN MOON (ages 5 and up)

840 Elm Grove Road, Suite 2, Building 2, Elm Grove, WI 53122; (414) 821–9829; e-mail: woaamilw@execpc.com. June.

Asian Moon was launched in 1994 and features music and foods from Chinese, Japanese, Hmong, Indian, Filipino, and other Eastern cultures. Dancers swirl with silk, songs touch on homelands, and foods move far beyond the standard fried rice and into such delicacies as sweet banana egg rolls, kung pao chicken, and spicy pork with green beans. The fest is sponsored by the Wisconsin Organization for Asian Americans. For more details call Summerfest at (414) 273–2680.

POLISH FEST (ages 5 and up)

6941 South Sixty-Eighth Street, Franklin; (414) 529–2140. Mid-June.

Join in the polka-ing and enjoy the intricate folk-dancing performed by Milwaukee and Chicago's finest Polish-dance ensembles in their handmade costumes. Milwaukee's top Polish restaurants serve up their mouthwatering pierogies and smacznego. Contemporary talent and top names in Polish-style polka music, such as Jimmie Mieszala and The Chicago Masters, get feet stomping. The annual egg-decorating extravaganza is always sure to bring out the Slavic creativity in anyone, especially kids.

SUMMERFEST (ages 5 and up)

200 North Harbor Drive, Milwaukee; (414) 273–3378. Held for eleven days from the end of June through the July Fourth weekend.

Summerfest, one of North America's largest music events, brings a wonderful range of music to the eighty-five-acre Lake Michigan Henry W. Maier Lakefront Festival showgrounds. Almost a million people attend each year. The tree-shaded site is named after a former Milwaukee mayor who enthusiastically got the fest scene up and running. Even a dad who refuses to ask directions can find the mile-long grounds by following the smiley faces along the freeway and surface streets to Harbor Drive. The fest is held where the I-794 spur cuts south across the harbor via the Dan Hoan Bridge. Follow the crowds. For parents with little kids, Summerfest is best attended during the day; the evenings jam up with folks packing the dozen-plus stages to hear rock, blues, jazz, and mainline acts. There is a large play area in the center of the grounds, but it is not a baby-sitting service. Wheelchairs are available to rent on a first-come basis, so it is best to bring your own, if needed. This can be very crowded, so choose a designated meeting place at a certain time for the all-important parental check-up when teens are along.

Amazing Wisconsin Facts The typewriter was invented in Milwaukee by Christopher Latham Sholes, with the help of Carlos Glidden and Samuel W. Soule. The device, the first practical machine of its kind, was developed in 1867. You can see a plaque dedicated to Sholes and his typewriter at the corner of West State and North Fourth Streets, behind the Milwaukee Arena and across the street from the *Milwaukee Journal-Sentinel* offices at 333 West State Street.

GREAT CIRCUS PARADE (all ages)

Downtown Milwaukee; (414) 273–7877. Mid-July.

The parade brings back the color and vibrancy of the good old days of the Big Top. The showgrounds on the lakefront can be toured for several days prior to the parade. Dozens of authentic circus wagons can be seen and photographed, and there are camel and elephant rides, circus performances and wandering clowns, plenty of cotton candy, and a petting zoo. It is a tradition for die-hard parade watchers to stake out sites overnight along the Wisconsin Avenue route and side streets on which the horses, acrobats, and bands will pass. A first-time visitor may wish to purchase a hotel package from the Pfister, Wyndham, or Hyatt hotels, which usually includes reserved seating in front of the property and a lunch. The wagons come to Milwaukee from the Circus World Museum in Baraboo, the former winter quarters for the Ringling Brothers Circus before it merged with Barnum & Bailey before the turn of the twentieth century.

BASTILLE DAYS (ages 5 and up)

c/o East Towne Association, 770 North Jefferson, Milwaukee, WI 53202; (414) 271–1416. July.

The city's French celebration on Cathedral Square, where all things French come together, is usually held the same weekend as the Great Circus Parade. There is usually a *voyageur* encampment, fire eaters, bowling-ball jugglers, and an amazing line of cajun, French-Canadian, zydeco, jazz, torch singing, and all manner of other sounds from several stages on the closed-off streets around the park. One entertainer has been

Amazing Wisconsin Facts

Wisconsin has about 110,000 miles of highways and paved roads. In 1917, the state was the first to adopt the number system for highways, a practice soon followed elsewhere.

returning for years. He tucks his bony frame into a 2-foot by 2-foot box and actually gets out again, to the amazement of onlookers.

FESTA ITALIANA (ages 5 and up)

c/o Italian Community Center, 631 West Chicago Street, Milwaukee, WI 53202; (414) 223–2180. Late July.

If you love fireworks and still more fireworks, Italian food, Sicilian brass bands, a Venetian boat parade, and entertainers singing "New York, New York," this is the festival for you. Festa prides itself on being a family-reunion type of event. Naturally guests munch pizza and all sorts of pasta possibilities. A religious procession through the grounds on the Sunday of the fest is great for the kids.

GERMAN FEST (ages 5 and up)

8229 West Capitol Drive, Milwaukee; (414) 464–9444. July.

This oompha event is North America's largest festival of authentic German traditions. From yodeling to tuba playing, German Fest definitely taps Old Country culture. While chewing a succulent rib-eye and spanferkel sandwich, tour the traditional German town square and browse in the marketplace for a new cuckoo clock or a colorful nutcracker. Dog lovers howl over demonstrations by the Badger Dachshund Club and their famous, ground-hugging Dachshund Derby. There is always plenty of lederhosen and polka bands, along with displays of Teutonic muscle autos such as the mighty Mercedes.

AFRICAN WORLD FESTIVAL (ages 5 and up)

2821 North Fourth Street, Milwaukee; (414) 372–4567. Early August.

To understand the wonders of the Black cultural experience, take in this African and African-American celebration. The opening ceremonies highlight rich African traditions, where native priests bless the water and earth and are accompanied by dancers, drummers, and singers. This authenticity continues throughout the festival. The motherland is re-created in an "African Village" and is also represented in ancient dances, music, and fine African cuisine, which includes peanut soup and other exotic dishes. The children's area, featuring African storytelling, talent contests, mime, magic shows, and hands-on experiments, leaves children and adults alike with an unforgettable cultural experience. Rap, blues, jazz, and bebop are on tap from afternoon to late at night. Vendors sell an amazing array of T-shirts, African and Caribbean crafts, records, and all sorts of other paraphernalia.

*B*ook Smarts! Take a reading on this. The largest libraries in Wisconsin are in Milwaukee and at the University of Wisconsin-Madison. Each has more than two million volumes.

Architectural tours of the century-old Milwaukee Central Library, 814 West Wisconsin Avenue, are occasionally available. Call (414) 286-3000 to check times and dates. Looking up at the inner dome, the sight is different than what is viewed from the street. An outer dome covers the main building, with an interior walkway allowing maintenance personnel to crawl around to change the light bulbs of the inner dome. Heady business, for sure.

Even without a tour, a visit to the Central Library makes for a great side trip in Milwaukee. What's especially nice for those who can't check out books is the Bookseller Used Book Store and Coffeeshop. Hours are 8:30 A.M. to 4:30 P.M. Monday through Friday; 9:00 A.M. to 2:00 P.M. Saturday. Call (414) 286-2142. Prices for used books are 25 cents and up, with a lot of children's books and paperbacks—perfect for the long car rides. Metered parking is available on nearby streets.

The state has 380 public libraries, which are part of Wisconsin's 17 regional library systems. State legislation authorizing free public libraries was passed in 1872. There are also many specialty libraries in the state. A reference library for state legislators in the State Capitol building was founded in 1901, the first of its kind in the nation.

The State Department of Public Instruction is responsible for promoting and developing the public and school libraries around Wisconsin.

WISCONSIN STATE FAIR (ages 5 and up)

8600 West Greenfield Avenue, West Allis; (414) 266–7000. End of July and early August.

This fair is more than one hundred years old, showcasing geese, horses, cheese, tractors, and geegaws. The best place to take a family— after watching the racing pigs—is the Family Center, where the Wisconsin Potato and Vegetable Growers Association serves up huge baked spuds, the honey folks have sweet taste tests, 4-H kids dish out enormous ice cream cones and sundaes (hint: the cherry topping is best), and the pork producers make sandwiches. This is eats on the cheap and probably better for the cholesterol level than some of the fried foods found on the midway.

MILWAUKEE IRISH FEST (ages 5 and up)

1532 Wauwatosa Avenue, Milwaukee; (414) 476–3378. Third weekend in August.

This is the world's largest Irish music and cultural event. The fest emphasizes that it is a family affair, with an entire Castle McFest devoted to kids' activities. Youngsters can learn Irish geography at the Lilliput mini-golf range, which is in the shape of Ireland (the holes mark the locations of major cities on the Emerald Isle). Teachers direct arts-and-crafts activities that range from making potato people to Irish drums. Often a play is commissioned for the children's stage (one of fifteen stages on the grounds). Troupes of young people dance, sing, and act. One of the most exciting presentations has been the regular appearance of the Trinity Irish Dance Company, with various African-American groups, such as the Nefertari Dancers of North Division High School, demonstrating a delightful mix of ethnic cultures and percussion styles. Most of the major Irish and Irish American entertainers in the world have performed at the festival. Teens can really get into the Irish rock stage, with its showcase of rising young Irish talent. Once hooked on the music, they can then pick up the more traditional sounds.

MEXICAN FIESTA (ages 5 and up)

1030 West Mitchell, Milwaukee; (414) 383–7066. End of August.

Olé! Our neighbors to the south greet guests with open arms for as much fun as a barrel of red-hot peppers. Musicians such as David Lee Garza and Elsa Garcia treat your ears while burritos and tortillas treat your mouth. The El Baile dance competition, El Grito Shouting Contest, and the Jalapeno Pepper Eating Contest all give people the chance to dance, shout, and—well—shout some more for cash prizes. Car lovers will jump when they see the low-rider car hopping competition. An unforgettable Mexican experience.

ARABIAN FEST (ages 5 and up)

200 North Harbor Drive, Milwaukee; (414) 342–4909. Held annually in September.

The newest festival to join the lineup of special lakefront ethnic festivals is Arabian Fest, featuring foods, music, and entertainment from the Middle East. The first event was held in 1998. Twenty-one Arab countries are highlighted, ranging from Saudi Arabia to the North African nations spreading along the warm shores of the Mediterranean Sea. There are extensive cultural displays, dancing, singing, readings, and visits from overseas dignitaries. The range of music styles covers pop, Arab jazz, and folk for a great mix of sounds. Numerous Milwaukeeans of Arab descent volunteer their services to showcase the best of their individual traditions.

INDIAN SUMMER (ages 5 and up)

7441 West Greenfield Avenue, Milwaukee; (414) 774–7119. Early September.

Colorfully costumed Native American dancers of all ages from around the country compete for top awards at this nationally recognized pow-wow. Before opening to the public, the fest hosts schoolkids from throughout the metro area for a full day of educational events, with music, drama, discussions, and exhibitions on the environment and native culture. Once it's open, however, everyone will realize that, from the intricate footwork of the competition powwow to the competition for knowledge of tribal attributes in the Princess contest, Indian Summer is packed with Native American fun. Cultural and contemporary Native American performers entertain as visitors enjoy a juicy buffalo burger. (Best of all, no one has to catch their own buffalo.) More than sixty vendors display a wide array of Native American wares, while skilled native demonstrators share their handiwork. Get the kids up close while the craftworkers show off their intricate finger- and basketweaving and the ancient skill of horsehair art. Walk through the four traditional tribal villages and soak in this rich heritage while looking over the various types of huts and tepees.

HOLIDAY FOLK FAIR (ages 5 and up)

c/o International Institute of Milwaukee County, 1110 North Old World Third Street, Milwaukee; (414) 225–6220. Mid-November.

The Folk Fair is a rainbow mix of all the ethnic traditions in the city, from Latvian to Serb and from Hungarian to Latino. Held in the Wisconsin Center complex downtown, Folk Fair is a food feast where you can turn the kids loose with a few dollars, and they can come back to the table with six varieties of munchables, a dozen desserts, and plenty of change. Matinees on the Saturday and Sunday of Folk Fair present youngsters performing traditional dances and songs, while evening shows feature major international entertainers and adult dance troupes. Many of the city's ethnic societies have stalls where they sell crafts. Many of these items are inexpensive; perfect for kids doing a bit of early shopping for Christmas. Folk Fair, the oldest such program in the nation, is one of the major events sponsored each year by the International Institute of Wisconsin.

And the Fun Continues In addition to those festivals covered here, there are many other events geared to families during the year. Don't forget **Juneteenth Day** (414-372-3770), celebrating the final liberation of slaves after the Civil War; **Rainbow Summer** (414-273-7206) on the grounds of the Performing Arts Center, a summerlong series of outdoor concerts, many of which are aimed at young people; **Milwaukee a la Carte** (414-256-5412); the **Grape Lakes Food and Wine Festival** (414-224-3850); **Briggs & Stratton Al's Run Marathon** (414-266-6320); the *Milwaukee Journal-Sentinel* **Rose Festival** (414-529-1870) in Whitnall Park; several **Greek** and **Serbian festivals** at outlying churches; and **Jazz in the Park** (414-271-1416), held every Thursday during the summer in the downtown Cathedral Square.

BREWERIES

All this partying is enough to work up a thirst. When visiting Milwaukee, one of the first questions always asked is "where are the breweries?" Although residents bemoan the title of Beer City, bestowed on it generations ago when a six-pack of America's biggest breweries once held sway here, they know they can't knock a good thing. Although many of the eighty breweries that "made Milwaukee famous" in the good old days are gone, Miller, Sprecher, and a couple of brewpubs remain. Tours are held at each plant, providing samples—beer for parents and sodas for kids—at the end of the educational walk. The tours are fun, however, and involve some strolling, so be ready to point out sights to little youngsters. They seem to be fascinated by the bottling and canning operations, the whirring conveyor belts, and all the clanking and clattering during the filling process.

MILLER BREWING COMPANY (ages 10 and up)

Visitor's Center, 4251 West State Street; (414) 931–2337. Tours are held Monday through Saturday from 10:00 A.M. to 5:30 P.M.; closed Sunday.

The plant is located on the city's north side, easily spotted via the huge billboards on top of the company's buildings and roadway signage, which proclaim, IF YOU'VE GOT THE TIME, WE'VE GOT THE TOUR.

SPRECHER BREWING CO. (ages 10 and up)

701 West Glendale Avenue, Glendale; (414) 964–2739. Tours are at 4:00 P.M., Monday through Friday. On Saturday, tours are held every half hour between 1:00 and 3:00 P.M. Reservations required.

Sprecher root beer, considered a "gourmet soda" by those who appreciate brown cows (root beer and vanilla ice cream), is so creamy it usually leaves a delicious foam mustache on your upper lip. There is great beer, too.

Ziggy Tale Of all the tales to come out of Milwaukee's Prohibition era is the one about Ziggy, an elephant that toured with Leo Singer's midget vaudeville troupe. Ziggy was quite talented: He could smoke cigarettes through a foot-long holder and play "Yes, Sir, That's My Baby" on a large harmonica. When his trainer, Charlie Becker, shouted, "Shake it up, Ziggy," the elephant wiggled and snorted loudly.

But back to Beer City and our story. While the midgets were staying in a Milwaukee hotel in the 1930s at the height of Prohibition, Ziggy spent the night in a nearby doctor's stable. The animal became restless and knocked down a wall while trying to get loose. Behind the wall was a secret stash of bootleg booze kept by the doctor for "medicinal purposes." The doctor, of course, was quite upset. To top it off, he was also the brother of a top police official. Subsequently, Ziggy and his midget friends hurriedly left town the next day. No one remembers if they paid for the damage.

LAKEFRONT BREWERY (ages 10 and up)

1872 North Commerce Street, Milwaukee; (414) 372–8800.

This small neighborhood brewery grew and grew and grew. It is now one of the more popular beverage providers in southeastern Wisconsin. Its plant is tucked away in the city's Riverwest neighborhood.

BREWPUBS

Milwaukee has several brewpubs that make their own beers to augment their menu items. Each has extra-special flavors that are quite a change from the more mass-produced beverages. Try one or all:

MILWAUKEE ALE HOUSE (all ages)

233 North Astor Street, Milwaukee; (414) 266–2337; www.ale-house.com. $$.

This hometown pub is located in Milwaukee's trendy Third Ward, a section of refurbished warehouses that now house galleries, offices, and restaurants. The pub is along the Riverwalk, linking it to the downtown about 3 blocks north. Live music almost daily.

ROCK BOTTOM RESTAURANT (all ages)

740 North Plankinton Avenue, Milwaukee; (414) 276–3030. $$.

The Rock Bottom is part of a national chain, but it fits in well along Milwaukee's Riverwalk in the downtown district. Enjoy the patio in the summer. Billiard tables and other games are in the basement for when it rains or snows.

WATER STREET BREWERY (all ages)

1101 North Water Street, Milwaukee; (414) 272–1195. $$.

This is one of Milwaukee's oldest brewpubs, opening in 1987. It features lunchtime sandwiches and a hearty nighttime menu. Many of its beers have won awards in regional and national competitions.

ON THE OUTSIDE

MILWAUKEE COUNTY ZOO (all ages)

10001 West Blue Mound Road, Milwaukee; (414) 771–3040. Open year-round.

From the living, breathing animal viewpoint, there is always plenty of interest here. The exotic collection of critters are kept in open-air enclosures. Each area is reminiscent of the animal's surroundings in nature.

MILLER LITE RIDE FOR THE ARTS (ages 10 and up)

All courses begin at the Performing Arts Center, 929 North Water Street, near the Milwaukee River; (414) 273–8723. Early June.

The Ride for the Arts is an exciting pedal-powered event that loops through downtown Milwaukee; this is a great urban biking experience. The ride is held rain or shine, so riders should dress accordingly. Participants can choose from 5-, 15-, 30-, or 50-mile-long routes, so there are opportunities for families as well as hard-core bikers. The ride is not only good exercise, but it benefits more than twenty performing arts groups in southeastern Wisconsin. The Ride for the Arts is one of the largest recreational bike rides in the country.

Amazing Wisconsin Facts Well before the Wisconsin Dells became one of Wisconsin's leading resort areas, Waukesha was the place to be. The village, just west of Milwaukee, was an ordinary place until Col. Richard Dunbar stopped over in 1868. He paused for a drink from a spring near the edge of town. The water was so pure, Dunbar thought it cured his diabetes. Dunbar settled down in town and immediately began promoting the spring's medicinal properties. Within a few years, Waukesha became a popular spa. During the 1880s and 1890s, the town bustled with outsiders seeking "the cure." One local company, White Rock, became nationally famous for its bottled water. All the old resort buildings are now gone, but Waukesha still retains the charm from those days, with its Victorian-era homes and central square.

LAKE MICHIGAN CRUISES (all ages)

Check out the city skyline from one of the city's cruise boats. All are kid-safe with railings and other safety devices, but parents certainly need to keep their own eyes on the tykes. Each boat offers onboard beverages, rest rooms, and plenty of deck space on which to loll while admiring the lakeshore and harbor. It is especially fun for kids who ride the *Iroquois;* when the tall boat heads out to the lake, a number of drawbridges elevate as the vessel passes underneath. Tell the kids to wave to the folks on shore.

All vessels have well-informed crews who should be able to answer questions about the height of the Dan Hoan Bridge over the harbor, how many freighters visit the city during an average shipping season, and the depth of the Milwaukee River mouth. (And no, there aren't any killer whales in Lake Michigan.) Boats leave from one of several docks in the downtown area. Call to confirm schedules. Tours are generally April through October.

Iroquois (414-384-8606). Docks downtown on the Milwaukee River between the Michigan and Clybourn Street bridges.

Celebration of Milwaukee (414-272-2628). Departs from 502 North Harbor Drive.

Edelweiss (414-272-3769). Departs from 1110 North Old World Third Street. Reservations are required for this boat, which serves lunch, brunch, and dinner.

*B*ridges of Wisconsin

Ever notice that the bridges on Wisconsin Avenue and the other streets crossing the Milwaukee River are set at angles? Naturally, there is a story to this. Let me tell you about the "Great Bridge War" of the 1830s. The following is a much simplified version, because the longer tale involves stolen construction plans, schooners running aground, horses falling into the river, fistfights, and lots of hoopla. Milwaukee was really quite wild in the old days, you see.

So settle for this: Disputes arose between settlers on both sides of the river, who made up two separate communities in those early frontier times. Boats coming upriver usually docked on the west bank due to the shape of the channel, which naturally aggravated the east siders who wanted a cut of the economic action. So they proposed to build a bridge so their teamsters would have an easier time picking up goods, rather than take a ferry. The west siders said they wouldn't object, as long as the bridge stopped in the middle of the river.

Discussions raged back and forth, and some options were tried, including a floating bridge (one bridge did just that; in the next spring's rains, it floated away). Neither side would budge on the location nor agree on who should ultimately pay for construction.

Tempers flared, and both sides took to their muskets and shotguns. A cannon was rolled out on the east side but never fired because no one had any cannonballs. A stalemate went on for some months, in which citizens from either bank had to carry a white flag if they wanted to visit the other side of the river. Eventually, the territorial lawmakers stepped in and passed legislation approving bridge projects in Milwaukee. As a compromise, the bridges were eventually built on angles, touching on what the residents of each shore felt was their best site. Wags subsequently have said that this planning actually would prevent the firing of a straight cannon shot through the heart of Milwaukee if another such disturbance ever occurred again. So far, it hasn't.

ON THE INSIDE

DISCOVERY WORLD (all ages)

712 West Wells Street, inside the Milwaukee Public Museum (800 West Wells Street), Milwaukee; (414) 765–9966. Open 9:00 A.M. to 5:00 P.M. daily. Admission is $5.50 for adults; $4.50 for seniors (sixty and older), and $3.50 for children four to seventeen. Children three and under are admitted Free.

Discovery World is a popular hands-on learning place for kids of all ages. Displays emphasize science, economics, and technology. Kids will be fascinated to learn how lightning discharges and how a laser can open an egg without breaking it. Discovery World interpreters are always on hand to help out. Visit Gizmo, The Scien-terrific Store, for educational games and science-oriented toys that help youngsters think as they play. It's all in good fun.

MILWAUKEE PUBLIC MUSEUM (ages 5 and up)

800 West Wells Street, Milwaukee; (414) 278–2702. Open 9:00 A.M. to 5:00 P.M. daily. Admission is $5.50 for adults, $3.50 for children four to seventeen, and $4.00 for seniors (sixty and older). Children three and under are admitted Free.

This museum brings together dinosaurs, the Streets of Old Milwaukee, Native Americans, African hunters, and a whole lot more. This is one of the country's premier natural history museums, and probably the only one with a full-blown buffalo stampede on an upstairs floor (have the kids look for the rattlesnake). A return visit always opens up a new door to discovery, especially with all the traveling exhibits augmenting the

Milwaukee's city hall is considered one of the world's best examples of Flemish Renaissance design. The building celebrated its 100th anniversary in 1995.

core collection. Youngsters will come away knowing more about life in rain forests, tundra, and deserts than they ever thought possible.

AMERICAN BLACK HOLOCAUST MUSEUM (ages 5 and up)

2233 North Fourth Street, Milwaukee; (414) 264–2500. Call for hours.

The museum is somber, tracing the pattern of discrimination and racial hatred in the United States. Yet the displays are powerful, serious, and point out the importance of learning from past mistakes. Kids, therefore, need to be exposed to such exhibits, so they can help prevent such abuses in the future.

 WISCONSIN BLACK HISTORICAL SOCIETY MUSEUM (ages 5 and up)
2620 West Center Street, Milwaukee; (414) 372–7677. Call for hours.

Black contributions to the state are highlighted in this facility, which provides an intimate glance at the African-American cultural experience of past generations.

SPORTS

For sports fans, Milwaukee has the **Brewers** baseball club (414-933-4114), the **Mustangs** for arena football (414-272-1555), and the **Admirals** for hockey (414-227-0550). Soccer fans enjoy the **Wave** (414-241-7500) for pro indoor matches and the **Milwaukee Rampage** (414-358-2655 or 414-964-7267) for pro outdoor games. Hoops fanatics love the the **Bucks** (414-227-0500) and the college basketball teams. Indoor events are generally held in Bradley Center, 1001 North Fourth Street in downtown Milwaukee. The hall is big enough to hold a 747 airplane. Even the nosebleed section provides great views. Giant television monitors mounted over the central floor help with close-up action.

PERFORMING ARTS

There are more than twenty theater, dance, and musical companies in town, including **First Stage** (414-273-2314), which gears its performances to children; The **Milwaukee Repertory Theater** (414-224-1761); **Skylight Opera** (414-291-7811); **Milwaukee Chamber Theater** (414-276-8842); **Florentine Opera** (414-291-5700); **Milwaukee Ballet** (414-643-7677); **DanceCircus** (414-277-8151); **Theatre X** (414-278-0555); and the **Next Act Theater** (414-278-7780). Irish, Native American, and African-American theater companies keep the ethnic performance world alive. Kids can really get into the live shows, which are far better than becoming absorbed in the hotel television set.

Teens have been become fond of "**poetry slams**," in which readers compete for applause at local clubs. For more than twenty-five years, the **Coffee House**, in the lower level of Redeemer Lutheran Church, 631 North Nineteenth Street (414-299-9598), has had open stages in addition to regularly scheduled performers. Kids and grown-ups can test their theatrical panache in front of live audiences.

HOTEL MILWAUKEE (ages 13 and up)

Held at various sites around Milwaukee, plus occasionally in other Wisconsin communities; (414) 276–7889, ext. 009; (414) 352–3331 (Hotel Milwaukee Hotline); www.hotelmilwaukee. com. Tickets are $5.00 for adults and $3.00 for seniors and students.

Mark your calendar for the live radio taping of regional and traveling talent at the *Hotel Milwaukee* radio show, "an old-time radio program with a '90s twist." The focus is on a mythical hotel with numerous poets, musicians, and famous personalities dropping by to talk and entertain. Taping is usually held at 5:00 P.M. on Sunday, and the shows are then aired on Ideas 90.7, WHAD-Wisconsin Public Radio, at 7:00 P.M. on Friday and at 4:00 and 10:00 P.M. on Saturday. Several programs are picked up for National Public Radio. Taping sites sometimes change, so call ahead.

Top Frozen-Custard Shops

The flavor of Milwaukee can be captured on many fronts, from art to sports to activities to landscape. The best in the eyes of the backseat gang, however, is probably frozen custard. The city is known for its smooth, creamy custards, served from stands dotting the city. Drive the car up to any one of a dozen stands (many of which look as if they date from the 1950s, which most do), unleash the munchkins, and march everyone up to the window to order a cone, shake, or sundae. Yes, plenty of napkins are provided. Those who have earned a place on the honor roll of top-notch buttery custards include:

- **Gilles.** 7515 West Blue Mound Road (414–453–4875)
- **Kopps.** 7631 West Layton Avenue (414–282–4080) and 5373 North Port Washington Road (414–961–2006)
- **Leon's.** 3131 South Twenty-seventh Street (414–383–1784)

Places to Eat

African Hut. *1107 North Old World Third Street, Milwaukee; (414) 765–1110.* Nigerian recipes predominate for a delightfully different cuisine. $$

Albanese's. *701 East Keefe Avenue, Milwaukee; (414) 964–7270.* The elite come here to eat spaghetti.

Beans & Barley. *1901 East North Avenue, Milwaukee; (414) 278–7878.* Vegetarian meals are always tops. $$

Benjamin's Deli. *4156 North Oakland Avenue, Shorewood; (414) 332–7777.* This is the place in town for corned beef and chicken soup. $

Places to Stay

County Clare. *1234 North Astor Street, Milwaukee; (414) 27–CLARE.* Touch of the Old World; Irish music. Great restaurant. Twenty rooms. $$

Hotel Metro. *411 East Main Street, Milwaukee; (414) 272–1937.* Renovated property in 1937 art deco office. On National Register of Historic Places. Sixty-four rooms. $$$

Hotel Wisconsin. *720 North Old World Third Street, Milwaukee; (414) 271–4900.* Funky and fun in the heart of downtown. Adjacent to Grand Avenue Mall. One hundred rooms. $$

Milwaukee Hilton Downtown. *509 West Wisconsin Avenue, Milwaukee; (414) 271–7250 or (800) 558–7708.* Elegant lobby and the fastest elevators in town. Five hundred rooms. $$

Park East Hotel. *916 East State Street, Milwaukee; (414) 276–8800 or (800) 328–7275.* Close to the lakefront and the festival grounds. One hundred fifty-nine rooms. $$

Pfister Hotel. *424 East Wisconsin Avenue, Milwaukee; (414) 273–8222 or (800) 558–8222.* The grandest hotel in town; it's more than a century old. Three hundred seven rooms. $$$

For More Information

Greater Brookfield Convention and Visitors Bureau, *405 North Calhoun Road, Suite 106, Brookfield, WI 53005; (414) 789–0220 or (800) 388–1835.*

Greater Milwaukee Convention and Visitors Bureau, *510 West Kilbourn Street, Milwaukee, WI 53203; (414) 273–7222 or (800) 231–0903.*

Waukesha Chamber of Commerce, *223 Wisconsin Avenue, Waukesha, WI 53188; (262) 542–4249*

Cedarburg

To see charming small towns north of Milwaukee, drive north on I–43 to State Highway 162. Turn west to State Highway 57. Turn north and drive into Cedarburg.

CEDAR CREEK SETTLEMENT (ages five and up)
N70W6340 Bridge Road; (262) 377–8020.
The **Cedar Creek Festival,** held throughout the year, is centered around the Cedar Creek Settlement in the historic village, which provides a jump back to the mid-1800s, when the town was established.

While in the neighborhood, visit the old **Cedarburg Woolen Mill** at the corner of Bridge Road and Washington Avenue, which now houses a warren of crafts shops, art galleries, and similarly trendy retail outlets. The original textile machinery, dating from the 1860s, provides the complex with a rustic look. It's a good idea to show the kids how cloth was made a century ago before turning them loose inside the building, with its numerous staircases and hide-and-seek hallways.

The Cedar Creek Winery, with a tasting room in the mill, is available for tours. The winery is one of America's most noted small regional wineries, which provides a chance to learn how vintners create their fine wines just like back home in Europe. The shop hosts a **Winery Open House** on the third full weekend in March, with special tastings and lectures on wine production as well as a grape-stomping contest for purple footers. White socks for participants are not encouraged.

CEDARBURG CULTURAL CENTER (all ages)

W62N56 Washington Avenue; (262) 375–3676.

Just a short walk from the mill is the Cedarburg Cultural Center, which features permanent and temporary exhibits exploring the community's history, heritage, and contemporary culture. The center also sponsors an outdoor concert series on the lawn of City Hall on Sunday afternoons in July, where visitors can sprawl on the grass and relax. Kids are welcome to turn somersaults, play tag and, of course, listen to the music. On the stroll to the center, shoppers are lured by the antiques shops, boutiques, and galleries lining the main street. For more information on Cedarburg and its festivals, call the Cedarburg Chamber of Commerce at (262) 377–9620.

Covered Bridge Park Stock up on goodies for a walk in Covered Bridge Park, where the kids can run though Wisconsin's last remaining original covered bridge. There is a comfortable picnic area alongside the bridge, which spans Cedar Creek. Take Washington Avenue north to Five Corners, then continue to the park via Covered Bridge Road. It's a leisurely, half-hour drive from downtown Cedarburg.

DAVID V. UIHLEIN RACING MUSEUM (ages 10 and up)

Hamilton Road; (262) 375–4032. Open Wednesday through Saturday from 10:00 A.M. to 5:00 P.M. and Sunday from 1:00 to 5:00 P.M.

For a speedier look at life, the David V. Uihlein Racing Museum houses a collection of antique racing cars dating back to the early twentieth century.

OZAUKEE COUNTY FAIR (all ages)

W67N866 Washington Avenue; (262) 375–6185. Late summer.

The 140th annual Ozaukee County Fair was celebrated in 1999, making it one of the oldest in the state. The fair keeps alive a wonderful rural tradition of rooster crowing, cow mooing, horse neighing, pig oinking, lamb bleating, kid yelling, and all-around fun that can be shared by urban folks. There are the usual giant vegetables, homemade pies at the church booths, merry-go-round fun at the carnival, and nationally known musical entertainment after dark.

Festival Fun

- **Strawberry Festival (ages 5 and up);** (262) 377–9620. End of June. The annual Strawberry Festival is always a "berry fun time" for families. Sample luscious strawberry desserts, take part in the strawberry pie-eating contests, and try the berry bob competition. There is also plenty of other fruity entertainment, with music and stage performances. A folk-art show, featuring more than fifty Midwest artists, is a popular draw during the festival weekend.

- **Wine and Harvest Festival (ages 5 and up);** (262) 377–8020. Third full weekend of September. The Wine and Harvest Festival offers pumpkin carvers, hayrides, wine tasting, blacksmiths pounding on forges, and music.

- **Winter Festival (ages 5 and up);** (262) 377–9620. First full weekend in February. Regardless of the season—even in the frostiest weather— the mill and winery, as well as the rest of Cedarburg, always bustles. A Winter Festival has bed races on the millpond, along with snow- and ice-sculpting competitions and indoor dramatic and musical entertainment.

BEERNSTEN'S CANDY (all ages)

W61N520 Washington Avenue; (262) 377–9512.

A must-stop to satisfy any sweet tooth in the crew is Beernsten's Candy, with its hand-dipped chocolates. The homemade hard candies, brittles, and fudge are worth walking across Wisconsin to get, to say nothing of the caramel corn and roasted nuts. Located in an old stage-coach inn, Beernsten's has been a Cedarburg landmark since 1932.

For More Information

Cedarburg Chamber of Commerce, *W63N645 Washington Avenue, Cedarburg, WI 53012-0204; (262) 377–9620.*

Port Washington

Port Washington is about 20 miles north of Milwaukee on I–43. Follow the signs and exit on State Highway 33.

Crowning Port Washington is St. Mary's Church, which sits atop a high hill overlooking the Lake Michigan harbor. Have the kids dash up the steps from the downtown streets to the ridgetop while you drive around the back of the hill and up to the church parking lot. See who gets to the church's front door first. Have the speedsters count the steps (which should slow them down a bit).

FROZEN FUN (ages 5 and up)

Winter does not put the deep freeze on Port Washington. **Cross-country excursions** at nearby Harrington Beach State Park feature **candlelight skiing,** with **ice skating** at Kolbach Park on East Whitefish Road and Hill School Park, at the corner of Grand and Spring Streets. (For details on ice skating conditions, check in with the city recreation department at 262-284-5881.) **Sledding** is popular at Hawthorne Hills Park on State Highway 1, with snowmobiling trails around town. Call (262) 284-8259 for locales.

HISTORIC BUILDINGS (ages 5 and up)

The first Yankee and Irish settlers in Port Washington were soon joined by Luxembourgians and Germans, all of whom put their ethnic stamp on the city. While a fire in 1899 destroyed many of the older downtown buildings, there are still plenty of pre–twentieth century structures that make a stroll along the downtown streets a photographer's delight.

A Hintz Adventure by Kate Hintz

Travel experiences opened my eyes throughout my childhood. I had the opportunity to experience many parts of the United States, Canada, and Jamaica. Having such exposure so early influenced many of my decisions later in life. I knew, firsthand, that the world had more to offer than I had ever imagined. From investigating crafts shops and candy stores in Wisconsin's Door County to sampling deliciously exotic alligator sausage in New Orleans, I knew as a child that I wanted to see it all.

With so many things to see and do and so many places to explore and discover, traveling has remained a top priority for me. It will take an entire lifetime to see and do it . . . and then some. Many of my most cherished memories have been acquired through travel. I fondly remember fishing and frog hunting at Hintz's North Star Lodge on Star Lake and listening to my mother tell the story of the giant muskie that tried to tip her boat. And, although cold weather and I do not mesh well, I even enjoyed cross-country skiing with my dad and brothers during snow-touched evenings.

I have explored Wisconsin with my family my entire life, and I have pleasant memories. It didn't make any difference if the memories were made of the delightfully silly, touristy fun at the Wisconsin Dells, with its water slides, petting zoos, and offbeat museums. And the state's historic sites provided insights on the past. Always, the opportunity to meet people on their hometown grounds helped me understand how thoughts, dreams, and feelings are the same everywhere.

(Kate Hintz completed her freshman year at Clark-Atlanta University in Atlanta and is now pursuing a degree in arts and psychology at the University of Minnesota. She is also a model.)

HARRINGTON BEACH STATE PARK (all ages)

531 County Highway D, Belgium; (262) 285–3015. Open 6:00 A.M. to 11:00 P.M. year-round. State-park vehicle pass required.

This 637-acre park, site of an old quarry and abandoned town, has seventy-one interesting trails, a picnic area, and a playground. The park is 7 miles north of Port Washington, off U.S. 43.

ALL THINGS FISHY

 CHARTER FISHING (ages 10 and up)

Port Washington has one of the finest harbors on the Great Lakes and is a center for many charter-fishing fleets. Kids can get the feel of being a captain for a morning or afternoon experience on the big water. Be sure they dress for the weather. A layered look is best, because sweatshirts and jackets can be peeled off as the day warms and the trout and salmon start flopping aboard. Among the top charter vessels using the Port are:

- *Fishing Pox,* (262) 284–7222

- *Foxy Lady,* (262) 258–0657

- **Lighthouse Charters,** (920) 854–4140

- *Nicky Boy,* (262) 284–9246

- *Night Flight,* (920) 994–8419

WORLD'S LARGEST ONE DAY OUTDOOR FISH FRY (all ages)

Fishing has long been a tradition in Port Washington; the city was chartered in 1848, the same year Wisconsin became a state. The World's Largest One Day Outdoor Fish Fry, therefore, is celebrated the third Saturday of each July in honor of that piscatorial heritage. Kids' games, fire-department water fights, music, and lots of fish make up the fun. A Fish Day 8-kilometer run kicks off the day's activities, with divisions for young, as well as old-timer dashers.

SMITH BROS. FISH SHANTY RESTAURANT (all ages)

100 North Franklin Street; (262) 284–5592. $$

With a name like this, you know Smith Bros. specializes in fish. Kids love to dig into the restaurant's "mile-high" lemon pie for dessert. A fish market is adjacent to the eatery for the take-home-and-cook set.

For More Information

Port Washington Chamber of Commerce, *P.O. Box 514, Port Washington, WI 53074-0514; (262) 284–0900.*

West Bend

West Bend is a 30-minute drive north of Milwaukee off I–45. Exit on State Highway 33 and follow signs.

GERMANFEST (ages 5 and up)

Held on the last weekend in August. Call the West Bend Chamber of Commerce at (262) 338–2666 for more information.

Since 1985 West Bend's annual Germanfest has offered enough sauerbraten and spanferkel to satisfy the hungriest burgermeister and his followers. The southeastern Wisconsin city of 25,000 persons proudly shows off its Germanic heritage during the festival, which is just large enough to enjoy but small enough not to worry about being lost in the crowd. On the festival's Saturday, a farmers' market near the grounds opens before dawn with tons of sweet corn and other fresh produce temptingly displayed from stalls and the back of trucks.

TOP FACTORY OUTLETS (ages 10 and up)

The kids might not appreciate the time it takes to hunt out bargains, but when they receive a new coin purse at Christmas, stuffed with dollar bills, the urchins should appreciate the earlier stopover. Check out these favorites:

- **Amity Leather Factory,** State Highway 33 West (262–338–6506). All the best in leather accessories can be found at Amity, from wallets to handbags.

- **West Bend Woolen Mills,** West Bend. On Washington Avenue along the Milwaukee River at Riverside Park, one block west of the Amity Outlet Store (262–334–7052). Try on the latest woolens.

- **Bierl's Cheese Mart and Factory,** 3721 County Highway P, Jackson (262–677–3227). Go for samples of award-winning baby Swiss, or have your car full of cheeseheads try the creamy Muenster and brick.

Riverwalk Art Fair

The Riverwalk Art Fair, held along the banks of the lazily flowing Milwaukee River, brings together dozens of regional fine-art and crafts artisans. Naturally, there is plenty of polka and waltz music, so you can work off the calories from German chocolate cake and other desserts. Best of all, the entire program is free. The fair is good entertainment for children ten years and up. Call (262) 338–3909 for details.

THE EMERALD NECKLACE (all ages)

The city calls its 600 acres of parkland The Emerald Necklace, with hiking, ice rinks, swimming, tennis, bike/hike trails, basketball courts, ball fields, and other outdoor amenities. Canoe launching on the Milwaukee River is permitted at Riverside Park, and there is a toboggan chute at Regner Park.

LIZARD MOUND COUNTY PARK (all ages)

Lizard Mound County Park is 2 miles north of West Bend on County Highway A, then east ½ mile.

This site is on the National Register of Historic Places, containing effigy mounds made between A.D. 500 and 1000. There is a self-guided nature trail that kids will enjoy, plus a picnic area.

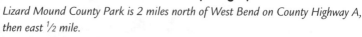

WEST BEND ROTARY SEAFOOD FEST (all ages)

West Bend Chamber of Commerce, 122 North Main Street, West Bend, WI 53095; (262) 338–2666. Held annually on Father's Day.

Kids should take Dad out on Father's Day to the West Bend Rotary Seafood Fest, with children's plates available. Seafood gumbo, shrimp, scallops, lobster (presold at $17.50 by ordering from the festival), an oyster bar, and smoked fish augment the usual brats, burgers, and corn-on-the-cob offerings. The pageant is held in Regner Park, at North Main and Silverbrook. Paddleboat rides, rock 'n' roll, country music, face painting, line dancing, and tons of kids' games round out the family day.

FAT DOG/FUNFEST FORTY (ages 5 and up)

c/o Race Coordinator Julie O'Halloran, N105 W14653 Wilson Drive, Germantown, WI 53022 (mail only). Late June.

The Fat Dog/Funfest Forty bicycle race has categories for kids (starting in the fourteen-to-nineteen age divisions for both girls and boys) and on to ages fifty-five and over, so Grandma and Grandpa could even pedal along. Awards are given to the top three finishers in each age category, with trophies for the overall men's and women's divisions. The 27½-mile race travels over the hilly Kettle Moraine countryside, kicking off at 10:00 A.M. in Jansen Park (on Schuster Drive in West Bend). Post-race events are held in Regner Park, with music, a carnival, food, and an awards ceremony as part of its annual Funfest. Approved helmets must be worn on the race course. The ride is fun, invigorating, and scenic, so prepare the family to pedal-hearty and think of the carnival rides at the end of the loop. Pedal Moraine of West Bend provides technicians to make last-minute repairs and adjustments on bikes, so if Junior has grown 3 inches overnight, his growth spurt can be accommodated.

The Historic Third Ward

The worst maritime tragedy to strike Wisconsin was the sinking of the *Lady Elgin* on September 8, 1860. The number lost was never finalized, but 290 bodies were recovered. The tragedy occurred late at night when the steamer was returning to Milwaukee from Chicago. Aboard were 550 passengers, mostly residents of Milwaukee's Third Ward, an Irish section of the city. They had gone to Chicago to hear a speech by fiery politician Stephen A. Douglas. A lumber boat plowed into the side of the ship near Winnetka, Illinois, and severely damaged the Milwaukee vessel. To compound the problem, a sudden storm rose shortly after the collision, making it impossible for the crew to stop the flow of lake water into the hull.

Decks were chopped up for life rafters to supplement the three small lifeboats. But that wasn't enough to save the hundreds who drowned. Historians say the entire political structure of Milwaukee changed due to the disaster, because many of those on board were political and cultural leaders in the community. The loss of the Irish presence in the city allegedly gave rise to the next wave of German immigrants who were coming into Milwaukee.

A large sign recapping the Lady Elgin disaster can be seen near the drawbridge where Water Street crosses the Milwaukee River, upriver from the city's harbor. To commemorate the event, the Emerald Society and other Irish organizations in Milwaukee annually drop wreaths into the lake around the anniversary of the sinking.

The Third Ward was also hit by another disaster on October 28, 1892, when some 16 square blocks in the neighborhood were destroyed by fire. Five persons died, and the property loss was estimated in the millions of dollars. A Milwaukee County Historical Society sign at the corner of Broadway and Chicago Streets describes the disaster.

The Third Ward has long since recovered and is now one of the trendier sections of the city, with theaters, restaurants, brewpubs, and galleries in the old warehouses that replaced the burned-out structures.

For More Information

West Bend Chamber of Commerce, *122 North Main Street, West Bend, WI 53095; (262) 338–2666.*

Hubertus

Hubertus is 30 minutes northwest of Milwaukee. Take I–45 to the State Highway 175 exit and follow the well-marked route.

 NATIONAL SHRINE OF ST. MARY (ages 10 and up)
1525 Carmel Road; (262) 628–1838 or (262) 673–3540. Open year-round.

On State Highway 167, 5 miles east of State Highway 83, is a sight directly from Gothic Europe. The spires of the National Shrine of St. Mary, crowning one of the highest peaks in southeastern Wisconsin, pierce the skies. From the distance, especially on a late afternoon with the rosy sun setting at its back, the shrine appears to be a shimmering castle in some far off Avalon. In 1855, Irish settlers around the town of Erin erected a cross on top of the hill. Shortly afterward, a wandering hermit said he experienced a miraculous cure while visiting there. This naturally drew a flood of the curious, the devout, the maimed, and the sick. A church was built and outbuildings added to accommodate the pilgrims. Eventually the Discalced Carmelites order of monks took over the site, now called Holy Hill by the neighborhood folks. The original cross that marked the hill can be viewed in a basement vault. Upstairs, near the main altar, hundreds of crutches and braces line the walls, attesting that at least some healing—physical, spiritual, or whatever—has taken place here over the generations.

Kids can climb the tall bell tower (more than one hundred steps) to get an even broader view of the world than what can be seen from the veranda in front of the church. The landscape below rolls out a colorful quilt regardless of the season, making for perfect photo opportunities. A cafeteria is on the grounds, as well as gift shop packed with religious mementos. Tours can be arranged by calling (262) 628-1838. The church is reached from State Highway 167 on the long, winding Carmel Road. Don't worry about getting lost; the steeples can be seen for miles from any direction. By keeping them in sight, you will be led directly to the front door, where there is ample parking in several lots. Be prepared to walk a lot and climb a great deal; however, the grounds are handicap accessible.

Places to Eat

Fox and Hounds. *1298 Friess Lake Road; (262) 628–1111.* Nestled amid the rolling Kettle Moraine Hills, the Fox and Hounds is for the romantic in you. Looking like an old hunting lodge, the restaurant is snug and warm in the winter, with fireplaces, walls framed by exposed timbers, and intimate rooms. It's a great stop on an autumn-color tour around the neighborhood, as well. And while we're at it, just add spring and summer for enjoyable dining. Order the roast goose. Yum. $$$

Hartford

Hartford is about twenty-five minutes northwest of Milwaukee. Take I–45 to State Highway 167, go west about 4 miles to State Highway 83, and turn north. Proceed to Hartford by following the signs.

HARTFORD HERITAGE AUTO MUSEUM (ages 5 and up)

147 North Rural Street; (262) 673–7999. Open 10:00 A.M. to 5:00 P.M. Monday through Saturday and noon to 5:00 P.M. Sunday, May through September; 10:00 A.M. to 5:00 P.M. Wednesday through Saturday and noon to 5:00 P.M. Sunday, October through April.

This museum honors the memory of the Kissel automobile, which was built in town between 1906 and 1931. Nash autos, also designed in Wisconsin, are displayed along with the many styles of the Kissel. There are some seventy cars and trucks at the museum.

W. B. PLACE & CO. (ages 10 and up)

368 West Sumner Street; (262) 673–3130 or (800) TAN–HIDE for national calls.

Kids who are into crafts will appreciate a stop at the W.B. Place & Co. leather factory outlet. Leather made from deer and cow hides are stacked in colorful profusion, ranging from purple to red to green, as well as the traditional brown. It's all the result of various types of tanning practices and dyeing. Leather goods are also sold in the shop. Place is the place for both extensive and more personalized tanning processes. (Local hunters regularly bring in their single deer hides for treatment.) Get enough leather so the kids can make their own moccasins and you can outfit yourself in a black leather motorcycle outfit.

PIKE LAKE STATE PARK (all ages)

3340 Kettle Moraine Road; (262) 670–3400. State-park vehicle stickers required.

Pike Lake State Park is only 2 miles south of town on State Highway 60. Powder Hill overlook is a prime spot for deer watching (these deer still wear their coats, of course). There are also campsites and nearby hiking opportunities along nature trails. The park is open year-round. Camping, however, is available only from May through mid-October. Be sure to call for reservations, because the park is a quick jaunt from major metro areas such as Milwaukee and can get crowded. The good news, though, is that other visitors won't be noticed much because of the extensive forestland and hills.

Places to Eat

The Country Retreat. *3461 High Road; (414) 673–9977.* The Retreat serves a general range of American-style dishes. You can't go wrong here. $$

North Lake

To reach North Lake from Milwaukee, drive west on I–94 and exit on State Highway 83. Go north on 83 about 10 miles.

KETTLE MORAINE SCENIC STEAM TRAIN (ages 5 and up)

P.O. Box 247, North Lake, WI 53064; (262) 782–8074. Open Sunday from the first weekend in June through mid-October. Closed holidays. Train departs at 12:30, 2:00, and 3:30 P.M.

Hop aboard the Kettle Moraine Scenic Steam Train for a ride through scenic glacier country. The rides, in old coaches pulled by a huffing, puffing locomotive, take passengers on an 8-mile-long round-trip. An 1890s depot in North Lake (look for the signs off State Highway 83) is the point of departure. The steam train, complete with bright red cowcatcher on the front of the engine, runs only on Sunday. Extra rides are offered in October to catch a glimpse of the brilliant crimson maples and golden oaks that cover the surrounding countryside.

Ashippun

Ashippun is on State Highway 67, about forty minutes northwest of Milwaukee. Drive west on I–94 to State Highway 16; turn north and connect with 67. Continue north for about another 8 miles.

HONEY ACRES (ages 5 and up)

State Highway 67; (920) 474–4411. Open 9:00 A.M. to 3:30 P.M. Monday through Friday year-round and noon to 4:00 P.M. Saturday and Sunday, mid-May through mid-October.

For a honey of a museum, sample a variety of the bees' sweet stuff at Honey Acres. The youngsters will learn everything they ever needed to know about the buzzers and beekeeping. Exhibits in the museum include spigots that drip clover and other flavors of honey for a tempting taste-bud treat.

Eagle

From Ashippun, take State Highway 67 directly south about 25 miles to the town of Eagle.

OLD WORLD WISCONSIN (ages 5 and up)

S103 W37890 Highway 67; (262) 594–2116. Open 10:00 A.M. to 4:00 P.M. Monday through Friday and 10:00 A.M. to 5:00 P.M. Saturday and Sunday, May through October. Winter skiing. Eagle is 35 miles from downtown Milwaukee via I–94 to State Highway 67 (follow signs), 55 miles from Madison, and 75 miles from Chicago.

Old World Wisconsin, one of six **living-history museums** operated by the Wisconsin State Historical Society, comprises 576 acres of **hills, forests, pastures,** and **cornfields** in the southern unit of the **Kettle Moraine State Forest.** Buildings at Old World were collected from around the state and placed in their appropriate ethnic site. Sites featured are German, Polish, Norwegian, and Danish farms, along with a crossroads Yankee village. Interpreters in period clothing perform the tasks done by rural residents in the nineteenth and early twentieth centuries. They care for the crops and rare breeds of animals in the same way as the early Wisconsin farmers. It is not uncommon to see Cotswold sheep, Ossabaw hogs, Lineback cattle, and Morgan-Percheron horses.

Even the visitors center has historical significance; the **octagonal Clausing Barn** (built in 1897) now houses a cafeteria-style restaurant with simple, inexpensive fare at a decent price. A museum, rest rooms, and theater are in the adjacent **Ramsey Barn,** built in 1841 in Fort Atkinson. Horse-drawn wagons make regular loops around the grounds, picking up and dropping off families who can explore the farm sites, talk with the interpreters, and learn more about life on the frontier. Each cluster of buildings is authentic, right down to the **original sauna on the Finnish farm site.** Kids enjoy poking around the **Raspberry School,** a one-room schoolhouse built in 1896 by three Scandinavian families in Bayfield County near Lake Superior's Raspberry Bay.

The grounds often host special programs, ranging from **traditional Fourth of July celebrations** complete with political speeches to uplifting holiday caroling in tiny St. Peter's Church (1839), the first Catholic church built in Milwaukee. **Cross-country skiing** is allowed every Friday, Saturday, and Sunday from late December through the first weekend in March as conditions permit, with hot cider and cookies often served from kitchens at the various homesteads. The trails range from easy to difficult (they are marked appropriately) and loop and swish over the low hills, leading through farmyards and even an open barn or two. Ski equipment rentals are available in the Ramsey Barn; lunches are offered in the Clausing Barn. The last ski tickets of the day are sold at 3:30 P.M., so be sure to get there early enough. It is an amazing feeling to swoop down off a maple-covered ridge with kids in tow and suddenly find your entire family in a different century.

The museum also hosts what it calls **"Homespun Journeys"** packages, which include tours and supper at Old World, an overnight at a local bed-and-breakfast inn, and a visit to the East Troy Trolley Museum, just to the south.

SWINGING "W" RANCH (ages 5 and up)

Take Wilton Road between State Highways 67 and 59; (262) 594-2416.

For modern buckaroos, the nearby Swinging "W" Ranch offers trail rides that can run up to 20 miles long or even overnight. Kids need to be good patient riders for the longer excursions. Riding lessons are also given, as well as hay and sleigh rides in their respective seasons.

Delavan

From Milwaukee, take I–43 southwest from the city and exit at Delavan on State Highway 11.

Between 1847 and 1894 this sawdust city was home to some twenty-six circuses that had winter quarters here. The Spring Grove and St. Andrew's Cemeteries in town have dozens of gravesites marking the final resting place of roustabouts, clowns, lion tamers, front office workers, acrobats, and showgirls. A rearing elephant statue in the downtown square is a reminder of its center-ring heritage and a perfect backdrop for family portraits, so don't forget the tripod and camera.

EARLENE'S DOLL HOUSE (all ages)

116 North Second Street; (262) 728–9500.

Be sure to look over the collection of antique dolls and check out the doll wigs, clothes, trunks, and patterns at this embroidery and sewing shop. If one of the youngsters has a broken doll, it can be repaired at Earlene's, which acts as an emergency clinic for tattered toys.

DAM ROAD BEARS (all ages)

Located in an old barn, 1 mile north of Walworth Avenue on North Terrace Street near Lake Comus; (262) 728–9417.

Kids can watch toy bears being custom-made. The shop is packed with fat little fuzzies.

FANTASY HILLS RANCH (ages 5 and up)

2430 Town Hall Road; (262) 728–1773.

Horseback trail rides, children's pony rides, buggy rides, hayrides, and sleigh rides should keep the kids busy.

Places to Stay

Delavan Inn. *215 East Walworth Avenue; (262) 728–9143.* Fifty-five rooms. $$

Lake Lawn Lodge. *2400 East Geneva; (262) 728–7950.* Two hundred eighty-four rooms. $$$

Royal Inlet Motel. *5560 State Highway 50; (262) 728–9399.* Thirty-eight rooms. $

Elkhorn

Elkhorn is forty minutes southwest of Milwaukee via I–43. Take the Elkhorn exit to State Highway 11.

WISCONSIN HIGH SCHOOL RODEO (ages 5 and up)

Elkham Area Chamber of Commerce; (262) 723–5788. Late May.

With plenty of bumps, whoops, and hollering, the Wisconsin High School Rodeo brings the Old West to southeastern Wisconsin. Bare-bronc riding, girls' and boys' cutting, barrel racing, calf roping, break-away roping, bull riding, team roping, saddle-bronc riding, goat tying, steer wrestling, and pole bending are among the rootin' tootin' events. Although there is admission, kids under five are admitted **Free**. A country round-up dance at the activity center of the Walworth County Fairgrounds is held on the Saturday night of the rodeo. Of course, there is line dancing, plenty of polkas, and usually even a bit of vintage rock 'n' roll.

GRANDPARENTS DAY (all ages)

Premium Green Farms, W6384 Sugar Creek Road, 5 miles north of Elkhorn; (262) 728–8810. Take either County Trunk O or H north of the city to Sugar Creek Road. It's the kids' job to watch for the signs from then on along the highway. Early September.

Kids are usually the apple of their grandparents' eye, so have them host their grandads and grandmas at the annual Grandparents Day. There is an apple pancake breakfast, along with pony rides, face painting, clowns, and a small animal display. Later in the month is Happy Birthday, Johnny Day in honor of Johnny Appleseed, followed in October by Apple Fest Weekend, Pumpkin Daze, and Sweetest Day. Whatever the celebration, though, there are always apples, apples, apples. The orchard has been in the same family since the 1840s and now grows almost twenty varieties of the juicy one-a-day-keep-the-doc-away fruit, from Paulared to Northern Spy, along with pears and plums.

East Troy

East Troy is 30 minutes southwest of Milwaukee. Take I–43 and exit at the East Troy off-ramp (State Highway 20).

EAST TROY ELECTRIC RAILROAD MUSEUM (ages 5 and up)

202 Church Street (twenty-four-hour information line, 262–548–ETER). The trolleys run from Labor Day weekend through the end of October.

The East Troy Electric Railroad Museum brings back the fun of smooth quiet travel on tracks that once linked small communities in southeastern Wisconsin with Milwaukee. Rides can be taken on **vintage trolleys** that scoot along through 10 miles of farmland. On Saturday and Sunday from mid-September through the end of October, the trolley ride stops at **The Elegant Farmer market,** where passengers can stop for a hayride, pick their own pumpkins and apples, or make fresh caramel apples. Everyone can then pick up a later train for the return to East Troy. (So if you happen to leave a kid behind while out looking for the Great Pumpkin, he or she will eventually show up.)

The museum is staffed by volunteers who are always eager to explain the finer points of trolley travel. While a peek inside the repair barns might be oily and messy due to the work being done on the cars, it is also a chance for kids to look at the inner workings of the machinery. Be sure they keep their hands to themselves, however, both for safety and cleanliness sake. Inside the old depot on Church Street is all sorts of memorabilia about trolleys as commuter transportation.

Throughout the summer the trolley museum sponsors special programs, such as its annual **Trolley Festival** in May, **June Dairy Month** (with **Free** ice cream with each paid fare), **Model Railroad Weekend** in July, **Dog Days of Summer** (**Free** hot dogs with each paid fare), and the **Fall Fun Days,** with its stop at the farmer's market.

 ## ALPINE VALLEY RESORT (ages 5 and up)

County Trunk D; (262) 642–7374. $$$.

 For winter fun in southeastern Wisconsin, stop by the Alpine Valley Resort on County Highway D off State Highway 20, which offers twelve slopes serviced by eleven chairlifts and five rope tows. Saunas, pizza parlors, a cafeteria, lounges, and whirlpools make Alpine Valley the closest thing to Aspen in these Dairy State parts. KinderKids meet daily at 10:30 A.M. and 1:30 P.M. for lessons and bunny-slope fun. ValleyKids is a six-week instructional program that starts in early January for older youngsters who want to perfect their skiing form. The resort also features an adult and youth race series that also begins in January, along with NASTAR racing open to all ages on Saturday and Sunday. Night skiing is available each evening until 11:00 P.M.

Waterford

Waterford is 20 minutes southwest of Milwaukee on State Highway 36.

 ### GREEN MEADOWS FARM (all ages)

Three miles west of Waterford on State; (262) 534–2891. Open from 10:00 A.M. to 1:00 P.M. daily from May through August; 10:00 A.M. to 3:00 P.M. Saturday and Sunday and 10:00 A.M. to noon Monday through Friday in October.

Green Meadows is a chain operation, with locations in California, Illinois, New York, Florida, New Jersey, and Maryland, as well as Waterford, but it is a great place to introduce youngsters to animals. More than 300 furry and feathery creatures can be fed, fondled, and befriended. Learn to milk a cow the old-fashioned way by hand, take a hayride, and put Junior and Missy on a pony.

 ### RAUSCH'S BEAR DEN GAME FARM AND PETTING ZOO (all ages)

6831 Big Bend Road; (262) 895–6430. Open 11:00 A.M. to 5:00 P.M. May through October.

Located on State Highway 64 in Tichigan near Waterford, Rausch's is another pet-and-cuddle place. Even Wilber, the thousand–pound pig, doesn't mind a pat on the head.

Places to Eat

Rivermoor Country Club. *30802 Waterford Drive; (262) 534–2500. The public is welcome to eat at the club. You don't even need to discuss golf.* $$

Lake Geneva

Lake Geneva is forty minutes south of Milwaukee via I–43. Exit at Lake Geneva.

 ### GENEVA LAKE CRUISE LINE (all ages)

Riviera Docks, 812 Wrigley Drive; (262) 248–6206 or (800) 558–5911. Mail runs sail forth from 10:00 A.M. to 4:00 P.M., mid-June to mid-September.

Cruises on 5,000-acre Lake Geneva have been a tradition for more than a century. Today's tours on the *Lady of the Lake* and other vessels range from one-hour to half-day jaunts, along with champagne brunches and lunch expeditions. Geneva Lake Cruise Line can help with details. Kids will enjoy a morning cruise that features mail girls who perform flying leaps from moving boat to resort docks to carry letters and packages to postal boxes. Between postal drops, they tell about the estates on the shoreline. Seldom does anyone slip and plop into the water.

SUNBIRD BALLOONS

2493 Crest Drive; (262) 249–0660. Open 9:00 A.M. to 5:00 P.M. Monday through Saturday and 10:00 A.M. to 5:00 P.M. Sunday. (Note: In order to participate, individuals must be at least 4 feet tall.)

For another perspective on life, sign the kids up for a balloon ride from Sunbird Balloons. There is little that can match looking down on a silent world as it slips below a balloon basket drifting in the wind. Flights are offered at sunrise and sunset from several locations, depending on both wind conditions and weather. If a ride cannot be taken, Sunbird will reschedule at no extra cost. For the early-morning flight, lay out clothes the night before, because passengers can't be late for the thrilling ride. As the pilots say, "the right weather waits for no one." Everyone can help inflate the balloons, too. Even the littlest kid can help straighten ropes or serve early-morning coffee.

LAKE GENEVA HORSE PARK AND PETTING ZOO (ages 5 and up)

 Corner of State Highways 50 and 67; (262) 245–7700. Open daily from May through October.

The stables offer tours, a petting zoo, and live animal displays, and the horse park has wagon rides and pony rides for young, adventurous types. Call for hours and rates.

Places to Eat

Annie's Ice Cream Parlor and Restaurant. *712 Main Street; (262) 248–1933.* Numerous flavors of the cool stuff from which to choose. Their burgers are pretty good, too. $

Hogs & Kisses. *Downtown Lake Geneva, 1 block from the waterfront; (262) 248–7447.* Hospitality and family prices make this eatery a vacation favorite. $$

Popeye's Gallery & Grog. *Downtown Lake Geneva; (262) 248–4381.* Family-style goodies, amid a nautical theme, are easy on the pocketbook. $$

The Red Geranium Restaurant. *7194 W150E; (262) 248–3637.* Steak and seafood are popular. Enjoy eating in the dining room overlooking the geranium-filled garden. $$

St. Moritz. *327 Wrigley Drive; (262) 248–6680.* Dress up the kids (or keep them at the campsite with a baby sitter while you go out) and make sure they don't drool on the brie. This is the fanciest place in town, located in a Victorian home on the National Register of Historic Places. And the food is great. Try the salmon Polignac. $$$

Places to Stay

Ambassador Inn. *415 Wells Street; (262) 248–3452.* Eighteen rooms. Children under eighteen stay 𝐅𝐫𝐞𝐞. $$

French Country Inn. *W4190 West End Road; (262) 245–5220.* Twenty-four rooms. $$

Grand Geneva Resort & Spa. *7036 Grand Geneva Way; (262) 248–8811.* Three hundred fifty-five rooms. $$$

Williams Bay

Williams Bay is on State Highway 67, about 2 miles south of Lake Geneva.

YERKES OBSERVATORY (ages 10 and up)

State Highway 67; (262) 245–5555. Tours are offered at 1:30, 2:15, and 3:00 P.M. Saturday from June through September; 10:15 and 11:15 A.M. Saturday from October through May.

If you want to do some stargazing, take the kids to Yerkes Observatory, which has the world's largest refracting telescope. The observatory is set amid the pines and aspen, out of sight of State Highway 67 but near enough to the resort community of Williams Bay on Lake Geneva to provide a neat getaway on a vacation day.

*S*ports and Recreational Activities

INDEPENDENCE First advocates sports and recreational activities through monthly newsletters, listings of activities, and referrals for those who are physically and mentally challenged. Contact INDEPENDENCE First at 600 West Virginia, Suite 301, Milwaukee, WI 53204 (414–291–7520). Office hours are 8:00 A.M. to 4:30 P.M. Monday through Friday.

Kenosha

Kenosha is 45 miles south of Milwaukee off I–94. Look for the exits.

Money magazine calls Kenosha one of the best places to live in America for its location along Lake Michigan, midway between Milwaukee and Chicago; its range of housing and accommodations; its business base; and all the cultural intangibles that contribute to the quality of life.

The **Wisconsin Information Center** (262-857-7164), at the I-94 rest area just inside Wisconsin near Kenosha, is a great place to pull over for a breather and pit stop. Plus the vacationer will find racks and racks of tourist literature, as well as knowledgeable staff behind the counter. For spur-of-the-moment side trips, or for added details on a planned getaway, the center can provide frontline help.

BRISTOL RENAISSANCE FAIRE (ages 5 and up)

12550 120th Avenue; (262) 396–4320. Open from the end of June until the end of August on Saturday and Sunday from 10:00 A.M. to 7:00 P.M. $.

Thundering hooves, a clash of steel upon steel, and merry minstrel tunes make for all the stuff of fantasy, fable, and kids' dreams. That's the Bristol Renaissance Faire, where those dreams come alive from the end of June through August. The actors and actresses who play the roles of knight, princess, beggar, or king certainly get into the swing of things, which makes the scenes very realistic. From jousting to juggling, from banquet table to royal court, the faire sweeps up its guests and plunks them down in another era. As they say at the faire, "Eat, drynke and be merrie." It's enough to make a kid want to scurry to the library for an added dose of Arthur and the Round Table.

CONGO RIVER ADVENTURE GOLF (ages 5 and up)

Easily accessible off I–94 via State Highway 50; (262) 857–PUTT. The course is open seasonally from May through October, with summer hours from 10:00 A.M. to late evening.

Congo River Adventure Golf challenges all duffers regardless of size or age. Waterfalls, deep pools, rock ledges, and jungles (all more or less real) provide a backdrop for a busy round of mini-golf. There aren't any hungry crocs, hippos, chest-thumping gorillas, or zebras, though, to distract the concentrating golfer. Adjacent to the Factory Outlet Centre with its dozens of stores, Congo River can fill in the time for the older kids while parents do some shopping.

***B*est Fruit and Vegetable Farms in Kenosha** You won't find any bananas on the Congo River palms, but visitors to the Kenosha area will find plenty of fruits and vegetables to pick. A number of truck farms are open seasonally during the harvest. Such a family adventure can stock the home shelves with peas, pumpkins, beans, and berries, as well as provide a fun-in-the-sun outing. Here are a few places where kids can pick apples, strawberries, or other fresh goodies: **Munster Apple Orchard**, Old State Highway 50, 1 mile west of New Munster (262–537–2664); **Oriole Springs Orchards**, 36116 128th Street, Twin Lakes (262–877–2436); **Smith Produce and Country Store**, 7150 Eighteenth Street, Kenosha (262–859–2645); **Szele Apple Orchards**, 11934 Twenty-eighth Avenue, Kenosha (262–694–8374); and **Thompson Strawberry Farms**, 14400 Seventy-fifth Street, Kenosha (262–857–2351). Smith Produce also has hayrides, carriage rides, and a petting zoo.

OLD LAKESHORE TROLLEY (all ages)

Downtown and weather permitting. The trolleys run from mid-May through Labor Day. Signage marks the stops.

One of the best ways to see downtown while taking a load off your feet is via the Old Lakeshore Trolley, which putters through the business district.

MINIATURE VILLAGE DOLLHOUSES (all ages)

1725 Fiftieth Street; (262) 656–0188 or (800) 383–0188. Open Monday through Saturday 10:00 A.M. to 5:00 P.M.

Tiny is really big at the Miniature Village Dollhouses. With one of the Midwest's largest collections of dolls and their teeny homes, along with roofing, lighting fixtures, and lumber, the shop is an eye-opener for little girls and dads or moms who love to tinker. More than one hundred dollhouses are in stock, with a second level of the shop packed with Barbie items.

 ### KENOSHA CHARTER BOAT ASSOCIATION (ages 10 and up)

To find out about available charters, contact the KCBA, P.O. Box 981, Kenosha, WI 53141; (800) 522–6699.

Charter fishing is big in this lakefront city. At least twenty boats belong to the Kenosha Charter Boat Association and are available to haul landlubbers out on the bounding waves in search of salmon and lake trout. All equipment is furnished by the licensed and insured captains. The boats put out from the several Kenosha marinas from April through October.

SOUTHPORT MARINA (all ages)

97 Fifty-seventh Street; (262) 657–5565.

This marina has a tot lot on which toddlers can play while one parent or the other works on the family yacht berthed nearby. The marina has 214 slips with water, power, telephone, and cable television hooks, as well as showers, laundry, and full marina services. With all that, a family doesn't even need to cast off.

STUNT EDUCATION SCHOOL (all ages)

10610 Burlington Road; (262) 859–2379.

For real thrills take the gang on a tour of the Stunt Education School, where trained staffers leap through fire, blow themselves up, toss themselves out windows, and generally tumble, fall, and flip around just like in the movies. Call in advance to check times for visits and warn the kids that under no circumstances should they ever try to do anything remotely similar to what these pros do for a living.

*B*est Musical Venues in Kenosha Kenosha does have a more genteel side, to calm even the antics of the wildest little one. Try the soothing effects of music from the **Kenosha Symphony Orchestra, Kenosha Pops Band,** and **Band of the Black Watch** (bagpipers can be genteel, really). (And don't forget the **Kenosha Public Museum** for a peek into the past.) Call the **Kenosha Area Tourism Corporation** for other suggestions (800–654–7309 or 262–654–7307).

Places to Eat

Brewmasters' Pub. *4017 Eightieth Street; (262) 694–9050.* Good suds, casual duds. You can't go wrong. $

Taste of Wisconsin. *7515 125th Avenue; (262) 857–9110.* You can get everything here but the moo from a Dairyland cow. $

Places to Stay

Best Western Inn. *7220 122nd Avenue; (262) 857–7699 or (800) 438–3932.* One hundred fifteen rooms. Children under eighteen stay **Free**. $$–$$$

Holiday Inn. *5125 Sixth Avenue; (262) 658–3281.* One hundred ten rooms. Children under eighteen stay **Free**. $$

For More Information

Wisconsin Information Center, *Rest Area 26, I–94, Kenosha, WI 53140; (262) 857–7164.*

Union Grove

Take I–94 south from Milwaukee to the Union Grove exit (State Highway 20). The city is about 5 miles west of the interstate.

GREAT LAKES DRAGAWAY (ages 10 and up)

Mail: 5279 North Fifty-fifth Street, Milwaukee, WI 53218; (414) 462–5520 or (414) 878–3783. Races are held from April through October.

Plug your ears, hold on to your hats, and count to ten. The nitro-fueled jet autos at the Great Lakes Dragaway make enough smoke, fire, and noise to rival a space-shuttle launch. Hurtling down the paved runway at lip-cracking, nostril-expanding speed, the dragsters will amaze any kid with their fast, faster, and fastest. Many even use parachutes to slow down at the end of their run. The track, on the east-side outskirts of Union Grove, has attracted car lovers from around the world for more than two decades. Under the flamboyant baton of Broadway Bob, the outgoing, white-haired, fast-car fanatic who owns the place, the reputation of Great Lakes has been well earned. By walking around the back lot, where mechanics tinker on the cars and drivers talk warp factors, it is obvious that anyone into these tangerine-colored, hot-purple land cruisers ain't into no Buicks.

Racine

Racine is easy to find from Milwaukee. Just drive south on I–94 and exit where it tells you.

Amazing Wisconsin Facts Racine businessman William Horlick invented malted milk in Racine in 1887.

GOLDEN RONDELLE THEATER (ages 10 and up)

1525 Howe Street; (262) 631–4001. Tours are given from 9:15 to 11:00 A.M. and from 1:15 to 3:00 P.M. Friday. Reservations required.

The Golden Rondelle Theater was originally designed as the Johnson Wax Pavilion at the New York World's Fair of 1964 and 1965. More than five million persons there viewed the film *To Be Alive,* which won numerous awards from the likes of the New York Film Critics and an Oscar for best documentary short subject in 1966. The theater was moved to Racine after the fair and rebuilt alongside the company's existing administration building, which was designed by Frank Lloyd Wright. **Free** thirty-minute tours of the theater and the Wright building are mostly offered Tuesday through Friday and include the showing of one of several films, *On the Wing, Living Planet,* and *To Be Alive.* Kids will be amazed at the visual effects in each movie, with their six-track wraparound sound and neck-craning giant screens. It is best to call ahead to confirm times, because the theater is often used for corporate and community meetings.

ALL-AMERICAN SOAP BOX DERBY (ages 10 and up)

All events, including the Badger State Challenge and the Border Clash, are held on Hoffert Drive off North Beach; (262) 767–8779.

The All-American Soap Box Derby spring rally receives young entrants from around the United States and Canada, with stock, kit, and master division races held over its early May weekend.

RACINE ZOO SNOOZE AND OTHER ZOO EVENTS
(ages 5 and up)

2131 North Main Street, Racine, WI 53402; (262) 636–9189. Open every day except December 25. Summer hours are 9:00 A.M. to 8:00 P.M. and winter hours are 9:00 A.M. to 4:00 P.M.

Now here is a great activity for the "bravest" kids, ages seven to eleven years old. The Racine Zoo Snooze is held early each July, with a sleepout amidst the lions and tigers. There is a scavenger hunt, nightwalk around the zoo to watch nocturnal animals go about their business, a behind-the-scenes tour, evening snack, and breakfast. In mid-August the zoological gardens also holds its Children's Zoo Debut to introduce kids to the resident beasties. (No petting, of course.) Clowns, magicians, an animal show, and a silent auction with some animal artifacts are on the agenda. In October the zoo holds Maze of Madness, with goofy monsters and other spine-tinglers, in time for Halloween.

> **Kringles** Kringles are a special Danish oval pastry usually made with layers of thin sweetened dough, nuts, and honey. Other kringles are made with fruit fillings. Hmmmm, good. Stop by any of these places to try the best:
>
> - **Racine Danish Kringle,** 2529 Golf Avenue; (262) 633–1819
>
> - **O&H Danish Bakery,** 1841 Douglas Avenue; (262) 637–8895
>
> - **Lehmann's Bakery,** 2210 Sixteenth Street; (262) 632–4636

Places to Eat

Kewpee. *520 Wisconsin Avenue; (262) 634–9601.* The city's best hamburgers. A Racine landmark since 1927. $

Pasia Grill. *340 Main Street; (262) 637–4340.* Party place for dinner and after hours. $$

Ron's Place. *3307 Fifty-second Street; (262) 657–4455.* $

Burlington

Burlington is southwest of Milwaukee via I–43. Exit at the Burlington ramp (State Highway 11).

 KANE'S CIRCLE K COACH AND CARRIAGE (ages 5 and up)
27535 Ketterhagen Drive; (262) 534–2771.

For a kicked-back, relaxing ride in old-time style, gallop up to Kane's Circle K Coach & Carriage. Draft horses the size of, well, Belgians and Percherons if not elephants, pull haywagons, sleighs, stage coaches, or covered wagons around the farm's meandering trails. The ranch also offers elegant carriage rides in downtown Lake Geneva during the summer when the weather permits. No need to fear the winter winds when Mr. Frosty sweeps down out of the North; monster lap robes are provided for sleigh rides, perfect for wintery snuggling. Families just need to provide their own long johns or red woolies.

CHOCOLATE FESTIVAL (all ages)

Grounds are 1 block east of State Highway 36, with parking on Maryland Avenue. Third weekend in May.

Designated as Chocolate City USA by the Wisconsin state legislature—a sweet kudo, indeed—Burlington is home to a Nestle Company chocolate factory. This is reason enough for the city to host a giant Chocolate Festival each year. The event consists of a parade, musical performances (past performers have included Blood, Sweat and Tears and similar major names) and kids' entertainment with magicians and a petting zoo. On display is the world's largest milk-chocolate sculpture, which usually tops out at more than 2,000 pounds. Dinosaurs, castles, and giant crunch bars have been subjects of chocolate artists in the past. No nibbling is allowed on the statues, but there is always plenty of chocolate around the grounds, because candy bars are passed out freely. Service clubs, nonprofit organizations, and restaurants always have calorie-sinful chocolate desserts to go along with the other fare at their booths.

The Burlington Liar's Club

The Burlington Liar's Club, dating from 1929, is famous for its yearly competition for the biggest, tallest tales that stretch the truth to the moon and back. Submissions are received from around the world from all ages of folks, with the winner announced on New Year's Eve. If interested in winning (you can always fib and say you did), send your submission by mid-December to Mitzi Robers, 332 Dardis Drive, Burlington, WI 53105 (262-763-4640).

An exhibit containing memorabilia and photos about the competition can be seen in the Chamber of Commerce office on East Chestnut Street. We wouldn't kid ya—really.

KIWANIS PANCAKE BREAKFAST AND FAMILY FAIR (all ages)

249 Conkey Street, Burlington, WI 53105; (262) 763–2555 or (262) 763–6060. Late February.

The Kiwanis Pancake Breakfast and Family Fair is held each year at Cooper School, helping tummies prepare for the summer chocolate extravaganza. Might as well start training early with syrup and butter.

SPINNING TOP EXPLORATORY MUSEUM (ages 5 and up)

533 Milwaukee Avenue; (262) 763–3946 or (262) 728–5623. Call for tour availability.

For a new spin on life, take the kids over to the Spinning Top Exploratory Museum, which exhibits more than a thousand antique and modern tops, gyroscopes, and tons of yo-yos. There is enough here to keep a tyke interested for several hours. Free demonstrations by champ yo-yo-ists show what can be done without knocking yourself on the head. Everyone is encouraged to try their own hands-on experiments. Of course, there is a museum gift shop with all shapes, sizes, colors, and styles of tops.

BONG STATE RECREATION AREA (ages 5 and up)

26313 Burlington Road, Kansasville; (262) 878–5600.

Only 8 miles east of Burlington near Kansasville is the Bong State Recreation Area on State Highway 142. The area offers camping, hiking, and plenty of fishing for walleyes, perch, bass, and northern pike. A swimming beach is great for little ones to splash around the shallows and pretend that toes are nibbled by underwater creatures. Cross-country skiing, horseback riding, snowmobiling, hunting, and even a sled-dog training area round out the recreational opportunities at Bong. During the summer, rangers conduct interpretive programs and describe the local flora and fauna. Numerous hot-air balloonists also find the Bong area perfect for lift-off points. The site was named after Richard Bong, a flying ace who died during World War II.

For More Information

Burlington Area Chamber of Commerce, *112 East Chestnut Street, Burlington, WI 53105; (262) 763–6044.*

Amazing Wisconsin Facts Kenosha newspaper editor Michael Frank lead the movement for free schools in Wisconsin in the 1840s. In 1845 he left journalism to start the first public school in the state. The state constitution, which was adopted in 1844, provided free schools for youngsters between four and twenty years of age. Frank's lobbying efforts contributed to the statewide schooling program.

Greendale

From Burlington, take State Highway 36 northeast about 20 miles to Greendale.

This Milwaukee suburb was built in 1936 as a U.S. Department of Agriculture experiment to showcase town planning while providing construction jobs for the unemployed and housing for moderate-income folks. One of three such towns built by the federal government in the 1930s (in addition to Greenbelt, Maryland, and Greenhills, Ohio), Greendale is modeled after an English garden town. Parks, flower beds, open spaces, and public walkways attest to the success of that theme. The streets are narrow, with numerous cul-de-sacs to ensure privacy and quiet.

Places to Eat

Broad Street, Greendale's major thoroughfare, is lined with shops and restaurants. You can't go wrong with these favorites.

Ferch's Malt Shoppe. *5636 Broad Street; (414) 423–1414.* Owner Diane Kruger is a whiz at hamburgers and makes a mean frozen custard every day.

Ricardo's Pizza. *5627 Broad Street; (414) 421–1980.* Ricardo's has been consistently voted among the top ten pizza houses in Greater Milwaukee. The restaurant has been around for more than twenty years, serving up giant pizzas the size of flying suacers. It's worth a drive through the town with the kids just to sample a Ferch's malt and a Ricardo's everything-on-it.

Menomonee Falls

Menomonee Falls is a Milwaukee suburb. From downtown, take I–94 west to I–45 north. Take I–45 for about 10 miles to the Menomonee Falls exit.

RECREATIONAL TRAILS (ages 5 and up)

Two of the state's most easily accessible recreational trails launch from this turn-of-the-twentieth-century community. The **Bug Line Trail** is a former railroad spur converted into a 10½-mile pathway that is available for hikers, bikers, snowmobilers, and cross-country skiers. Pick up the Bug Line on Shady Lane in downtown Menomonee Falls, which is on the far northwest side of Milwaukee. The **Wild Rice Trail** is just a little more than 2 miles long and provides a scenic stroll along the Menomonee River, which eventually feeds into the Milwaukee River. Both trails are marked. If that isn't enough walking for the kids, take them on a tramp around the 1890s town using the self-guided strolling tour of original historic buildings.

OLD FALLS VILLAGE MUSEUM (ages 5 and up)

N96 W15191 Country Line Road; (262) 255–8346. Open May through September.

The Old Falls Village Museum is a re-creation of the original Menomonee Falls and features a number of historic buildings that have been moved to the site. A gazebo there was built in 1980 by trade classes from local high schools, with design and funding provided by the Menomonee Falls Garden Club.

For More Information

Menomonee Falls Chamber of Commerce and Industry Office, *W168 N8936 Appleton Avenue, Menomonee Falls, WI 53051; (262) 215–2430.*

A Month-by-Month Guide to Fun

Regardless of the season, it seems that Wisconsin has something going on almost every minute. There are festivals, parades, parties, gatherings, and all-around fun. The visitor can't go wrong in a state that capitalizes *Celebration* and takes it to the ultimate.

Check with visitors information centers for the latest details on any local whoop-de-do. The folks at each facility will be pleased and eager to send fliers, pamphlets, calendars, brochures, and all manner of promotional material. Many of the events have their own public relations and marketing personnel or promotions agencies. They can also provide information prior to a visit. All you have to do is ask.

Naturally, you should always call in advance for last-minute confirmations. Sometimes bad weather means a concert postponement. Maybe an event has been canceled. So plan for contingencies and consider the options. Take in a nearby gallery or a theatrical production instead. You won't have to go far to find all sorts of exciting things to do in the Badger State.

Maybe we'll see you in the timbered Northland, the river borderland of the West, the rural farmland of southern Wisconsin, or somewhere in a cityscape. There's so much happening!

January

■ **Northern Exposure/Wolf River Rendezvous,** Shawano; (715) 524– 2139 or (800) 235–8528. Early January.

Top sled-dog racers from Europe, Canada, and the United States compete in junior and amateur events. There are mutt sled-dog races, snowshoe races, a buckskinners' encampment, candlelight skiing, chainsaw carving, and sleigh rides.

- **Farm Expo,** Fond du Lac; (715) 723–5061. Mid-January.

  Hundreds of displays of farm and dairy equipment and seed and agri-business materials, along with farm safety and health clinics.

- **Maple Syrup Tasting,** Elmwood; (715) 639–3792 (Elmwood town clerk). Mid-January.

  An all-you-can-eat pancake lunch follows discussions on syrup making and technology.

- **Championship Snowmobile Derby,** Eagle River; (715) 479–4424. Mid-January.

  The pro event is internationally recognized as one of the largest gatherings of "sledders" in the world. More than 300 racers compete for titles and prizes.

- **U.S. International Snow-Sculpting Competition,** Milwaukee; (414) 476–5573. Late January.

  Teams from around the world compete on the grounds of the Marcus Center for the Arts to produce abstract designs and other snow forms. On the last day, spectators (including kids) can vote for the People's Choice Award.

February

- **Hot Air Affair,** Hudson; (888) 247–2332. Early February.

  More than 400 balloons from across the nation launch and race over the St. Croix River Valley. There is also a torchlight parade where balloon pilots and crews light up the night with blasts of fire from their baskets.

- **Snowflake International Ski Jump Tournament,** Westby; (608) 634–3211. Mid-February.

  Olympic-caliber participants from eleven countries soar more than 300 feet after jumping down Timber Coulee, a 90-meter hill.

- **Dyno American Birkebeiner,** Hayward to Cable; (800) 722–3386 in Wisconsin and (800) 872–2753 out of state. Mid-February.

The "Birkie" is the nation's longest and most prestigious cross-country ski marathon, running for 52 kilometers. Watch for many ski-related events and festivities.

■ **Klondike Days/World Championship Oval Spring,** Eagle River; (715) 479–6400. Late February.

The rendezvous features the winter's only winter horse-pull in the Midwest, along with sled-dog racing.

■ **World Championship Water Skipping Contest,** Siren; (715) 349–7399. Late February.

Professionals and amateurs attempt to leap water obstacles on their snowmobiles.

March

■ **Wollersheim Winery Open House,** Prairie du Sac; (608) 643–6515. Early March.

Tour the wine cellar, fermentation room, and other areas of the winery and enjoy wine tasting, wine-cooking demonstrations, grapevine-pruning demonstrations, and eagle watching from nearby ridges.

■ **Victorian Tea & Entertainment,** Superior; (715) 394–5712. Mid-March.

Enjoy turn-of-the-twentieth-century entertainment followed by high tea at Fairlawn Mansion and Museum. Wear a Victorian costume and win a prize.

■ **Cedar Creek Winery Settlement Open House,** Cedarburg; (262) 377–8020. Mid-March.

Taste samplings of new vintages, tour the cellar, and watch wine cooking demonstrations.

■ **St. Patrick's Day Parade,** Milwaukee; (414) 77-IRISH. Mid-March.

The wearin' o' the green comes alive as the Irish maintain a parading tradition that dates back to the mid-nineteenth century. A party at the Irish Cultural and Heritage Center follows.

- *Milwaukee Journal-Sentinel* **Sports Show,** Milwaukee; (800) 472-2070. Mid-March.

  Gear up for summer by attending the sports, travel, and boat show, with lumberjack events, fishing demonstrations, and wildlife art, rock climbing, and archery exhibits.

April

- **Airo Pow-Wow,** Stevens Point; (715) 346-3576. Early April.

  A variety of Wisconsin tribes put together a traditional feast, with dancing and other cultural activities.

- **Annual Crazy Quilters Show,** Mukwonago; (262) 392-3223. Early April.

  More than 200 quilts and wall hangings are displayed at this nationally known, judged show in Mukwonago High School.

- **Midwest Horse Fair,** Madison; (800) 373-6376. Mid-April.

  More than 500 horses of all breeds are showcased in a long weekend of family fun including seminars, demonstrations, vendors, and barn displays.

- **Taste of Scotland,** Racine; (414) 639-7824. Mid-April.

  Scottish culture is celebrated through Highland flings, scones and meat pies, and music.

- **Fort McCoy Earth Day/Volksmarch and Bike Tour,** Fort McCoy; (608) 388-3517 or (608) 388-4375. Mid-April.

  Educational activities and displays include birds of prey, reptiles, a Woodland Volksmarch, a bike tour, and more family events and games.

- **Spring Muster,** Greenbush; (414) 526-3271. Late April.

  This Civil War reenactment of camp life features Union and Confederacy troops performing military drills, a swearing-in ceremony, musket- and cannon-firing demonstrations, and domestic living.

May

■ **Mississippi Valley Archaeology Center (MVAC) Archaeology Day,** Hixton; (608) 785-8454. Early May.

Guided tours of rock shelters, interactive events, spear throwing, and archaeological displays bring ancient times alive.

■ **Cinco de Mayo,** Milwaukee; (414) 671-5700 or (414) 389-6003. Early May.

Mexican festival features an open-air mass, music, and cultural dance groups and displays.

■ **Folk Festival,** Ashland; (715) 682-1289. Early May.

Lots of activities for the kids and food, crafts, concerts, and daytime workshops that present a traditional look at spring.

■ **Spring Fling,** Necedah; (608) 565-2789 or (608) 565-3583. Mid-May.

Plenty of fun games, sing-a-longs, musical entertainment, bonfires, and food light the spark of spring in the North Country.

■ **Chocolate Festival,** Burlington; (262) 763-3511. Mid-May.

Carnival rides, arts and crafts, a parade, a bike ride, a walk, a pancake breakfast, and lots of chocolate are guaranteed for a sweet getaway.

■ **Automation,** Wisconsin Dells; (800) 223-3557. Mid-May.

More than 700 antique, street, and classic cars are displayed. Events include a swap meet, live entertainment, a parade, and kids activities.

■ **Syttende Mai,** Stoughton; (608) 873-7912. Mid-May.

This is the longest running Norwegian Independence Day festival held outside of Norway, featuring cultural booths, parades, costumes, rosemaling exhibitions, an ugly-troll contest, and food.

■ **Sunfish Days,** Onalaska; (608) 783-1110. Late May.

This festival offers a parade, a run and walk, a kids' fishing derby, a men's and women's softball tournament, volleyball, food, beer, entertainment, clowns, a petting zoo, a carnival, music, and dancing.

- **Broiler/Dairy Days,** Arcadia; (608) 323-3645. Late May.

  A farm-style celebration includes tractor pulls, a horse pull, softball, music, a parade, hot-air balloon rides, a carnival, and delicious charcoal-broiled chicken.

- **Festa Italia,** Madison; (608) 251-1880. Late May.

  Food, entertainment, rides, and fireworks showcase Italy's culture.

June

- **Farm 'n' Feather Fest,** Barron; (715) 537-5631. Early June.

  A parade, a carnival, kids' games, music, street dances, and a young'ns' parade greet the month.

- **RiverSplash,** Milwaukee; (414) 273-7222 or (414) 297-9527. Early June.

  This 10-block long celebration along the Milwaukee River features food, entertainment, and fireworks.

- **Walleye Weekend,** Fond Du Lac; (262) 923-6555. Early June.

  A ton of activities coincides with the Mercury Marine National Walleye Fishing Tournament, including Familyland attractions, sporting events, five music stages, and the "world's largest fish fry."

- **Great Wisconsin Cheese Festival,** Little Chute; (920) 788-7390. Early June.

  Includes a parade, children's activities, and cheese carving and tasting.

- **Tri-County Thresherman's Show,** Plainfield; (715) 335-6575. Early June.

  Visit Wisconsin's farming past with demonstrations on corn shredding, sawmills, blacksmithing, and threshing. Farm antiques, a kids' tractor pull, and a power parade are also featured.

- **Aquafest,** Rice Lake; (715) 234-2126. Mid-June.

  There's no damper on fun with this water fest, featuring an aqua bug hunt, street dances and bands, parades, kids' games, art-in-the-park, rubber-duck races, and golf and softball tournaments.

- **Asian Moon Festival,** Milwaukee; (414) 521–9829. Mid-June.

  This cultural festival of different Asian countries features food, dance, and fun from Chinese, Thai, Japanese, Korean, Filipino, Hmong, Indian, Pakistani, and related cultures.

- **Lakefront Festival of Arts,** Milwaukee; (414) 224–3850. Mid-June.

  A family art festival on Lake Michigan featuring kids' activities, a silent auction, performing arts, and close to 200 artists and their works.

- **Wonago Rodeo,** Milwaukee; (800) 357–6336. Mid-June.

  More than $22,000 in prize money and world championship points to be given away in rodeo's most popular events, featuring more than 150 top cowboys and cowgirls.

- **Juneteenth Day Celebration,** Milwaukee; (414) 273–7222. Mid-June.

  Food, music, and informational booths commemorate African-American freedom.

- **Polish Fest,** Milwaukee; (414) 529–2140. Late June.

  Contemporary and historical Polish culture is celebrated through food, music, dancing, and an outdoor mass.

- **Children's Day, Old World Wisconsin,** Eagle; (262) 594–6300. Late June.

  Enjoy the work and play of nineteenth-century Wisconsin youngsters re-enacted in a hands-on look at chores, washboard washing, making textiles, working in the garden, and the hoop-and-stick game.

- **Summerfest,** Milwaukee; (414) 273–2680 or (800) 273–FEST. Late June.

  A huge variety of music, food, and family activities includes many national acts and nonstop action. This is one of the nation's largest music festivals.

- **Strawberry Festival,** Cedarburg; (800) 827–8020. Late June.

  Family fun with minnow races, pie-eating and bubblegum-blowing contests, a pig roast, bands, hayrides, a crafts show, a fine-arts show, strawberry desserts and delicacies, strawberry wine, and a pancake breakfast.

July

- **Fourth of July Powwow,** Lac de Flambeau; (715) 588-3346.

  Music, food, a parade, kids' games, sidewalk sales, a special powwow, and fireworks keep guests going through the day and into the night.

- **Umbrella Daze,** Cambridge; (608) 423-3780. Early July.

  Look for a great chicken barbecue, plus a carnival, a parade, fireworks, and reunions. Held in Riverview Park.

- **The Great Circus Parade,** Milwaukee; (414) 273-7877. Mid-July.

  The circus train comes to town. The event features the World's Greatest Breakfast, Circus in the Sky fireworks, and the excitement of the Big Top.

- **Bastille Days,** Milwaukee; (414) 271-1416. Mid-July.

  French lifestyle is re-created in this free street festival with music, a marketplace, can-can dancing, food, and a cultural area.

- **Annual Art Fair Off the Square,** Madison; (608) 798-4811. Mid-July.

  This festival of art showcases the works of more than 125 artists and craftspeople, along with music, munchies, and children's activities.

- **Salmon-A-Rama,** Racine; (262) 634-1931. Mid-July.

  The bait here is fun for this family fishing contest and its displays, food, and drinks.

- **Festa Italiana,** Milwaukee; (414) 223-2193. Late July.

  Italian-style festival at the lakefront features national and international acts, food, games, fireworks, and fun.

- **Twin-O-Rama,** Cassville; (608) 725-5855 or (608) 725-5121. Late July.

  Don't think twice about missing this festival of multiple births, complete with twin judging, a parade, a chicken barbecue, entertainment, fireworks, a carnival, dances, and games.

- **Paperfest,** Kimberly; (262) 788-7507. Late July.

  This arts-and-crafts festival for families includes entertainment, athletic competitions, kids' games, food, and drinks.

- **Greek Fest,** Madison; (608) 244-1001. Late July.

  Celebrate Greek culture through exhibits, games, food, music, and a marketplace.

- **German Fest,** Milwaukee; (414) 464-9444. Late July.

  The Germans take over the lakefront for four days of traditional fun, dachshund racing, polkas, and yodeling.

- **River Falls Days,** River Falls; (715) 425-2533 and www.rfchamber.com. Late July.

  This community festival hosts the best outdoors dancing in the state, plus a marathon, a petting zoo, a carnival, and a parade.

- **Wisconsin State Fair,** Milwaukee; (414) 266-7188. Late July.

  The biggest family event in the state offers livestock judging, youth exhibits and games, rides, entertainment, food tasting, pig racing, exhibits, and lots more.

- **International Fly-In,** Oshkosh; (262) 426-4800. Late July.

  The annual Experimental Aircraft Association air show brings in 11,000 planes of every size, shape, and description from around the world. There are also educational forums, seminars and workshops, air shows, and fly-by performances.

August

- **African World Festival,** Milwaukee; (414) 372-4567. Early August.

  The Old and New Worlds come alive with traditional and modern African and African-American exhibits, entertainment, shops, peanut soup and other traditional foods, and music, including reggae, hip-hop, blues, and jazz.

- **Annual Great River Jazz Fest,** Friendship; (608) 784-7575. Early August.

  Four stages of music, a youth jazz workshop, and food nourish the spirit of music.

- **Fun Days,** Bangor; (608) 486-4082. Early August.

  Marathon runs, a parade, and numerous other activities are featured.

- **National Mustard Day,** Mount Horeb; (608) 437-3986. Early August.

  The local Mustard Museum shares its hot-stuff collection with the public. Try chocolate-fudge mustard and sesame, ginger, peanut, and scallion mustards.

- **Milwaukee Irish Fest,** Milwaukee; (414) 476-3378. Mid-August.

  The world's largest Irish cultural event brings together top entertainers from Ireland and America for a weekend of good fellowship, music, dance, theater, poetry, and sports.

September

- **Wisconsin State Cow Chip Throw,** Prairie du Sac; (608) 643-4317. Labor Day weekend.

  The competition is open to the public for a day of family fun. The event includes a nationally sanctioned tug-of-war competition, a running race, arts and crafts, and a bovine bingo.

- **Wilhelm Tell Festival,** New Glarus; (608) 527-2095. Early September.

  Swiss independence is celebrated with yodeling, flag throwing, and alpenhorn-tooting.

- **Indian Summer,** Milwaukee; (414) 273-FEST. Early September.

  Native American tribes from across the United States participate in the annual powwow and celebration of Native American culture at the Lake Michigan lakefront.

- **Arabian Fest,** Milwaukee; (414) 342-4909. Mid-September.

  This annual festival features foods, music, and entertainment from the Middle East.

- **Watermelon Seed-Spitting and Speed-Eating Championship,** Pardeeville; (608) 429-2873. Mid-September.

  Thousands of visitors converge each year in Pardeeville to witness seed-spitting competitions, munch free watermelon, indulge in a pancake breakfast, and enjoy the waterskiing show, melon sculptures, and music.

- **Laura Ingalls Wilder Festival,** Pepin; (715) 442–2461 or (715) 442–2147. Late September.

  This annual festival celebrates the author of the Little House books and features displays and events showcasing life in the mid-1800s.

- **Annual Cranberry Festival,** Warrens; (608) 378–4388. Late September.

  This harvest festival includes tours of cranberry bogs, cranberry products for sale, a parade, 700 booths of antiques and arts and crafts, and a farm market.

- **Oktoberfest,** La Crosse; (608) 784–FEST. Late September.

  This annual fall harvest is an Old World German celebration complete with music, entertainment, arts and crafts, ethnic food, carnival rides, Maple Leaf and Torchlight parades, the Miss La Crosse/Oktoberfest pageant, the Festmaster Ball, and a 100-mile bicycle tour and race.

- **Annual Gays Mills Apple Festival,** Gays Mills; (608) 735–4341. Late September.

  The largest and most concentrated apple-orchard area in the Midwest hosts a variety of apple-related events and activities, including the Wisconsin State Apple Recipe Contest, arts and crafts, a flea market, a parade, and fireworks.

October

- **Spectacle of the Geese,** Horicon Marsh, Horicon; (800) 937–9123. Throughout October.

  Tours, harvest specialties, hayrides, naturalist lectures, and other events celebrate this resting spot for more than 200,000 geese as they fly south for the winter.

- **Applefest,** Bayfield; (715) 779–3335. Early October.

  This festival offers a heritage-and-talent show, an apple peeling contest, a pet parade, Big Top Chautauqua performances, carnival rides, kids' contests, and country dancing.

■ **Annual Cranberry Fest,** Eagle River; (715) 479-8575 or (800) 359-6315. Early October.

The "World's Largest Cranberry Cheesecake" will be served. Also included are crafts shows, a photography contest, weaving and quilt exhibits, an auction, and music along with hundreds of other cranberry events.

■ **Swan Watch at Rieck's Lake Park,** Alma; (608) 685-4249. Mid-October.

Almost 2,500 migrating tundra swans and other waterfowl find protection in these waters during the month of October.

November

■ **Fall Polka Fest,** Wisconsin Dells; (608) 846-3835. Early November.

Learn the polka, Wisconsin's unofficial State Dance, with the aid of six dance bands.

■ **Jule Fest Breakfast,** Kenosha; (262) 657-9781. Early November.

A Danish crafts fair, with special foods. Try a breakfast of *aebliskiver* (pancake balls) and *medestopoise* (sausage).

■ **Holiday Folk Fair,** Milwaukee; (414) 225-6220. Mid-November.

This annual festival is the nation's largest and oldest multiethnic indoor festival, featuring dance, music, costumes, foods, and crafts.

■ **Santa Exhibition,** House on the Rock, Spring Green; (608) 935-3639. Mid-November to January.

Each year, more than 6,000 Santas of all shapes and styles are displayed at the Christmas-themed House on the Rock.

■ **Festival of the Trees,** Racine; (262) 634-6002. Mid-November.

Dazzling decorated Christmas trees are displayed in the city's Festival Hall.

■ **Puerto Rican Independence Day Celebration,** Milwaukee; (414) 278-2700. Late November.

A weekend honoring the city's Puerto Rican families is hosted by the Milwaukee Public Museum.

December

- **Wisconsin Special Olympics Fall Sports Tournament,** Milwaukee; (608) 222-1324. Early December.

  This statewide sports competition for more than 900 athletes brings spectators from around the state.

- **Sinter Klausen Christmas Koncert,** Germantown; (262) 255-2590. Early December.

  This annual concert showcases Wisconsin's German heritage with carols sung by children's choirs.

- **Capitol Christmas Pageant,** Madison; (608) 233-9165. Mid-December.

  Christmas carols are sung by area high school and college students in the state capitol rotunda.

- **Annual Chocolate Festival,** American Club, Kohler; (800) 344-2838 or (414) 457-8000. Mid-December.

  A chocolate-lovers dream getaway features crystal, candlelight, and *tons* of chocolate candies, tortes, cakes, cookies, and other delicacies at the Midwest's only five-star resort.

- **Torchlight Cross-Country Skiing,** Crivitz; (715) 757-2467. Late December.

  Family ski social gets the entire clan out for skiing, a bonfire, hot dogs, and other refreshments.

Index

W

Y

Z

About the Authors

MARTIN HINTZ, a member of the Society of American Travel Writers, has been a travel writer for three decades. Hintz has more than sixty books to his credit, some of which are other travel-related books published by Globe Pequot, and he has written hundreds of magazine and newspaper articles. He also publishes *The Irish American Post,* an international news magazine, and is director of the Mountjoy Writers Group, an international news syndicate. In addition to his son Stephen, son Daniel and daughter Kate have collaborated with him on writing projects.

STEPHEN HINTZ graduated from the University of Wisconsin-Milwaukee in 1996 and is working toward his Masters. He has coauthored five books with his father and is currently working on a film screenplay and a novel. Hintz started a mentoring program for court-ordered youth, which he runs full-time,

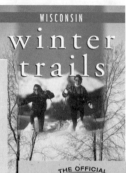